The
Popular Press Companion
to
Popular Literature

The Popular Press Companion to Popular Literature

Victor Neuberg

Bowling Green State University Popular Press
Bowling Green, Ohio 43403

Copyright ' 1983 by Bowling Green State University Popular Press

Library of Congress Catalogue Card No. 82-074162

ISBN: 0-87972-233-9 Clothbound

List of Illustrations

Acknowledgements

The original idea for this book must surely date from my purchase of a Catnach broadside in the Portobello Road more than 30 years ago. Its writing has occupied me for three. Debts incurred in its making are therefore mostly personal – and can never be adequately repaid. My wife Anne has provided the atmosphere in which sustained work was possible; Barbara Gilbert, competent and critical, has kept me (mostly) on the right path and typed the manuscript; my daughter Caroline Robertson and her husband Brian have always been encouraging, and their daughters Katherine and Alison have provided the distractions that every writer needs.

For various things – things which those concerned may well have forgotten – I am grateful to John Adlard; Stanley Brett; Tony Brown; Gillian Dickinson; Frank Hoffmann; John Lazar; Chris Needham; Rudolf Schenda; Brian Southam; Graham Scott; Margaret Spufford; C. Wellesley-Smith; Natascha Würzbach.

Librarians, especially those in the School of Librarianship at the Polytechnic of North London, have been more helpful to me in this enterprise than I can say.

Finally, and with great pleasure, my especial thanks are due to Muriel Pettman, who always replied with unfailing generosity to my many queries about the life and career of her mother, the novelist Grace Pettman. Muriel Pettman, more than anyone else, has enabled me to understand the world of the popular novelist at the turn of the century. My gratitude to her is enduring.

Introduction

The aim of this book is, quite simply, to provide a guide to popular literature, printed mainly in English, from earliest times to the present day. Inevitably, because the subject is so wide and to a large extent ill-defined, some selection will be necessary. 'Completeness' in a literal sense would be impossible to achieve; and in another sense the very notion of finality implied by such a description would be seriously misleading. However we approach the subject, there does seem to me to be a pretty basic corpus of knowledge which might be both useful and interesting to a whole range of readers with widely differing needs; but so much of it is hard to find, outside a scattered area of often obscure reference material. To take just a first point of contact with the general reader, there are many characters in popular literature who have become household names – Mickey Mouse, Sherlock Holmes, Dick Turpin, Simple Simon, for instance; and information about them in an immediately accessible form could be welcome, or could indeed prove valuable.

A look at some forerunners and contemporaries in this field seems necessary. The *Enzyklopädie des Märchens*, edited by Kurt Ranke at Göttingen University and currently appearing volume by volume, is staggering both in its length and in its scope. For many years it will remain a standard reference work, even though at the time of writing it is far from completion. At the other end of the scale are works which attempt to cover a discrete subject. *The Oxford Book of Nursery Rhymes* by Iona and Peter Opie was first published in 1951, and after more than a quarter of a century it is far from being superseded. It represents the fruits of a long devotion to the theme, and is in most ways a satisfactory work of reference. Clearly it is open to criticism on several counts, notably the lack of a bibliography; but this is of marginally less importance than its overall excellence as a guide to the subject. Other guides to clearly defined branches of popular literature that I have found useful include Chris Steinbrunner and Otto Penzler (eds.), *Encyclopedia of Mystery and Detection* (1976); Maurice Horn (ed.), *The World Encyclopedia of Comics* (1976); and H. J. Crawford, *Crawford's Encyclopedia of Comic Books* (1978). Peter Nicholls (ed.), *The Encyclopedia of Science Fiction* (1981), was published when the bulk of the work for the present volume was completed, but I have no doubt of the usefulness of Nicholls's work.

Somewhere between the universally magisterial Göttingen enterprise and the specialized worlds of nursery rhymes, detective stories, comics and science fiction, there is, I believe, need for a more general, and necessarily more selective, reference book to the entire field of popular literature. It is this which I have attempted to provide.

In Western Germany there is an excellent guide to contemporary popular culture which covers a good deal of what is called *Trivialliteratur*. This is G. Seesslen and B. Kling, *Unterhaltung* (2 vols., 1977), an admirable and attractive work. Clearly the authors were faced with a tremendous problem of selection. It is a problem that I have shared.

What does one include? More important perhaps, what does one leave out? Is there some crucial point of principle involved here, or is it a matter of empiricism? Both temperamentally and intellectually I am drawn to the latter. Principles in popular literature, no less than in real life, are not easy to live with. This does not, of course, mean that principles, however uncomfortable, are not important, and I have certainly been guided by the notions of reliability, utility and readability; but there must also be a high degree of empiricism, or the whole exercise might well degenerate into a narrow selectivity which demonstrates a theoretical grasp of priorities at the expense of the subject itself.

It follows, then, that some users (readers, should I say?) may be disappointed because a particular favourite is omitted, or because one topic receives more attention than they feel it deserves. Clearly this is a matter of taste, and more especially of judgment, and in no sense can I take it to invalidate the general guideline of presenting the wide spectrum of the subject.

Some entries will be self-selecting – broadsides, dime novels, comics, Marie Corelli, are obvious examples. But how does one decide (although ultimately, of course, considerations of space might be the criterion!) between, say, Jane Porter and Elizabeth Helme? Both were extremely popular novelists in their day, and no vital issue of taste appears to be at stake. A glance at S. A. Allibone, *A Critical Dictionary of English Literature* (vols. 1 and 2, Philadelphia, 1882), will show that the latter has a four-line entry while the former has a considerably longer one. The problem of selection is confounded by the sheer number of nineteenth-century and twentieth-century popular novelists, each of whom has an equal, or nearly equal, claim to inclusion. I have no wish to make too much of this, and have in fact included a number of popular novelists for no better reason than that they appear to me to be important for one reason or another. Perhaps something more than personal preference is involved here, and it becomes a matter of just how useful the book is.

A fairly persistent problem – so far as contemporary writers are concerned – has been that of dates. When was X or Y born? If the information is not readily to hand either in a reference book or a publisher's handout, then I have let it go. It seems an unwarrantable intrusion upon a stranger to write and ask when they were born!

For the many minor novelists of the eighteenth and nineteenth centuries who are excluded from these pages there are often relevant entries in Allibone – five portly volumes in all, and readily available in a facsimile reprint. Then there is R. Watt, *Bibliotheca Britannica*, originally published in 1824 in Edinburgh. These four volumes are also easily accessible in facsimile. A. Johannsen, *The House of Beadle and Adams*, contains a wealth of detailed information about novelists who were once household names. Alas, this is not readily available. Volumes 1 and 2 were published in 1950, and a supplementary volume appeared in 1962; but since publication in Norman, Oklahoma, not many copies have found their way into this country.

To indicate the existence and the excellence of such works as these three may appear an uneasy compromise – and so it is; but there really is no satisfactory alternative if a general reference book is to be kept within reasonable bounds. There is no doubt at all that specialists in various fields will experience some pleasure in discovering items that I have not mentioned, whether intentionally or just because I did not know about them. On the other hand, the less specialized and curious reader will, I hope, find this book useful.

Amongst the topics that I have, with a great deal of regret in most cases, felt bound to omit are newspapers and most magazines; the popular literature of sport; political ephemera; books on home medicine, including dieting; manuals of self-help and instruction. In some cases these are too complex to permit of brief and selective treatment; while in others I may lack the competence to venture beyond the blandest of generalities.

In fact, the last category in this list of omissions does constitute an important part of the subject as a whole. I would like to suggest here a three-part definition of popular literature which is, I believe, sufficiently broad to encompass the subject and at the same time imprecise enough to permit both modification and development. First, it is what unsophisticated readers choose, or have chosen, to read for pleasure. Then, it includes what one group – I refrain purposely from introducing the concept of class into this discussion – have thought that another group ought to be reading for its own good. Religious tracts, temperance literature and political material come into this category. Finally, there is the popular literature of self-improvement, including cheap reprints of the classics, manuals of self-instruction and the like. In the nineteenth century publishers like John Cassell of London built the fortunes and the reputations of their firms upon such literature. There is a close connection here with the Puritan work ethic, and a popular book of the 1880s exemplifies this: *From the Loom to the Lawyer's Gown; or Self Help that was not all for Self*. Exhortations to the young to improve themselves and rise in the world were often couched in evangelical language; but the mass of self-improvement literature, reflected in publishers' lists of cheap, wholesome, improving books – Shakespeare's plays included – with a coloured cover and offered at one penny a time, was very much more impressive.

Because we can learn so much about the development of popular literature from a study of these publishers' lists, and of the fortunes of the publishing firms concerned, one aim of this companion must be to provide information about the most important members of the book trade. But the search for this information is not easy. There are, it is true, dictionaries of printers; but these are not always as helpful as one might wish, for only a minority of them may have been involved in catering for the popular market, and many of those who were thus involved left scant records behind them other than their products – and these were often undated. Then, besides production, a book trade requires distribution – and of the chapmen and shopkeepers who effected this we know even less. What might be termed the 'socio-bibliographical' aspects of popular literature have so far received comparatively little attention.

I have, therefore, touched upon that section of the book trade which produced and distributed popular literature so far as this is possible; and where it is not, I hope to indicate at least by implication the gaps in our knowledge. There is, of course, a third indispensable element in this trade – the reader. The relationship between printed artefact, producer and recipient underlies any fruitful approach to the subject. I am conscious that the 'common reader', however we define him or her, has received short shrift in these pages. There is an entry on 'Literacy'; but the fact is that the reader of popular literature remains a shadowy and insubstantial figure. There are some records of what others thought that he or she should – or should not – be reading; but if the readers themselves are inadequately represented here, it is because I have been unable to locate personalities as precisely as I would have wished.

The fascination and the importance of popular literature are obvious. The difficulties inherent in writing this sort of guide are, I hope, equally obvious; but a start has to be made somewhere, or there is a danger that we shall remain at a primitive level of debate over definitions and models.

Finally, a note on the arrangement of entries. It is alphabetical in its coverage of genres, and lists publishing firms or individuals under surname. Where fictional characters are concerned, however, the alphabetical position relates to the first word in the character's name – there seemed to be something essentially improbable in the idea of entries such as 'Mouse, Mickey', 'Bill, Buffalo', 'Holmes, Sherlock' or 'Capp, Andy'!

V.E.N.

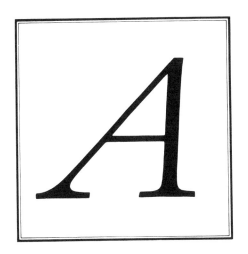

AINSWORTH, William Harrison (1805–1882). British author of some 40 popular novels. Among the best were *Rookwood* (1834), which featured Dick Turpin (qv), and *Old St. Paul's* (1841).

S. M. ELLIS, *William Harrison Ainsworth and His Friends* (2 vols., 1911).

ALGER, Horatio (1834–1900). American author of some 135 books for young readers on the theme of 'rags to riches', with such titles as *Fame and Fortune*; *Struggling Upward*; *Strive and Succeed*. The heroes of such books – and each had a different one – give rise to the myth that any boy, provided that he was intelligent, hardworking and honest, could become either a millionaire or President of the USA.

RALPH GARDNER, *Horatio Alger* (1964).
J. G. CAWELTI, *Apostles of the Self-Made Man* (1965), contains an account of the 'rags to riches' theme in popular literature.
I. G. WYLLIE, *The Self-Made Man* (1954), is also useful.

ALLINGHAM, Margery (1904–1966). British writer, creator of the detective Albert Campion, who appeared in 21 novels between 1929 and 1965. After Margery Allingham's death her husband, Philip Youngman Carter, wrote two further novels which featured Campion. *The Tiger in the Smoke* (1952) is considered to be her best novel.

Ally Sloper, comic cartoon character created by Charles Henry Ross. His full name was Alexander Sloper F.O.M. (Friend of Man), and his partner in various adventures was Isaac Moses, better known as Ikey Mo. Both were seedy con-men whose plans to become rich invariably came to nothing.

He made his first appearance in a full-page strip entitled 'Some of the Mysteries of Loan and Discount' published in a comic paper called

Judy on 14 August 1867. He soon became a weekly feature in the magazine, and a paperback reprint of his exploits, *Ally Sloper: a Moral Lesson* (1873) was probably the first comic book to appear.

The following original publications featured the character: *Ally Sloper's Comic Kalendar*, 1874–1887; *Ally Sloper's Summer Number*, 1880–1884; *Ally Sloper's Comic Crackers*, 1883; *Ally Sloper's Half-Holiday* – this was a weekly comic paper which ran from 3 May 1884 to 30 May 1914. The title was changed to *Ally Sloper*, and ran from 6 June 1914 to 9 September 1916. *Ally Sloper's Half-Holiday* was revived and ran from 5 November 1922 to 14 April 1923. There were also annual extra editions – *Ally Sloper's Christmas Holidays*, 1884–1913 and a short-lived weekly paper, *Ally Sloper's Ha'porth*, which ran from 23 January to 21 March 1899. Attempts were made in 1948 and 1949 to revive Ally Sloper, but they did not succeed.

Ally Sloper was the first comic strip hero to be exploited commercially: there was the 'Sloper Keyless Watch', a Sloper Insurance Scheme, a Sloper Club with a bronze medallion, and the 'Sloper China Bust'. There were songs about him, colouring books for children featured him, and he was portrayed in several early films; he was a character in a Drury Lane pantomime, *The Forty Thieves*; and there was a set-piece Ally Sloper display in fireworks at the Crystal Palace. In addition, Ally Sloper umbrellas, walking sticks, pipes, toys, sweets, kites and fireworks were offered for sale. C. H. Ross made little out of all this exploitation, for he had sold the copyright to Gilbert Dalziell, the engraver who became a publisher. Ross, however, did become Editor of *Judy*, and his son Charles Jr wrote for *Ally Sloper's Half-Holiday* under the pseudonym 'Tootsie Sloper'.

Several artists were involved. As soon as the character was established, Marie Duval (Mrs C. H. Ross) took over; later W. G. Baxter drew him; and finally W. F. Thomas took the strip into the 1920s. (I am grateful to the late Charles Ross, son of Ally Sloper's creator, for most of these details.)

Almanacs. The word 'Almanack' was first used in Britain in 1267 by Roger Bacon. He used it to describe tables showing the apparent motions of heavenly bodies; and indeed almanacs, known in manuscript before the beginning of printing, provided information about the conjunctions and oppositions of the sun and moon, dates of eclipses and moveable feasts. The two earliest known survivals, both of them in fragments, date from about the 1490s – one was printed by Caxton's successor, Wynkyn de Worde.

Printed almanacs, therefore, are pretty well as old as the history of printing itself. They began with a minimum of information printed on a single sheet, but variations were soon introduced, and some almanacs burgeoned into pamphlet form – a form in which they are still available each year in Britain and the USA.

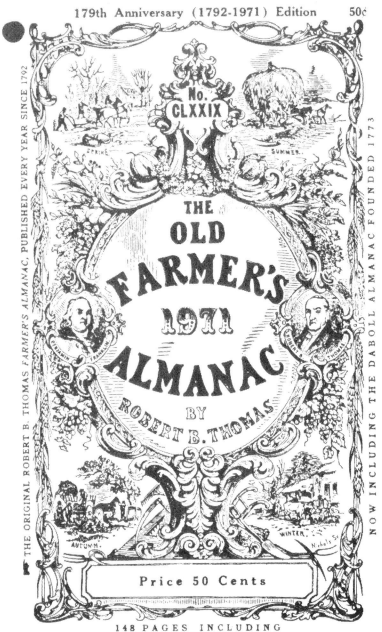

THE ORIGINAL ROBERT B. THOMAS *FARMER'S* ALMANAC, PUBLISHED EVERY YEAR SINCE 1792

No.
CLXXIX

SPRING SUMMER

THE
OLD
FARMER'S
1971
ALMANAC
BY
ROBERT B. THOMAS

BENJAMIN FRANKLIN ROBERT B. THOMAS

AUTUMN WINTER Nichols Sc

NOW INCLUDING THE DABOLL ALMANAC FOUNDED 1773

Price 50 Cents

148 PAGES INCLUDING
Weather Forecasts For All of the U.S.A.
PLANTING TABLES, ZODIAC SECRETS, RECIPES, ETC.

1 A modern American Almanac (1971)

With additional pages, the traditional material could be expanded to include prognostications, religious and political comment, and other assorted items. The seventeenth century was probably the golden age, but almanacs have been popular for very nearly five centuries.

What has contributed mostly to this continuing popularity has been, I think, the extremely powerful attraction which the pseudo-science of astrology, with its concomitant notion of fortune-telling, has always had. Almanac makers, particularly in early modern Europe when ideas of magic and religion were inextricably intertwined, took advantage of this, and exploited it with considerable success. The residual success of the almanac today is hardly surprising, for in the scientific, industrial twentieth century an interest – to put it no higher – in astrology and fortune-telling is still widespread.

BERNARD CAPP, *Astrology & the Popular Press* (1979) is the standard work.

ROB SAGENDORPH, *America and her Almanacs* (1970) is good.

For early almanacs see E. F. BOSANQUET, *English Printed Almanacks and Prognostications. A Bibliographical History to the Year 1600* (1917).

G. L. KITTREDGE, *The Old Farmer and His Almanack* (1920) is an attempt to see the role of the almanac in early American life.

DEREK PARKER, *Familiar to All. William Lilly and Astrology in the Seventeenth Century* (1975) is a biography of a noted almanac maker.

CYPRIAN BLAGDEN, 'The Distribution of Almanacks in the Second Half of the Seventeenth Century' published in *Studies in Bibliography*, Vol. XI (1958), pp. 107–116, remains a pioneer study on how these ephemeral items reached their readers.

Alternative press. 1968 was the year of student revolt in the USA and in Europe. It was also the year which gave currency to the term 'alternative society'. The idea itself was not new, but the phrase was; and the phenomenon which characterized it was a rash of radical publications known variously as the 'alternative' or the 'underground press'. The extent to which so loosely defined a movement was a reaction to the affluence of the sixties, or to American involvement in the Viet Nam War, is uncertain. Looking back, the late sixties do seem to be the point at which post-war material prosperity reached its climax, and the war in the Far East, with its bombing of civilian targets, deeply offended the sensibilities of the young in both continents. Other factors were, of course, involved. Student riots in Berlin, Paris and California, the troubles at Warwick University and Hornsey College of Art in Britain, and the shooting of students at Kent State College in Ohio, were all, in a sense, results and causes of social unrest. This complex pattern gave rise to an equally complex literature.

Such a literature – the alternative press – would not have assumed the physical form that it did had it not been for the fact that developments in printing and reprography at this time made it possible for individuals or groups to publish their own papers and magazines at a fairly small cost. The result was that the alternative publications looked different from more orthodox publications. They were usually very much more amateurish in appearance – and always more outspoken. The point of view of the alternative press was uniformly radical. Radicalism, however, speaks with many different (not always mutually exclusive) voices, and the range of topics was wide. It included Black protest, vegetarianism, pacifism, socialism, Eastern religion, local issues, attacks upon the political establishment, exposé journalism, and so on.

The problem with which the myriad publications had to cope was fundamentally that of distribution. This was the rock upon which so many of them foundered. Many died after only a few issues (sometimes only one or two) had been published, and the numbers of each issue were usually quite small – nearly all were run on a shoestring. New titles, however, continued to appear throughout the early seventies, and to a lesser extent in subsequent years. The alternative press still maintains a fairly vigorous life in Britain and in the USA.

A tiny sampling of titles current in early Summer 1974 includes the following: *Nola Express* (New Orleans); *Amex Canada* (Toronto); *High Times* (New York); *Rising Up Angry* (Chicago); *Movement* (London). There were also at this time alternative magazines which emanated from Wellington, New Zealand, *Itch*; from Italy, *Ca Bala*; and *Hi* was printed in Bombay. The alternative press was then, and probably still is, pretty universal. Its tone is neatly caught by the *Nola Express*, which was described as being 'suspended temporarily whilst Darlene and Robert intervene against the Louisiana Power and Light Company's proposed nuclear-fission power plant.'

In Britain specifically, alternative publications have increasingly involved themselves with local issues and are published as community papers which challenge the established orthodoxy of the commercial local press. Examples include *Exeter Flying Post*; *Brighton Voice*; *Sheffield Free Press*; *Leeds Other Paper*; *Coventry Workshop Bulletin*; *Islington Gutter Press*. There are many others.

Since the survival of so many alternative publications is problematic – it is, for example, by no means certain that national libraries have complete runs of every, or even most, titles – books about them, and in particular anthologies of their contents, are of especial value. ROBERT J. GLESSING, *The Underground Press in America* (1970), is scholarly in its approach and contains a directory of titles. ROGER LEWIS, *Outlaws of America* (1972), is a very good survey and also has a list of titles and addresses. Nothing similar, so far as I know, exists for Great Britain.

'MINORITY PRESS GROUP', *Here is the Other News* (1980), is briefer and deals only with community papers and magazines. It is essential reading, and does contain a listing of publications.

So far as anthologies are concerned, there are two substantial American ones with illustrations and facsimiles. These are: JOSEPH BERKE (ed.), *Counter Culture* (1969); and MITCHELL GOODMAN (ed.), *The Movement Toward a New America* (1970). The latter is in large format and contains 752 pages. Indispensable.

Less ambitious is P. STANSILL and D. Z. MAIROWITZ (eds.), *BAMN. Outlaw Manifestos and Ephemera 1965–1970* (1971). The scope is international.

Half a dozen other American anthologies are interesting: J. HOPKINS (ed.), *The Hippie Papers* (1968); R. S. GOLD (ed.), *The Rebel Culture* (1970); E. G. ROMM (ed.), *The Open Conspiracy* (1970); P. SAMBERG (ed.), *Fire!* (1970); J. BIRMINGHAM (ed.), *Our Time is Now* (1970) – with an Introduction by K. VONNEGUT, Jr; and T. K. FORCADE (ed.), *Underground Press Anthology* (1972).

There is an exploration of the background in RICHARD NEVILLE, *Play Power* (1970).

In Britain, an alternative magazine called *Oz* ran foul of the law and a court case ensued. One of the defendants was Richard Neville. TONY PALMER, *The Trials of Oz* (1971), throws light upon the atti-

Volume 1 Number 17 • A Liberated National Publication • February 10, 1971 / 25¢

LIBERATED *Guardian*

ISLINGTON GUTTER PRESS (5p)

2 Alternative press publications from Great Britain and the United States of America (1971 and 1974)

tude of British authorities to the alternative press.

In 1974 an attempt was made in Britain to produce an *Alternative Press Digest.* I have traced only two numbers of it, which appeared in July and August of that year.

On radical publishers themselves, the best thing I know is an article by one of them, STUART CHRISTIE, whose 'Freedom is a Fiction' was published in *The Times Higher Education Supplement*, 16 October 1981. Other items include M. HOEY, *The Alternative Press in Britain* (1973), an 8-page pamphlet; J. NOYCE (ed.) *The Directory of British Alternative Periodicals 1965–74* (1979).

Amalgamated Press. Between about 1893 and 1960 the London publishers Amalgamated Press issued a vast amount of weekly fiction in paperback series and in periodicals (the distinction is often hard to draw) at prices which ranged from one penny to seven pence. The ramifications and complexities of such publishing are baffling. Not the least of the problems is the scarcity of such material and its physical fragility when located. The British Library has copies of most of the Amalgamated Press output.

Even when location is no problem, however, the authors remain almost without exception shadowy figures about whom nothing substantial is known. The firm itself, now subsumed (since 1960) with other enterprises under the title International Publishing Corpora-

tion (IPC), has sold many (?all) of its file copies. Fortunately, when the women's fiction was disposed of in the late 1970s, the booksellers who purchased it, John Benjamins of Amsterdam and Harold A. Landry of London, issued an illustrated sale catalogue (October 1979) which was in fact a valuable checklist of the material they were offering for sale as a collection. It consisted of 24,945 individual issues bound in 1,241 volumes, and there was also a quantity of ephemera which had been originally issued with the magazines. Thirty-two separate publications are listed; in some cases 'New Series' were begun and in others, titles were modified or changed completely. It is clear, too, that at some point Amalgamated Press took over the successful late Victorian enterprises 'Bow Bells' and 'Horner's Penny Novels'. No doubt they were absorbed into the larger firm just as Amalgamated Press itself was later taken over by IPC!

The following list, adapted from Benjamins & Landry, covers the bulk of Amalgamated Press's publishing in the field of women's fiction: *Answers Library*, later *Home Stories*, 1910–1923; *Bow Bells*, 1919–1925; *Companion Library*, 1919–1924; *The Cosy Corner Novels* (various modifications of this title), later *The Ladies Home Paper*, 1905–1909; *The Daffodil Library*, later *The Daffodil Novels*, 1906; *Eve's Own Stories*, 1923–1939; *Fanny Eden's Penny Stories*, 1905–1913; *The Fleetway Novels*, later *The Violet Novels*, 1919–1933; *FMN*

Handy Stories, later *Handy Stories*, 1906–1928; *The Girls' Best Friend*, later *The Girls' Friend*, 1898–1931; *The Girls' Friend Library*, 1907–1939; *The Girls' Home*, 1910–1915; *The Girls' Reader*, 1908–1915; *Golden Stories*, later *Golden Hours*, 1898–1913; *The Handy Library*, 1901–1906; *The Heartsease Library*, 1897–1917; *The Home Circle*, later *New Home Circle*, later *Home Circle and Family Fun*, 1901–1915; *The Home Companion*, later *New Home Companion* (modifications of this title), finally *The Home Companion*, 1897–1956; *Home Sweet Home*, 1893–1901; *Horner's Penny Stories*, later *Horner's Penny Stories and Woman's Own*, later *Horner's Stories*, c. 1894–1940; *Horner's Pocket Library*, later *Horner's Pansy Library (Stories)*, 1900–1911; *Lucky Star*, 1935–1960; *Mizpah Novels*, 1919–1922; *The Oracle*, 1933–1958; *Our Girls*, 1915–1918; *Peg's Paper*, 1919–1940; *Poppy's Paper*, 1924–1936; *Silver Star*, later *Silver Star and Golden Star*, later *Silver Star and Lucky Star*, 1937–1960; *Sunday Companion Library*, c. 1910; *Sunday Stories*, 1896–1940; *The Violet Magazine*, 1922–1939; *Woman's Magazine and Girls' Own Paper*, later *Woman's Magazine*, 1928–1940.

Amalgamated Press also published comics and story papers which were designed for children. Memorable characters in them who were enjoyed by a much wider public included 'Weary Willie and Tired Tim' (qv) and the famous fat boy, Billy Bunter (qv), who was created by Charles Hamilton (qv).

Amazing Stories. See *Gernsbach, H.*

AMBLER, Eric (1909–   ). British writer who published 22 novels – mostly spy stories – between 1936 and 1974. *The Mask of Dimitrios* (1939) – American title *A Coffin for Dimitrios* – is one of his best novels. It was filmed under the British name by Warner Bros. in 1944. Ambler also wrote film scripts, and was active in television.

Andy Capp. British comic strip character created by Reginald Smythe. He first appeared in the *Daily Mirror* (Northern Edition) on 5 August 1957, and on 14 April 1958 he spread to the National Edition. In 1960 he made his debut in a sister paper, the *Sunday Pictorial*.

Andy Capp is a truculent, male chauvinist layabout who wears a cloth cap too big for him. He has a long-suffering wife Florrie, and a friend called Chalky (the adventures of his son appear in a children's comic, *Buster*, dating from 28 May 1960). With his drinking, smoking and betting on dog races, Andy Capp struck an immediate and responsive note amongst Northerners, Scots – Britons generally; and thence throughout the world, where his exploits appear in thirty-four countries in thirteen languages! He is known in Austria as 'Charlie Kappl'; in Denmark as 'Kasket Karl'; in West Germany as 'Willi Wacker'; in Finland as 'Latsa'; in Holland as 'Jan Met de Pet'; in Italy as 'Carlo'; in France as 'Milord'; in Portugal as 'Jose Do Bone'; and in Sweden as 'Tuffa Viktor'. In 1963 he

The PRINCESS OF the LOOM

A Thrilling Story of Mill Life by Annie O. Tibbits.

No. 41.—" Sunday Companion " Library. . . Threepence.

3 Amalgamated Press fiction c. 1910

began a triumphant career in the USA. There have been various paperback reprints of his adventures.

Archie. US comic strip character. He was created by Bob Montana and first appeared in December 1941. The strip features, with Archie, such characters as Jughead, Reggie, Betty, Veronica and Moose; and following its immediate success, its fame became world-wide.

There have been several comic books based upon the strip, and one of them in 1969 was selling one million copies a month. This portrayal of American teenagers as they are apparently seen by adults has gone beyond comic strips and books, for there have been toys, games, merchandising material and commercial gimmicks of all kinds.

Arsène Lupin. Brilliant rogue created by Maurice Leblanc (qv). He pursues a criminal career for the sheer joy of it, and never for personal gain. Young, handsome, brave, he is also a master of disguise. So good is he at this that for a period of four years he became Lenormand, Chief of the Sûreté, and investigated his own criminal activities! At the end of a long and successful career in crime he becomes a private detective.

The first book about him was *Arsène Lupin Gentleman-Cambrioleur* (1907) – American title *The Exploits of Arsène Lupin* (1907). This was later reissued in Britain as *The Seven of Hearts* (1908), and in the USA as *The Extraordinary*

Adventurs of Arsène Lupin, Gentleman Burglar (1910). In some of the stories an English detective 'Herlock Shomes' appears.

Arsène Lupin was featured in both novels and short stories, and there have been many screen versions of his adventures made in Europe and in the USA.

Arthur Crook. Lawyer and detective created by Anthony Gilbert (qv). A burly, beer-drinking man with red-brown hair and a ruddy complexion, he was designed by his creator as a contrast to the aristocratic and patrician detectives who dominated the mystery novel in Britain in the 1930s. He appeared in 51 books published between 1936 and 1973. In some years two books were published, and in 1944 there were three.

ARTHUR, Timothy Shay (1809–1885). Voluminous and bestselling American temperance novelist. According to J. D. Hart in *The Popular Book* (1950), p. 109, he wrote 'over five per cent of all the volumes of fiction published in the 1840s.' This statement refers to American editions of his work, but he was also extremely popular in Great Britain where most of his novels were published after their appearance in the USA.

His best-known novel, *Ten Nights in a Bar-Room* (1854), was successfully adapted for the stage by W. S. Pratt, and featured the song which became famous, 'Father, dear father, come home with me now'.

ASHTON, John (1834–1911). British compiler of more than 30 books dealing with folklore, social history and related themes. He spent an uneventful life in London occupied with his literary activities. Several of his works touch upon popular literature, the most important of these being *Chap-books of the Eighteenth Century* (1882); *Humour, Wit and Satire of the Seventeenth Century* (1883); *Modern Street Ballads* (1888); and *Real Sailor Songs* (1891). Many of his books have been reissued in facsimile reprint editions.

JOHN ASHTON, *Gossip in the First Decade of Victoria's Reign* (1903). Reissued by Singing Tree Press, Detroit, in 1968 with a biographical introduction and bibliography by Leslie Shepard.

ASIMOV, Isaac (1920–   ). Prolific American author of science fiction. His first story, 'Marooned off Vesta', was published in the magazine *Amazing* in 1930, but he became widely popular when his story 'Nightfall' was published in *Astounding Stories* in 1940. A trilogy which established his reputation appeared first in this magazine: *Foundation*(1951); *Foundation and Empire* (1952); and *Second Foundation* (1953). Its theme was a million-year-old empire threatened with collapse into thirty thousand years of war. In 1963 Asimov received an award for 'adding science to science fiction' in his monthly column in *The Magazine of Fantasy and Science Fiction.*

Besides developing the 'Foundation' theme in three further novels, he produced many other works of fiction, including a series of 'Lucky Star' juvenile science fiction tales originally published under the pseudonym Paul French. Asimov has also written books on the popularization of science.

NEIL GOBLE, *Asimov Analysed* (1972).
JOSEPH F. PATROUCH Jr, *The Science Fiction of Isaac Asimov* (1974).
J. D. OLANDER and M. H. GREENBERG (eds.), *Isaac Asimov* (1977).

Auguste C. Dupin. First important fictional detective. He was created by Edgar Allan Poe (qv), and his adventures, recounted by an anonymous friend, were told in three stories: *The Murders in the Rue Morgue* (1841); *The Mystery of Marie Roget* (1842); *The Purloined Letter* (1845 – actually published in October 1844). The stories were collected in *Tales* (1845). Dupin was an intellectual detective, and his contempt for the official police and their methods reflected an attitude that was much copied by later writers of crime and mystery.

AYRES, Ruby M. (1883–1953). Best-selling British romantic novelist. The first of her 143 novels was published in 1917. During the 1950s she answered readers' problem letters in *Home Companion.*

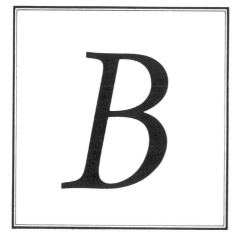

BAILEY, H(enry) C(hristopher) (1878–1961). British creator of Reggie Fortune (qv). Another of Bailey's characters was Joshua Clunk, a shyster lawyer who appeared in novels from 1930 onwards. Bailey's mysteries, in which he always plays fair with the reader, are complicated puzzles, and the solutions are logical. Because of elaborate plots and careful characterization, his short stories tend to be rather longer than those of other writers.

Ballad. A poem in short stanzas often sung to a traditional tune, and telling a popular story. As such it predated the printing press; but by about 1500 it was established in print in the form of the broadside ballad, the main characteristic of which was that the text was printed in black-letter on one side of a flimsy sheet, which was then hawked about the streets. This represented the earliest form of ephemeral popular literature. The subject matter comprised satirical comment on men and affairs of the day, romance, invective, jocular and religious themes. Broadsides were printed in enormous numbers. In 1520 John Dorne, an Oxford bookseller, had more than 190 different ballad sheets in stock, and by 1543 'An Act for the Advancement of True Religion and for the Abolishment of the Contrary' attempted to restrain the publication of 'printed books, printed ballads, plays, rimes, songs and other fantasies. . . .'

The popularity of broadside ballads continued into the seventeenth century. According to the poet George Wither, there were 'thousands of vain songs and profane ballads stored up in Stationers' warehouses'. There is a story told by John Aubrey (*Brief Lives*, ed. O. L. Dick, 1960) that Dr Richard Corbet (1582–1635), poet and divine, met a ballad seller in Abingdon Market who 'complained he had no custome; he could not putt-off his Ballads. The jolly Dr. putts-off his Gowne, and putts-on the Ballad-singer's Leathern jacket, and being a handsome man, and had a rare full Voice, he presently vended a great many, and had a great Audience.'

After about 1640, when printers began to change to the more modern whiteletter type, traditional black-letter was used for ballad sheets until the end of the century. Thereafter, ballads still maintained their vogue during the eighteenth century. Printers/publishers like Dicey (qv) turned them out in large numbers. They were referred to by their producers as Slips (i.e. slip songs), and in a catalogue issued by Cluer Dicey and Richard Marshall in 1754 twelve and a half pages of 'Old Ballads' are listed, with a concluding note: 'There are near three thousand different Sorts of SLIPS; of which the new Sorts coming out almost daily render it impossible to make a Complete Catalogue.' In addition to single sheets, collections of songs and ballads known as 'garlands' were issued in large numbers. There was, too, a growth during the eighteenth century of topical political ballads. Towards the end of the period ballad sheets, together with chapbooks (qv), began to go out of fashion; and indeed, as the industrial revolution was changing the structure of society, popular taste was shifting in a number of ways. A public which had long been content with a largely traditional popular literature became more sophisticated; and at the same time changes in printing techniques, an increase in the size of the population and growing facilities for elementary education all led to the production and wide circulation of new forms of popular literature.

Amongst the early nineteenth-century flood of cheap fiction and popular magazines, the chapbook survived as reading matter for children. That the ballad continued to flourish was largely due to James Catnach (qv) and John Pitts (qv), who issued large numbers of street ballads in the early years of the century from their respective printing offices. Their productions, usually illustrated with woodcuts, were characterized by topicality and sensationalism, both of which qualities were cleverly and profitably exploited by these entrepreneurs, and by a host of others. Catnach, however, was pre-eminent in this field, and the firm that he founded lasted for about 70 years. Murder, particularly of a revolting kind, was always grist to the ballad printer's mill, and equally to those who sold them. 'There's nothing beats a stunning good murder after all', a ballad seller in London told Henry Mayhew in the 1850s. It is, of course, true that traditional and popular songs still appeared on single sheets, and there were printers/publishers of these in most of the towns and cities of the British Isles.

It should be stressed that street ballads were sold in the streets. There were itinerant vendors who would attract attention with their cries of 'Three Yards a Penny' (i.e. several columns of ballads printed parallel upon long sheets). There were 'pinners up' who exhibited their wares on walls – as Words-

25

worth put it in *The Prelude*, 'Here files of ballads dangle from dead walls'; and there were street stalls where such things could be bought. A. J. Munby visited one of them on 19 July 1861:

I walked up to the New Road, and had a long talk with the old ballad seller opposite St Pancras Church. A very respectable intelligent man, of some education: said he had been there 20 years and brought up a family of nine children on the proceeds. The trade, he said, was never so good as now. . . .

He went on to say that servant girls amongst his customers would buy the old ballads when they first came up from the country to London, but later they chose the popular songs which they heard being played and sung in the drawing rooms of the houses where they worked.

At the close of the nineteenth century the street ballad petered out. The premises used by Catnach's successors in the trade were pulled down in 1883, and by then the days of the street ballad were almost done, although one or two printers survived in London. The ballad sheet was finally killed off by the cheap illustrated magazine and the newspaper.

In the later twentieth century there have been several rather self-conscious attempts to revive the street ballad, but none has been entirely successful. They have been connected with the revival of folksong, itself a sometimes questionable phenomenon. The last genuine ballad seller was James Smith, a one-armed, one-legged man who wrote and published his own ballads and sold them from the kerbside in

Place where can be seen | Tune I come from the Country. | or Post to Someone

DON'T STEAL A GOOSE.

I come from the country, my tale I will tell
For stealing a goose, in prison I fell
When I've told you my story, I will on
my way wend
You will find a good joke, when it gets
to the end.

I went to a wealthy estate one fine day
I said I was hungry, they said go away
We get all our wealth from the workers
we fleece
If you steal a goose, we'll ring up Police.

Soon out of my sack, some wire I did take
To catch a fine goose, a snare I did make
To prison the Police said you'll have to go
To keep you quite honest, mail bags you
must sew.

So never you try a goosling to take
But be clever enough to steal the estate
Then to prison in motor, you won't have
to whirl
They will make you a Lord, or a Duke
or an Earl.
THE END.

In 1510 a meek hungry workman was hung for stealing a goose from the common land, but there never was a wealthy man hung for stealing the common land from the goose Now as always the greedy landowners want more land that will give them more wealth, so they want the workers to take the Eastern Countries for them. But the meek have found strength in their unity to resist, and the call has gone throughout the world Workers of the World Unite for Peace Land & Prosperity. Then the meek shall inherit the Earth, not the warmakers & their Fascist friends. Think it over Conscription is a law of force against the meek.

Composed & issued by J. Smith, 3, Ropley St., Bethnal Green.

The Hackney Press 407 Hackney Road E.2

4 One of James Smith's ballads

26

Oxford Street and elsewhere in London. He called himself 'The Pavement Poet', and died in the 1950s. The last of the firms producing street ballads and ephemera was S. Burgess, whose premises were at 8 York Place, Strand, London. The business was still active just after the Second World War, and the shop and printing office were eventually demolished to make room for a new development. Rumour had it that in the cellar there were large numbers of traditional woodblocks used for illustrating ballad sheets, but I was never able to discover whether this was true or not.

Sources
There are ballad collections in the major libraries of Britain and the USA. So far as printed texts are concerned, there are several books by H. E. ROLLINS (qv). LESLIE SHEPARD, *The Broadside Ballad* (1962) is excellent. V. E. NEUBURG, *Popular Literature* (1977), contains a critical bibliography which lists a number of ballad reprints. Amongst the most important are:
FRANCIS CHILD, *The English and Scottish Popular Ballads* (5 vols., 1882–1898). A facsimile edition is available.
THOMAS PERCY, *Reliques of Ancient English Poetry* . . . (3 vols., 1886). (The best edition of a work first published in 1765. Other reprints are available).
JOSEPH LILLY (ed.), *A Collection of Seventy-Nine Ballads and Broadsides* (2nd Edition, 1870). A facsimile edition is available.
W. CHAPPELL and J. W. EBSWORTH

(eds.), *Roxburghe Ballads* (8 vols., 1871–1899). A facsimile edition is available.
W. W. WILKINS (ed.), *Political Ballads of the Seventeenth and Eighteenth Centuries* (2 vols., 1860).
MILTON PERCIVAL (ed.), *Political Ballads Illustrating the Administration of Sir Robert Walpole* (1916).
CHARLES HINDLEY (ed.), *Curiosities of Street Literature* (1871). Two reprints are available.
See also *Ballad collections*; *Furnivall, F. J.*; *Hindley, C.*; *Pepys, S.*; *Rollins, H. E.* For ballad printing specialists in the seventeenth century, see *Ballad partners*.

A note on the ballad in the USA
The development here was rather different. During the eighteenth century, as printers gradually set up their businesses in the colonies, both ballads and broadsides (qv) became part of their stock in trade. The revolutionary period saw a considerable increase in the production of such ephemera, which was invariably topical and sharply political. The more traditional ballad sheet, however, maintained its popularity alongside the political one, well into the nineteenth century, and was similar to the street ballad in Victorian England.

Sources
There are collections in major libraries. The reprinting of ballads has not been as widespread as it has been in England (but see *Broadsides (Broadsheets)* for two examples). Amongst useful books are:

w. c. FORD (ed.), *The Isaiah Thomas Collection of Ballads* (1924).

E. WOLF 2nd (ed.), *American Song Sheets Slip Ballads and Poetical Broadsides* (1963).

L. C. WROTH, *The Colonial Printer* (1964 (1931)) is excellent on early printers.

R. WRIGHT, *Hawkers and Walkers in Early America* (1965 (1927)) is about the 'Yankee peddlers' (q.v.) who sold ballad sheets, amongst other items, in colonial times.

Ballad collections. Samuel Pepys (qv) was not the only collector of ballads. Robert Harley (1661–1724), First Earl of Oxford, was another, and his collection, plus a few additions made by a subsequent owner, is now in the British Library, where it is known as the Roxburghe Ballads. Three volumes of ballads collected by John Bagford (1650–1716) are also there, and in the Bodleian Library at Oxford there are the remains of Anthony à Wood's (1623–1695) ballads. In the University of Glasgow Library there is the Euing Collection of seventeenth-century ballads. Other collections of ballads from the seventeenth and eighteenth centuries are to be found in the Harvard Library, the Public Record Office, the Madden Collection in the University of Cambridge, the John Rylands Library and the Chetham Collection at Manchester. The collection formed by the late Professor C. H. Firth is divided between the Bodleian Library and the University of Sheffield.

So far as nineteenth-century street ballads are concerned, the Baring-Gould and the Crampton Collections in the British Library are considerable. Locally printed material is to be found in many provincial libraries in Britain. The Library Company of Philadelphia possesses an extensive collection of nineteenth-century song sheets and poetical broadsides.

This partial description of some ballad collections both reflects and reinforces the need for a list of libraries in Great Britain and the USA which possess holdings not only of ballads, but also of all kinds of ephemeral popular literature.

Ballad partners. The production of ballads in the seventeenth century (and, indeed, in the sixteenth) could be an extremely complicated affair. Some, of course, were issued by a single printer; but many were the result of partnerships between several printers. An imprint might, for example, read like this one from the years 1680 to 1682: 'Printed for M. Coles, T. Vere, J. Wright, J. Clarke, W. Thackeray and T. Passinger'. The complexity of the ballad trade and its many partnerships is made all the more interesting by the fact that some of the men (and occasionally widows) concerned were substantial members of the book trade. This indicates that from a fairly early period involvement in popular literature was regarded as a profitable enterprise.

Much research is needed in the tangled field of partnerships and shifting relationships. A start,

A pleasant Countrey new Ditty :

Merrily shewing how

To driue the cold Winter away.

To the tune of, *When Phœbus did rest, &c.*

ALl haple to the dayes,
That merite more praise,
  then all the rest of the yeare:
And welcome the nights,
That double delights,
  as well the poore as the Peere:
Good fortune attend,
Each merry mans friend,
  that both but the best that he may:
Forgetting old wrongs,
With Carrols and Songs,
  to driue the cold winter away.

Let misery packe,
With a whip at his backe,
  to the deep Tartarian flood:
In the Lethe profound,
Let enuy be drown'd,
  that pines at another mans good:
Let sorrowes expence,
Be banded from hence,
  all payments of griefe delay:
And wholly consort,
With mirth and with sport,
  to driue the cold winter away.

Tis ill for a mind,
To anger inclind,
  to ruminate iniuries new:
If wrath be to seeke,
Doe not let her thy cheeke,
  nor yet inhabite thy brow.
Crosse out of those bookes,
Maleuolent lookes,
  both beauty and youthes decay:
And spend the long night,
In honest delight,
  to driue the cold winter away.

The Court in all state,
Now opens her gate,
  and bids a free welcome to most:
The City likewise,
Though somewhat precise,
  doth willingly part with her cost:
And yet by report,
From City and Court,
  the Countrey gets the day:
More Liquor is spent,
And better content,
  to driue the cold winter away.

The Gentry there,
For cost do not spare,
  the Yeomanry fast in Lent:
The Farmers and such,
Thinke nothing too much,
  if they keep but to pay their Rent:
The poorest of all,
Do merrily call,
  want, beares but a little sway:
For a Song or a tale,
Ore a Pot of good Ale,
  to driue the cold winter away.

Thus none will allow,
Of solitude now,
  but merrily greets the time :
To make it appeare,
Of all the whole yeare,
  that this is accounted the Prime,
December is seene,
Apparel'd in greene,
  and Ianuary fresh as May:
Comes dancing along,
With a Cup and a Song,
  to driue the cold winter away.

---

5 A seventeenth century ballad

however, has already been made. The following titles are essential:

CYPRIAN BLAGDEN, 'Notes on the Ballad Market in the Second Half of the Seventee..th Century' in *Studies in Bibliography. Papers of the Bibliographical Society of the University of Virginia*, vol. 6, 1953–1954, pp. 161–180.

ROBERT S. THOMSON, *The Development of the Broadside Ballad Trade and its Influence on the Transmission of English Folksongs*, University of Cambridge Ph.D. Thesis (1974, unpublished). BLD 12831/75. See especially pp. 39–69.

MARGARET SPUFFORD, *Small Books and Pleasant Histories* (1981). Chapter IV, 'The fortunes and the volume of stock of the chapbook publishers' pp. 83–110 is especially relevant but see *passim*.

BARCLAY, Florence (1862–1953). Romantic British novelist whose books had a strong and pervasive religious interest. A parson's wife, she wrote less than a dozen novels, the first being *Guy Mervyn* (1891). Her most famous work was *The Rosary* (1909), which sold more than 150,000 copies within nine months of publication and was still a best-seller in 1928.

The Life of Florence L. Barclay: a Study in Personality by One of Her Daughters (New York, 1924).

BARNABY ROSS. See *Ellery Queen*.

Batman. Comic strip hero created by Bob Kane and Bill Finger in response to the popularity of Superman (qv). Batman first appeared in *Detective Comics*, 27 May 1939, and subsequently on film, radio and television. He had no super powers, but an acute mind and a good physique. In real life he was the millionaire Bruce Wayne; at night he spent his time, suitably dressed in a bat-like cape and cowl, combating crime. This he did because his parents had been murdered when he was a child; and his partner Robin the Boy Wonder, in daily life Dick Grayson, circus performer, was also an orphan.

Beadle and Adams. New York publishers of dime novels (qv).

BENTLEY, E(dmund) C(lerihew) (1875–1956), British writer. Bentley's novel *Trent's Last Case* (1913) was described by *The New York Times* as 'one of the few classics of detective fiction'. He was also famous for the invention of the 4-line verse called a 'clerihew' which at one time was nearly as popular as the limerick. The first book of these verses, *Biography for Beginners* (1905), appeared under the pseudonym E. Clerihew; and this was followed by *More Biography* (1929); *Baseless Biography* (1939); *Clerihews Complete* (1951); and *The Complete Clerihews of E. Clerihew Bentley* (1981) which is the best edition and has an Introduction by Gavin Ewart. Bentley published *Those Days: an Autobiography* in 1940.

Bestsellers are more easily recognized than defined; but what they all have in common is the large number of copies sold. The implications of this – the reasons why so many individuals want to read the publication in question – are another matter. A book may be borrowed from a library, in which case it will have been purchased on behalf of those who have shown a desire to read it; or it may be purchased, mostly in paperback form, by individual readers.

If we assume that this desire to read is a determining factor in the definition of a bestseller, then publications like *The Bible*, *The Highway Code*, political pamphlets or religious tracts cannot strictly be included, although they are undoubtedly distributed, for one reason or another, very widely. Most bestsellers are in practice fiction. There is a category which comprises books on cookery, slimming, gardening, self-help, popular psychology, religion and sociology, medical manuals and school textbooks, all of them potentially bestsellers; but the compulsions to read are a little different in such cases, and do not necessarily have to be based upon pleasure.

Let us return to the question of numbers. How many copies of a book have to be sold before it can be considered a bestseller? And over what period of time? There seem to be no precise answers to these questions, and when one thinks of the problem of cumulative sales the issue becomes more intractable. One attempt to provide a formula was made by F. L. MOTT in *Golden Multitudes* (1947). He defined the overall bestseller in the USA as a book which was 'believed to have had a total sale equal to one per cent of the population of the Continental United States . . . for the decade in which it was published.' To qualify in these terms, a book had to have the following minimum sale:

1910–1919	900,000
1920–1929	1,000,000
1930–1939	1,200,000
1940–1945	1,300,000

The disadvantage here is that a steadily selling book can become a bestseller, whereas in today's publishing practice the essence of the bestseller is fast turnover.

Essential to the bestseller is a keen production and marketing mechanism. To some extent it will share these with other books on a publisher's list, but the bestseller is made rather than born, and the mechanisms are enhanced and sharpened to ensure success. Increasingly, too, the bestseller is being seen in international terms, and this means American domination because publishers there are more ready to spend money on promotion and advertising, and sales figures are considerably greater.

Some sales figures for bestsellers in the 1970s were enormous. Erich Segal, *Love Story* (1970), sold over 400,000 copies in hardback and over nine million in paperback; Peter Benchley, *Jaws* (1974), 200,000 copies in hardback and over nine million in paperback; James A. Michener, *Centennial* (1974), over 400,000 copies in hardback, more than five million in paperback. Such figures – and they are by no means atypical – make nonsense of definitions. We are thinking of ten-million-sellers in the USA and two-million-sellers in Britain. As JOHN SUTHERLAND, *Bestsellers* (1981), put it: 'The sales apparatus of bestsellerdom (lists, tie-ins) is now enormously rationalized. Bestsellers are produced with consummate efficiency, and on scales we have never witnessed before.' (p. 247).

Sutherland's book is the best discussion of the phenomenon that I know. F. L. Mott's book has been mentioned; there is also J. D. HART, *The Popular Book* (1950), which is a study of American literary taste; and S. E. GREENE, *Books for Pleasure. Popular Fiction 1914–1945* (1974), contains valuable lists of bestsellers. An earlier pamphlet by DESMOND FLOWER, *A Century of Best Sellers 1830–1930* (1934), provides much needed historial perspective for Britain. See also Q. D. LEAVIS, *Fiction and the Reading Public* (1932), a pioneer study which remains essential reading.

BIGGERS, Earl Derr (1884–1933). American creator of Charlie Chan (qv), the Chinese detective. Biggers also wrote a mystery novel, *Seven Keys to Baldpate* (1913), which was an immediate success. In the mid-1920s he hit upon the idea of using an 'amiable' Chinese character rather than the 'sinister and inscrutably wicked ones' which were almost a literary convention of the time. The result was Charlie Chan, who achieved great popularity in novels and films.

Biggles. Full name Wing Commander James Bigglesworth, DSO, DFC, MC, a fictional, ageless aviator created by William Earle Johns (1893–1968). The adventures of 'Biggles' were told in various boys' story papers and in 96 books written between 1932 and 1968. Most of those adventures featured his companions Ginger and Algy.

During the Second World War, in order to stimulate recruiting to the Women's Auxiliary Air Force, Johns was commissioned to create a female counterpart to Biggles, and the result was 'Worrals of the WAAF'. Although successful, she was retired in 1945, while Biggles took on a new lease of life when he was seconded to Interpol as the Air Detective.

JOHN PEARSON, *Biggles. The Authorised Biography* (1978).
P. B. ELLIS and P. WILLIAMS, *By Jove, Biggles! The Life of Captain W. E. Johns* (1981).

Billy Bunter. Fat boy at Greyfriars School, created by Charles Hamilton (qv) using the name 'Frank Richards'. He made his first appearance in February 1908 in a story called 'The Making of Harry Wharton' published in the first number of a weekly story paper called *The Magnet*, which was to specialize in stories about Greyfriars School. With its sister paper *The Gem* (commenced Spring 1907; Hamilton's pseudonym 'Martin Clifford', school St Jim's), it ceased publication in 1940.

Bunter was extremely popular. Indeed, his popularity grew to such an extent that in May 1919 a weekly story paper, *The School Friend*, was started for girls. The long story featured in the first number was *The Arrival of Bessie Bunter*; the school was Cliff House; and the author was Charles Hamilton as 'Hilda Richards'. In fact he wrote only the first six stories, but the series continued and Bessie was a success. Over the years she changed from being merely fat and stupid into a lovable duffer.

Billy was always lazy, greedy, stupid and dishonest. His one talent was ventriloquism. He was forever trying to borrow money against the arrival of a postal order from Bunter Court – which never arrived. His speech was simple, often prefaced by 'I say, you fellows . . .', and when his misdeeds were discovered and punished, characterized by 'Yarooh!', 'Beasts!' and 'Oh, crikey!'.

He had a revival after the Second World War. Between 1947 and his death in 1961, Hamilton turned out over thirty Bunter books. There were four Bunter Christmas plays on the London stage between 1958 and 1961, and he appeared on television in a number of Greyfriars stories in 1960, with Gerald Campion playing Bunter. Although by no means the only fat boy in English literature, Billy Bunter is certainly the most famous and the longest-lived.

Black Mask. Most important of the pulp magazines (qv) published in the USA. Founded in 1920 by H. L. Mencken and George Jean Nathan, it published adventure stories and traditional thrillers. It is, however, chiefly recalled today for its stories featuring the 'hard-boiled school' of tough private detectives. Writers like Caroll John Daly (qv), Dashiell Hammett (qv), Erle Stanley Gardner (qv), Raymond Chandler (qv), George Harmon Coxe (qv), Frank Gruber (qv) and others wrote fast, violent, cynical yet romantic tales of crime. The magazine achieved its highest point between 1926 and 1936 under the editorship of Capt. J. T. Shaw (1874–1952). It survived into the forties, ceased publication and was incorporated into *Ellery Queen's Mystery Magazine* (qv) in 1953.

Blackshirt. Gentleman crook created by Bruce Graeme (qv). He breaks the law and solves crimes. The first of Graeme's dozen thrillers about him was *Blackshirt* (1925). Writing as Roderic Graeme, Bruce Graeme's son Roderic Jeffries has written some 20 Blackshirt novels.

BLAKE, Nicolas (1904–1972). Pseudonym of C. Day Lewis, British writer who became Poet Laureate in 1968. He published 20 volumes of verse, several works of criticism and an autobiography. Twenty mystery novels were written under his pen-name, 17 of them featuring the detective Nigel Strangeways. He also reviewed this kind of fiction in *The Spectator*.

Blind Beggar of Bethnal Green, The. Subject of an early broadside ballad where the story was told in over 60 doggerel verses. The first part was about Bessy, the beggar's beautiful daughter, and her search for a husband; and the second described her wedding feast, at which the beggar told the story of his life.

The popularity of the ballad was such that by 1624 two others, current at the time, were intended to be sung to the same tune. It was reprinted many times in varying versions, and one was on sale in the streets of London in the early nineteenth century. There were stage versions, the first by Henry Chettle and John Day in 1600; an anonymous novel was published in 1848; and the story was retold for children. When Bethnal Green became a Metropolitan Borough in 1899, it adopted as its emblem a picture of the Beggar, his dog and his daughter. There is still a public house called The Blind Beggar, and nearby Bessy Street takes its name from the daughter.

The best – indeed only – comprehensive account of the subject known to me is to be found in *The Green. A History of the heart of Bethnal Green and the Legend of the Blind Beggar*, by A. J. ROBINSON and D. H. B. CHESSHYRE (Tower Hamlets Central Library, 1978).

Blondie. US comic strip character created in September 1930 by Murat (Chic) Young. At first Blondie Boopadoop was a scatter-brained young woman pursued by Dag- wood Bumstead, playboy and son of an industrialist. On 17 February 1933 the two were married, and Dagwood was disinherited by his father. Since then the strip has remained half-way between humour and a family series. It has a simplicity and an optimistic outlook which have made it internationally popu- lar. It is probably the most widely circulated comic strip in the world, and has been translated into most languages. Its international audience numbers hundreds of millions.

Between 1938 and 1951 28 films were based upon it, with Penny Singleton playing Blondie and Arthur Lake, Dagwood. There has also been a television series in the USA, and one novel.

BLOOM, Ursula (1895–   ). British writer whose pseudonyms include Lozania Prole, Sheila Burnes, Mary Essex. Prolific author of 468 books, mostly romantic novels, of which 420 have been published. The first, *Tiger*, was privately published when she was seven! A friend of the family, Marie Corelli the novelist (qv), paid the printing costs; and in later life the friendship between the two writers provided the raw material for some of Ursula Bloom's novels.

Amongst her output are ten volumes of autobiography and memoirs, and a book called *The ABC of Authorship* (1938). The novels, all of which have strong moral undertones, include *Tomor- row for Apricots* (1929), *Price Above Rubies* (1965), and *Twisted Road* (1975).

BLOUNT, Margaret (*fl.* 1855–1900). Prolific American author of popular fiction from the late 1850s to the 1890s. She spent some time in England, and her work was published in both countries – some of it in the London periodical *Reynolds Miscellany* (see *Reynolds, G. W. M.*). Amongst her many novels, and typical of her stories, were *Once Wooed, Twice Won: The Story of a Woman's Heart* (1861), and *Barbara Home* (3 vols., 1864).

Bodice rippers (sometimes 'hot historicals'). A term used to describe novels of sex, violence and passion set within a recognizable historical period. Novels of this kind gained popularity in the mid-1970s in Britain and the USA; and what is different about them is that men are the sex objects, rather than women. *Paxton Pride* by Shana Carrol is described by the publisher (Arrow) as 'A sweeping saga of turbulent love, harsh vengeance and raw passion.' This seems entirely typical – and so does the heroine:

Her body demanded this man, and . . . her mind accepted her body's knowledge. She was close to him now and his naked torso glistened with sweat. He smelt of heat, of animal strength . . .

The heroines of novels like this are made of stern stuff. They have to be, in order to survive not only poverty, desertion and a stolen birthright, but also rape, torture and brutality at the hands of assorted marauding males who might be a pirate crew or members of an Indian tribe.

Some 'hot historicals' are long, up to 125,000 words, and sales can top a million copies. One of the most successful authors, Christina Nicholson (in real life Christopher Nicole), says about his work: 'There is no real formula to these books, but they must all have certain essential ingredients – a rape or seduction near the beginning, a man the heroine really loves, a spell for her as a mistress . . . and so on.'

Another writer, Annette Motley, took about eight months to write her first novel, *My Lady's Crusade*. As soon as it was finished the American rights were sold for $250,000.

Boone, Daniel. See *Western novels.*

BOS. See *Prest, Thomas Peckett.*

Boston Blackie. Ex-convict and cracksman created by Jack Boyle. *Boston Blackie*, 1919, is the only book about his adventures, but the character has featured in numerous films and in radio and television series. Despite his name, Blackie lived in San Francisco.

BOSWELL, James (1740–1795). Biographer of Samuel Johnson. Also a collector of chapbooks, some of which he describes purchasing in *Boswell's London Journal 1762–1763*, ed. F. A. Pottle (1950) p. 289:

Sunday 10 July [1763] . . . some days ago I went to the old printing-office kept by Dicey [qv], whose family have kept it fourscore years. There are ushered into the world of literature *Jack and the Giants, The Seven Wise Men of Gotham,* and other story books. . . . I bought two dozen . . . and had them bound up with this title *Curious Productions*.

This volume, with two others which Boswell collected later, is now in the Child Memorial Collection of chapbooks in Harvard College Library. The two later volumes contain a number of chapbooks printed by James Magee of Belfast. Two of them, rather unusually for chapbooks, are dated – one 1759 and the other 1764. Most of them contain eight pages, a few 24 pages, and only one 16 pages. One eight-page chapbook, *The Dead Man's Dream*, has the imprint 'Belfast: Printed for R. McConnel 1768'. In appearance it is similar to the Magee chapbooks and it is likely that he printed it.

BRADDON, M(ary) E(lizabeth) (1837–1915). Bestselling British author of about 60 novels, of which 13 – in three volumes each – were published during the seven or so years which followed the appearance of her most successful novel, *Lady Audley's Secret* (1862). This is the story of a beautiful woman, with the face of an angel, who murders her husband by pushing him down a well. The story had begun in 1861, after a false start in a paper which failed, as a serial in the *Sixpenny Magazine* published by John Maxwell, whom she subsequently married. A year later the Tinsley Brothers published it in three volumes, and its success was immediate and phenomenal. Three editions were sold out in ten days, and five more were called for within three months. The profits were such that one of the publishers established a villa at Barnes in Middlesex called 'Audley Lodge'. The successful formula was high life and crime without sexual irregularity and without corruption, and Miss Braddon repeated it in subsequent novels. Nevertheless, the sentiment and the melodrama with a dash of religion did not prevent her from gently satirizing both affectation and hypocrisy in society; and besides being an acute observer of contemporary manners, she was also strong on background.

Someone who knew her towards the end of her life said of her that 'She was a woman of the world with plenty to say and could say it amusingly'. The source of this quotation is *Queens of the Circulating Library* (1950), edited by F. ALAN WALBANK, whose brief introduction to 'Miss Braddon' is excellent. A good deal of obscurity surrounds M. E. Braddon's life. She began writing while she was still in her teens, and as early as 1860, for an unspecified reason, was separated from her family and supporting herself by hack writing and, for a time at least, as an actress under the name of 'Seaton'. She may have been a contributor to *Reynolds' Miscellany* (see *Reynolds, G. W. M.*), either anonymously or under an assumed name. Even her relationship with Maxwell was clouded by the fact that when she met him he was a married man with a wife in a mental home. Not until the wife died in 1874 were they able to marry.

There is a sensitive and informed

essay on M. E. Braddon in MICHAEL SADLEIR, *Things Past*, 1944.

BRAND, Christianna. Pseudonym of Mary Christianna Milne Lewis (1907–   ). British writer of detective fiction. Her best known detective is Inspector Cockrill of Kent County Police, who made his first appearance in *Heads you Lose* (1941). The best known of her novels was probably *Green for Danger* (1944) in which the victim dies on the operating table in front of seven witnesses, and this is the only one which has been filmed.

BREAN, Herbert (1907–1973). American author of mystery stories, some of which featured Reynold Frame, freelance writer, as detective. Also edited *The Mystery Writer's Handbook* (1958), and produced two books on jazz. His most popular works were *How to Stop Smoking* (1951); *How to Stop Drinking* (1958); *The Only Diet that Works* (1963).

BRETT, Edwin James (1828–1895). British publisher. Little is known about Brett's early life. He began his professional career as an artist, then became a journalist before turning to publishing. As a publisher he produced quantities of sensational fiction, much of it – like the Jack Harkaway series – for the juvenile market. Among his periodicals were *Young Men of Great Britain*, *Boys Comic Journal*, *Halfpenny Surprise* and *Our Boys Journal*. He was one of the most successful in this field, and was extremely wealthy when he died. Both his career and his publications would be well worth serious investigation.

Bringing up Father. American comic strip created by George McManus, appearing first in 1913. The chief characters are Jiggs, who was once a mason, and his wife Maggie, a former washerwoman. They have become wealthy as a result of winning the Irish Sweepstake. Jiggs wants to carry on as before, his only wish being to hobnob with his cronies at Dinty Moore's tavern enjoying a game of cards and a dish of corned beef and cabbage. Maggie, on the other hand, is the epitome of snobbishness and egotism, and the humour of the strip arises from this conflict, revolving round a continuing and often-hilarious battle between the sexes. After the death of McManus in 1954 the strip was continued. Bill Kavanagh wrote the story, and Vernon Greene drew the pictures until his death in 1965, when he was succeeded by Hal Campagna (drawings signed 'Camp').

This was the first comic strip to become internationally popular. It has been translated into many languages; and there have been films, animated cartoons and stage versions.

Broadsides (Broadsheets). Also known as fly-sheets, *feuilles volantes*, *fliegende Blätter* or *pliegos cueltos*. A large sheet of paper printed on one side only, used for announcements, proclamations and ballads (qv) from the earliest days of printing. The broadside/broadsheet was essentially the earliest form of the popular press, and as its alternative names show, it had an international quality. It performed something of its function during the American Revolution; and in the last quarter of the twentieth century it maintains a vigorous life, in both Great Britain and the USA, as an advertising medium – though purists may object that contemporary examples put through letter-boxes or distributed in the streets are printed on *both* sides of the paper!

For the sheer variety in contents of early sheets, ROBERT LEMON, *A Catalogue of a Collection of Broadsides in the Possession of the Society of Antiquaries of London* (1866). Examples from the late eighteenth century in the USA are to be found in JOHN DUFFY (ed.), *Early Vermont Broadsides* (1975); and M. I. LOWANCE Jr and G. B. BUMGARDNER (eds.), *Massachusetts Broadsides of the American Revolution* (1976).

BROOKS, Edwy Searles (1889–1965). Prolific British writer of popular fiction. The son of a minister in North London, he began writing as a young man and his published output has been calculated at 36,135,000 words. He wrote for Amalgamated Press (qv) and for D. C Thomson (qv). Between 1917 and 1933 Brooks wrote 900 adventure stories of 20,000 words each, a total output over these years which is about half as much again as Edgar Wallace wrote in his entire career. Many of Brooks's tales were pub-

lished in boys' weeklies, and occasionally he substituted for Charles Hamilton (qv) and wrote school stories.

He was the creator of a popular character in the Sexton Blake (qv) series, Waldo the Wonderman. In all, Brooks wrote 76 Blake stories of about 28,000 words each for a magazine called *Union Jack*. In later life he wrote over 60 adult crime novels. Under the pseudonym 'Berkely Gray', he created Norman Conquest – known as '1066' – an adventurer in the same tradition as The Saint (qv) or The Toff (qv). Conquest has a beautiful girlfriend called Joy Everard, and their adventures are told in 50 novels, the first of which was *Mr Mortimer Gets the Jitters* (1938). The last one, *Conquest in Ireland* (1969) was completed by Brooks's widow.

WILLIAM VIVIAN BUTLER, *The Durable Desperadoes* (1973).
C. STEINBRUNNER and O. PENZLER (eds.), *Encyclopedia of Mystery and Detection* (1976).

BROUGHTON, Rhoda (1840–1920). British romantic novelist whose first three books, *Not Wisely, But Too Well* (1867), *Cometh Up as a Flower* (1867) and *Red as a Rose is She* (1870) were published anonymously. She had a long writing career, and her novels sold well – the second of those mentioned sold 2,500 copies in the year of publication and a further 8,000 by 1874.

Her earlier work was characterized by an indiscriminate zest and an obvious infatuation with the senses

J. C. Seekatz inv.

Johann Conrad Seekatz
(1719 Grünstadt – 1768 Darmstadt)
Gravure en taille-douce (23,5 x 18,1 cm)
c. 1766

6 A seller of broadsides c. 1766

which struck some of her contemporaries as unusual and unmaidenly; but her readers loved it. She was also both caustic and flippant – qualities which were much less common in later Victorian popular fiction than they are in much of today's.

It was Rhoda Broughton's earlier novels which established her reputation, among them *Good-bye Sweetheart* (1872), *Nancy* (1873), *Joan* (1876) and *Second Thoughts* (1880). Critics, with few exceptions, had little good to say about her work: she was a novelist of notoriety. She continued writing beyond the first decade of the twentieth century, but by then she was writing tales about the contemporary scene and the English character rather than the romances which had established her as a best-selling novelist.

F. ALAN WALBANK, *Queens of the Circulating Library* (1950); and MICHAEL SADLEIR, *Things Past* (1944) – which contains a perceptive essay on Rhoda Broughton.

BROWN, Frederic (1906–1972). American writer of detective and science fiction. His best novel, *What Mad Universe* (1949), is a picture of the world where science fiction happenings are reality. He is also credited with having written the shortest science fiction story ever in three sentences:

After the last atomic war, Earth was dead; nothing grew, nothing lived. The last man sat alone in a room. There was a knock on the door. . . .

(Its claim, however, to be the shortest is rivalled by this one: 'As the sun set slowly in the East. . . .')

BRIAN ASH, *Who's Who in Science Fiction* (Revised Edition, 1977, from which both texts are taken).

BUCHAN, John (1875–1940). British diplomat, journalist, lawyer, publisher. As a writer of popular fiction Buchan was the creator of Richard Hannay, adventurer and sometime officer in the British Army. His exploits appeared in *The Thirty-Nine Steps* (1915); *Greenmantle* (1916); *Mr Standfast* (1919); *The Three Hostages* (1924); *The Rungates Club* (1928) (a collection of short stories featuring Hannay).

Buck Rogers. The first American science fiction comic strip appeared on 7 January 1929. It had been adapted by Phil Nowlan from his own novel *Armageddon 2419*, and drawn by Dick Calkins. It was called 'Buck Rogers in the Year 2429 AD', later 'Buck Rogers in the 25th Century', and finally 'Buck Rogers'.

Former US Air Force Lieutenant Buck Rogers wakes from a five-century sleep to find himself in an America devasted by war and overrun by Mongol invaders. With the help of young, pretty Wilma Deering, who becomes Buck's constant companion, he defeats the invader and liberates America almost single-handedly. New enemies appear, however – the tiger-men of Mars, pirates from outer space and Killer Kane with his accomplice Ardala Valmar. With the help of scientific genius Dr Huer, Buck triumphs over all his foes.

Buck Rogers remained popular for a long time. There were comic book versions and a radio series, while the earliest film version was made in 1939 with Buster Crabbe as Buck.

The Collected Works of Buck Rogers in the 25th Century (1969). Preface by Ray Bradbury.
Buck Rogers 1931–32 (1971).
Adventures in the 25th Century (1974).

Buffalo Bill. See *Western novels.*

Bulldog Drummond. Captain Hugh Drummond, gentleman adventurer created by H. C. McNeile (qv) who used the pseudonym 'Sapper'. Drummond, to whom peace is dull after his service during the Great War, continues to defend Britain against various German and Russian adversaries. In several books he encounters the arch-villain Carl Peterson. Six feet tall, broad and muscular, Drummond is intensely patriotic, and for love of his country will break the law or risk his own life – or even that of his beautiful wife Phyllis. His closest associates were Tenny, his valet; Algie, an aristocratic friend; and a Scotland Yard policeman, Colonel Neilson.

Drummond's adventures were told in ten novels by 'Sapper' published between 1920 and 1937: *Bulldog Drummond* (1920); *The Black Gang* (1922); *The Third Round* (1925) – US title *Bulldog Drummond's Third Round*; *The Final Count* (1936); *The Female of the Species* (1928); *Temple Tower* (1929); *Return of Bulldog Drummond* (1932) – US title *Bulldog Drummond Returns*; *Knockout* (1933) – US title *Bulldog Drummond Strikes Back*; *Bulldog Drummond at Bay* (1935); *Challenge* (1937). After the death of the original author seven further Drummond novels were published by Gerald Fairlie, a friend of McNeile: *Bulldog Drummond on Dartmoor* (1938); *Bulldog Drummond Attacks* (1939); *Captain Bulldog Drummond* (1945); *Bulldog Drummond Stands Fast* (1947); *Hands Off Bulldog Drummond* (1949); *Calling Bulldog Drummond* (1951); *The Return of the Black Gang* (1954).

Bulldog Drummond featured in films from 1922 to 1971.

C. STEINBRUNNER and O. PENZLER (eds.), *Encyclopaedia of Mystery and Detection* (1976).

BUNYAN, John (1628–1688). Author of *The Pilgrim's Progress* (qv). Bunyan, however, has another claim upon our attention. He is the earliest Englishman of humble birth, so far as I know, to describe (and repent!) the reading of his childhood:

... give me a Ballad, a News-book, *George on Horseback* or *Bevis of Southampton*, give me some book that teaches curious Arts, that tells of old Fables; but for the Holy Scriptures, I cared not. And as it was with me then, so it is with my brethren now. (*Sighs from Hell*, Second Edition (1666?) pp. 147–148).

7 *a)* *A twopenny edition of* The
   Pilgrim's Progress (*right*)
  b) *This edition was one of*
   Frederick Warne and Co.'s
   'Marvels of Cheap Litera-
   ture' (below)

BURKS, Arthur J. (1898–1974). Prolific American author of adventure, mystery, science fiction and detective stories for pulp magazines (qv). Under the pseudonym of Esther Critchfield he also wrote love stories. His output was phenomenal. During the 1930s he would sometimes have nearly two million words in current publication (and this disregards material written but rejected, either by himself or by editors!). At this period he aimed to produce 18,000 words a day. He described it thus:

Editors would call me up and ask me to do a novelette by the next afternoon, and I would, but it nearly killed me . . . I once appeared on the covers of eleven magazines the same month, and then almost killed myself for years trying to make it twelve. I never did.

There is a good chapter on Arthur J. Burks in R. K. JONES, *The Shudder Pulps* (1978).

BURROUGHS, Edgar Rice (1875–1950). American creator of Tarzan (qv) and author of stories many of which were first published in pulp magazines (qv). Notable amongst these was a Martian series; and another which featured the underground lost world of Pellucidar had Tarzan as a central character in one tale, *Tarzan at the Earth's Core* (1930).

H. H. HEINS, *Golden Anniversary Bibliography of Edgar Rice Burroughs* (1964).
R. A. LUPOFF, *Edgar Rice Burroughs: Master of Adventure* (1965).
I. PORGES, *Edgar Rice Burroughs: The Man Who Created Tarzan* (2 vols., 1976).

BURTON, Miles. See *Rhode, John.*

BUSH, Christopher (1888?–1973). British writer, real name Charlie Christmas Bush; and since he was illegitimate, the precise date of his birth is not known. He used the pseudonym Michael Home when he wrote about English country life. As Christopher Bush he wrote numerous mystery stories, 61 of which dealt with the adventures of Ludovic Travers, a wealthy, successful amateur detective. The titles of all except the first five Travers books began *The Case of the* . . . Bush's writing career spanned 42 years. *The Plumley Inheritance* (1926) was his first novel and *The Case of the Prodigal Daughter* (1968) his last.

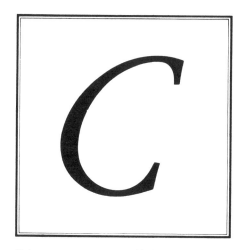

CAIN, James M(allahan) (1892–
). American author of hard-
boiled crime novels. Magazine articles and stories by him began to
appear in the 1920s. His first and
most famous novel, *The Postman
always Rings Twice*, was published
in 1934, and it was made into a
successful film starring Fred Mac-
Murray, Barbara Stanwyck and
Edward G. Robinson in 1944. Two
of his other novels, *Mildred Pierce*
(1941) and *Double Indemnity* (1943)
were filmed, and a two-hour version
of the latter was made for television
in 1973. *Serenade* (1937) was re-
leased as a romantic film starring
Mario Lanza in 1956. Altogether
Cain published 15 novels, an omnibus volume and a book of short
stories between 1934 and 1975.

CAINE, (Sir) Hall (1853–1931).
British author of numerous popular
novels with a strong religious bias.
The best known are *The Scapegoat*
(1891) and *The Eternal City* (1901).
   Marie Corelli (qv) never really
forgave him for recommending the
rejection of her first novel, *A
Romance of Two Worlds*, when he
was a publisher's reader for the firm
of Richard Bentley.

CAMPBELL, John W., (Junior)
(1910–1971). Influential American
writer and editor. He brought a
greater sense of accuracy to inter-
planetary tales, and his first, 'When
the Atoms Failed', was published in
Amazing Stories in 1930. In 1937 he
became Editor of *Astounding Stories*, a magazine which had made its
first appearance in January 1930;
and he held this post until his death.
During his editorship the magazine,
which became *Analog Science Fic-
tion/Science Fact* in 1960, was the
dominant periodical in science
fiction. Campbell introduced many
writers who later became famous in
the field, notably Isaac Asimov (qv)
and Robert Heinlein (qv).

Captain and the Kids, The. See
Katzenjammer Kids, The.

CARR, John Dickson (1906–   ).

44

American detective story writer whose best known character, Dr Gideon Fell, appeared in 26 books and was modelled upon G. K. Chesterton. He was also the creator of Sir Henry Merrivale, who featured in 24 books, and of Henri Bencolin (5 novels) and Colonel March of Scotland Yard. Carr also used the pseudonyms 'Carter Dickson' and 'Carr Dickson'.

Carr's plots were often improbable, and proved extremely popular. He also wrote historical novels, and of these *The Devil in Velvet* (1951) sold better than any of his books except for *The Life of Sir Arthur Conan Doyle* (1949), the official biography based upon documents made available by Sir Arthur's youngest son, Adrian Conan Doyle.

In 1932 Carr married an English wife, and has spent long periods living in Britain.

CARR, Philippa. See *Hibbert, Eleanor.*

Carson, Kit. See *Western novels.*

CARTLAND, Barbara (1900–). British writer. Occasional pseudonym Barbara McCorquodale. Author of more than 230 romantic novels with total sales of over 70 million copies. She is a best-seller in Europe, North America, Turkey, Singapore, India, the Philippines and Sri Lanka.

Her father was killed in Flanders in 1918, and she was one of the 'bright young things' of the post-war period. But as she says, 'Writing is my life', and she began her first novel when she was twenty. She also worked as a journalist for a time, and was encouraged by Lord Beaverbrook.

Barbara Cartland has a great facility for storytelling, and handles historical background with great skill. Her novels are always very moral – all her heroines are virgins; and much of this, of course, is totally at variance with some contemporary attitudes, and with the ideals of Women's Liberation. 'Men', she wrote in *The Times*, 17 January 1977, 'since the beginning of time, have been the hunters, the providers, the protectors, the masters in their own houses.' Explicit notes of sexual morality and male domination are continually struck in her books; and the fact that they remain extremely popular makes her an interesting, and perhaps an embattled, author.

No satisfactory study of her work exists. HENRY CLOUD, *Barbara Cartland, Crusader in Pink* (1979), is the only one to date.

Casey Court. Not quite a comic strip, but a large panel drawn by J. S. Baker which first appeared in *Illustrated Chips* on 24 May 1902. It ran for more than half a century: including a few reprints, there were 2,385 episodes, all describing the adventures of the back street urchins called the Casey Court Kids.

They were the only British comic strip characters who appeared on the variety stage. In the 1906 tour one of the chief characters, Billy Baggs, was played by Charlie Chaplin.

CASPARY, Vera (1899–   ). American writer of novels, film scripts and mysteries. *Laura*, her first and best crime story, was published in 1943 – an unconventional detective investigating a murder falls in love with the victim.

Vera Caspary has provided the basis for a number of mystery and romantic films. *Laura* was filmed in 1944.

CASSELL, John (1817–1865). British temperance reformer who became a publisher with a special interest in popular education. In 1850 he started a penny weekly called the *Working Man's Friend and Family Instructor*, and also a sixpenny monthly periodical, *John Cassell's Library*.

Two undertakings exemplify his firm's preoccupation with providing cheap editions of good books. The first was Cassell's 'Library of English Literature', which began in 1875 and went on for nearly six years. Issued originally in 282 separate parts, it was eventually published in five substantial volumes, and represents the most complete attempt that there has ever been to present both major and minor figures in English Literature, with substantial extracts from their work. The second was the 'National Library', started in 1886, which reprinted a wide range of literary classics in books which were issued at regular intervals, price threepence bound in paper, and sixpence bound in cloth. This series was an important forerunner of Pelican books and other paperback series which have appeared during the twentieth century. In their own day the titles of Cassell's 'National Library' were imitated by other firms (see *Cheap reprints of literary classics*).

SIMON NOWELL-SMITH, *The House of Cassell 1848–1958* (1958). This is extremely good on John Cassell and on the publishing activities of the firm.

V. E. NEUBURG, *Popular Literature* (1977).

Catchpenny prints. Popular illustrated prints which were being widely circulated in Europe very soon after the establishment of the printing press. They are sometimes known as broadsides (qv), but the distinction between the two is hard to define with any precision, particularly as the earliest use of the term 'broadside' was 1575, while the 'catchpenny print' dates from 1759. It is therefore – like the term 'chapbook' (qv) – a term applied by posterity to a literary phenomenon from an earlier period.

The literature on the subject is, as one might expect, sparse. *Catchpenny Prints. 163 Popular Engravings from the Eighteenth Century* (1970) contains a 'Publisher's Note' by way of brief introduction, but it is unsigned. There is also THOMAS GRETTON, *Murders and Moralities. English Catchpenny Prints 1800–1860* (1980).
In 1976 the Rijksmuseum in Amsterdam mounted a major exhibition of such material. The catalogue, *Centsprenten / Catchpennyprints*

(1976), has many illustrations, some in colour, and an excellent introduction in Dutch and in English by C. F. VAN VEEN. A marvellous selection of examples from c. 1450 to 1825 is to be found in DAVID KUNZLE, *The Early History of the Comic Strip* (1973).

CATNACH, James. (1791–1841). British printer and publisher, born in Alnwick, Northumberland. His father was a printer who had been associated with William Davison the Alnwick printer and Thomas Bewick, famous wood engraver. The family moved to London, where the older Catnach died after various ups and downs in business, leaving his son little more than a press and a small supply of type. With this equipment he set up his own business at 2 Monmouth Court, Seven Dials in 1813.

He demonstrated both his vision and his enterprise in two directions simultaneously. At a time when the chapbook had lost favour with adult readers, he saw its potential as children's literature and produced a considerable range of extremely attractive illustrated books for young readers, sometimes priced as low as one farthing each. These were sold in large numbers. Their subject matter was traditional, and these little books provided a refreshing antidote to the heavy-handed piety which characterized so many early children's books.

His other success – the one with which his name is chiefly associated – was with street ballads. They ranged in subject from gruesome murders to romantic songs, and sold quite literally in their millions. One of his most successful ventures was the *Confession and Execution of William Corder, Murderer of Maria Marten*. Catnach's sheets were printed on very thin paper, and were usually illustrated with woodcuts.

Although there were other producers of street literature in London and the provinces, Catnach's sheer output made him the most prominent. At a time when newspapers were highly priced, he provided something of a service, even if only with the more sensational items of news. As a printer and publisher of juvenile literature he has been greatly overlooked.

He retired from business in 1838, but the firm he had founded continued under a variety of names until 1883.

CHARLES HINDLEY, *The Life and Times of James Catnach* (1878 – a facsimile reprint is available).
P. C. G. ISAAC, *William Davison of Alnwick. Pharmacist and Printer. 1781–1858* (1968).
V. E. NEUBURG, *Chapbook Bibliography* (2nd Edition, 1972).

Catnach Press, The. Founded by James Catnach (qv) in 1813. Ballad sheets of all kinds, and children's books, were put out by the firm.

When the founder retired in 1838 the business was taken over by his sister, Mrs Ryle, and she was assisted by James Paul, who had risen from being Catnach's apprentice to the position of manager. He left the business in 1845, and several years later it was bought by W. S. Fortey, who carried it on until 1883. Fortey died in 1901, and his stock was sold as a lot at Sotheby's in 1906. It is now on permanent loan to the Printing Library of the St Bride Foundation in London.

See also *James Catnach*, *Seven Dials*, *Street Literature*.

CHARLES HINDLEY, *The Catnach Press* (1869), and *The History of the Catnach Press* (1887).

CHAMBERS, William and Robert (1800–1883, 1802–1871). British publishers. Edinburgh brothers who made a determined and successful attempt to reach a mass public with 'improving' publications. Their *Chambers's Edinburgh Journal* was first published on 4 February 1832, price three halfpence, and the circulation was soon 80,000 copies per issue. They published numerous cheap, serious books; and the firm they founded is still in existence.

Two autobiographical studies are useful: W. CHAMBERS, *Story of a Long and Busy Life* (1882); and W. CHAMBERS, *Memoir of Robert Chambers with Autobiographic Reminiscences of William Chambers* (6th Edition, 1872).

HENRY CURWEN, *A History of Booksellers*, ND (*c.* 1875).

F. A. MUMBY, *Publishing and Bookselling* (New and Revised Edition, 1949).

V. E. NEUBURG, *Popular Literature* (1977).

CHANDLER, Raymond (1888–1959). American writer. After service in World War One and a variety of jobs, Chandler sold his first detective story to a pulp magazine in 1933. He went on to write 20 novelettes for *Black Mask* (qv) and similar publications, and 12 of these were reprinted in *The Simple Art of Murder* (1950) long after he had become famous with the publication of his first novel, *The Big Sleep*, in 1939. The remaining eight novelettes were 'cannibalized' to form parts of later novels.

Chandler's most famous creation, Philip Marlowe (qv), developed in these novelettes. Sometimes he was anonymous: at others he was called Carmody, Dalmas, Malvern or Mallory. In the later ones he became Philip Marlowe, and as such featured in seven novels.

DOROTHY GARDNER and KATHERINE SORLEY WALKER, *Raymond Chandler Speaking* (1962).
FRANK MACSHANE, *The Life of Raymond Chandler* (1976).
J. SPEIR, *Raymond Chandler* (1981).

Chapbook printing (Great Britain). The printing of chapbooks was originally centred upon the capital, London, where a number of printers were engaged in turning them out from the seventeenth century and throughout the following one. During this period the trade was located mainly in the following areas: London Bridge, Bow Churchyard, Little Britain, Pye Corner. Few, if any, printers dealt exclusively with chapbooks. For nearly all of them these ephemeral publications represented a profitable sideline which could be easily produced and sold direct from the 'printing-office' to the chapmen (qv) who called there to purchase, at wholesale terms, a stock of titles which they offered to the public.

These are the most important London chapbook printers:

Ballard, Samuel	Early eighteenth century
Bates, Charles	c. 1700–c. 1720
Sara	Widow, c. 1720
E.	Son?
Blare, Josiah	d. 1706
Elizabeth	Widow?
Brooksby, Philip	d. 1696
Elizabeth	Widow, d. 1703
Conyers, George	c. 1697–c. 1709
Crowder, Samuel	c. 1759–c. 1770
Dicey, William	See Dicey, William
Cluer	
Thomas	
Hodges, James	c. 1732–c. 1758
How, Larkin	c. 1780
Marshall, Joseph	c. 1679–c. 1725
William	
John	?
Richard	c. 1764

(Many chapbooks were issued by one Marshall or another. In 1764 Richard Marshall was in partnership with Cluer Dicey, and was later named as a friend in Cluer Dicey's will.)

Midwinter, Edward	c. 1710–c. 1732
Norris, Thomas	c. 1695–1732
Onley, William	c. 1697–c. 1709
Sabine, T.	Late eighteenth century?
Sawbridge, George	c 1692–c. 1712
Hannah	Widow?
Woodgate, Henry	c. 1760

Provincial Imprints.
One of the most important cultural developments of the eighteenth century was the establishment of printing presses in a number of provincial towns and cities. The following is a chronological list of places where chapbooks are known to have been produced. Important centres of production are marked*: *Newcastle-upon-Tyne, *York, Birmingham, Northampton (see *Dicey, William*), Sheffield, Worcester, Tewkesbury, Leicester, Banbury, Nottingham, Carlisle, Coventry, Manchester, Durham, Whitehaven, Bath, Stockton.

Scottish Chapbook Printers
In Scotland chapbooks seem to have lingered longer as adult reading matter than they did in England. This, at least, is the inescapable conclusion to be drawn from a survey of chapbook printers there, some of whom were producing chapbooks as late as the second half of the nineteenth century – though it seems probable that these productions would have been intended for the juvenile market.

The following is a list of towns where chapbooks were printed. Those marked * apply to the eighteenth century: Aberdeen, Airdrie, Ayr, Banff, Beith, Crieff, Dalkeith, *Dumfries, *Dunbar, Dunfermline, *Edinburgh (with Glasgow, the largest centre. The earliest chapbooks were printed here by A. Anderson, c. 1671), Elgin, *Falkirk, Glasgow (with Edinburgh, the largest centre. The earliest printer of chapbooks here was R. Sanders, 1668–1726), Greenock, *Hawick, Kelso, *Kilmarnock,

Kirkcudbright, Kirkintilloch, Leith, Montrose, Newton Stewart, Paisley, Peterhead, Perth, Pittenweem, *Stirling, Wigtown. Many Scottish chapbooks do not show a place of origin, and are described as 'Entered according to order', 'Printed for the flying Stationers', 'Printed for the booksellers' or 'Printed in this present year'. J. Chalmers and Company (no place of business given) issued chapbooks in 1777, 1785, 1803, 1810.

For further details of English chapbook printing, see the present writer, *Chapbooks* (2nd Edition, 1972), and *Popular Education in Eighteenth-Century England* (1971). For Scottish chapbooks, see ALISTAIR R. THOMPSON, 'Chapbook Printers', printed in *The Bibliotheck. A Scottish Journal of Bibliography and Allied Topics*, vol. 6, 1972, no. 3.

Chapbook printing (USA).

Although chapbooks never achieved in America the enormous popularity that they enjoyed in England and Scotland, they were widely read between about 1725 and about 1825. Large numbers were imported from England. Andrew Stewart, who printed chapbooks in Philadelphia between 1763 and 1765, almost certainly imported some, and newspaper advertisements indicate that other firms of printers and booksellers did the same. In the *Patriot and Patrol* dated 18 August 1818 William Williams, printer of Utica, New York, advertised for the wholesale and retail trades '8,000 Chap Books, 60 kinds.'

Apart from large-scale importation of chapbooks, many were printed in Boston, Philadelphia and New York, and printers were to an increasing extent setting up their presses in smaller towns as well. For the most part American chapbooks were identical with their English counterparts; but one characteristically American chapbook would deal with the frontier, and this usually took the form of a horrifying 'Indian Captivity' story. There were many of these, and they enjoyed a wide circulation.

The main chapbook printers were:

Boston

Fowle and Draper	*c.* 1755–*c.* 1760
Barclay, Andrew	*c.* 1767
Fleet, T. and J.	*c.* 1770
Coverly, Nathaniel	1770

(Coverly moved on to other towns where he set up as a printer. In 1795 his son, also Nathaniel, was taken into partnership. After founding several newspapers in different places, father and son were back in Boston in 1805 and published from several addresses. Some time between 1814 and 1818 Coverly senior went out of business, and his son died in about 1823. His widow, Eunice, succeeded to the business in 1824. Nothing further seems to be known about the Coverlys).

Russell, Ezekiel	*c.* 1786
White, J.	*c.* 1795
Philadelphia	
Steuart, Andrew	*c.* 1763–*c.* 1765
Miller, Henry	*c.* 1767
Walters and Norman	*c.* 1779
Spotswood, W.	*c.* 1786
Green, Henry	*c.* 1790
Lawrence, Daniel	*c.* 1792

Bailey, Francis	*c.* 1793
Wrigley and Berryman	*c.* 1794
Johnson, B. and J.	*c.* 1800
New York	
Tiebout	*c.* 1796
Mott, Jacob S.	*c.* 1798
Totten, John C.	*c.* 1814
Borradaile, W.	*c.* 1823
Smith and Carpenter	*c.* 1838

For a general survey of chapbook printing in America see the present writer, *Chapbooks* (2nd Edition, 1972). There are detailed lists of printers, and surviving chapbooks are described, in the *Catalogue of English and American Chapbooks and Broadside Ballads in Harvard College Library*, Library of Harvard University Bibliographical Contributions no. 56, Cambridge, Massachusetts, 1905 (Reprint Detroit, 1968). Equally important is HARRY B. WEISS, *A Catalogue of the Chapbooks in the New York Public Library* (New York Public Library, 1936). The same author has also written *American Chapbooks* (100 copies, privately printed, Trenton, New Jersey, 1938). The best historical account of early American printing is LAWRENCE C. WROTH, *The Colonial Printer* (1964) (1931; Revised and enlarged edition 1938). A much older book, ISAIAH THOMAS, *The History of Printing in America* (1810) was reprinted by Weathervane Books (New York, 1970).

Chapbooks. Chapbooks – or 'penny histories', as contemporaries called them – formed the most important element in the reading matter available to the poor in eighteenth-century England. These paper-covered books, approximately $3\frac{1}{2} \times 6$in, consisting usually of twenty-four pages including woodcut illustrations, had begun to replace ballads (qv) in the public's favour in the last decades of the seventeenth century, when a number of printers/publishers in London began to issue them in considerable quantities. They remained popular amongst the adult poor until the turn of the eighteenth century; and during the nineteenth century chapbooks continued to flourish, but by then as part of a wider literature for children.

Eighteenth-century chapbooks intended for an adult market consisted almost entirely of the traditional lore of the English and European peasantry stretching back to a distant past. There were hero tales, ballads, folklore, tall stories, recipes, prophecies, weather lore, riddles. There were also, it is true, chapbook versions of popular novels like *Moll Flanders*, *Robinson Crusoe* and, of course, *The Pilgrim's Progress*, but in their severely truncated form they bore little relationship to the originals from which they were quite illegally derived. There was no reflection of any political awareness in chapbooks, despite the fact that royalty in the form of Queen Elizabeth and Charles I ('the Royal Martyr') was occasionally the subject. For the most part, then, penny histories preserved a great deal of traditional fiction (Guy of Warwick, for example, or Tom Thumb) and other material which would probably not otherwise have survived in any recognizable form.

The importance of the eighteenth-century chapbook is that it provided the means by which unlettered men and women were able to make the leap into literacy, and thus cope with the printed word as it began to be used in other ways. Basic educational facilities for the poor were not unknown, and the charity school movement of the eighteenth century enabled many poor children at least to modify their ignorance. Once they had learned their letters, chapbooks were the most attractive and widely disseminated secular popular literature available to them – the only inexpensive alternatives being political street ballads and sterile religious tracts. Thus the eighteenth-century chapbook became a crucial factor in the making of a working-class reading public.

All this presupposes a well organised book trade and an efficient system of distribution. So far as the trade is concerned, an increasingly large number of printers/publishers became involved in producing chapbooks throughout the eighteenth century. London was the major centre of printing and dominated the book trade, but there were more and more printers at work in provincial towns as the century went on, and for many of them the production of chapbooks was a profitable sideline. The growth of provincial printing in this century is an important cultural phenomenon, with implications for popular culture in its widest sense.

The eighteenth century was also notable for the fact that the first major entrepreneur in popular literature was in business early in the period. This was William Dicey (qv), who had connections with London and Northampton. The firm which he founded published vast numbers of chapbooks during the eighty or so years of its existence.

Evidence for the output of eighteenth-century chapbook printers/publishers comes mainly from their own printed wares. So far as distribution is concerned the evidence is much less straightforward, but the outlines are fairly clear. In the absence of shops in out-of-the-way villages, and with the isolation of some farms and small communities and the consequent difficulties for many people of 'going shopping', the man with something to sell went to his customers in rural districts, and even 'cried his wares' in town and city. The pedlar, hawker or chapman, as he was variously called, was an important and well-known figure in the eighteenth-century economy, providing an essential link between the producers of many goods and the customer. On foot, sometimes with a pack animal, more rarely with a cart, he would visit villages, fairs, outlying farms and isolated communities with a wide selection of small goods which people could not provide for themselves. Part of his stock in trade consisted of chapbooks which had been purchased wholesale from the printer/publisher. This travelling fraternity had its own circuits, and

FAIRY STORIES.

Containing, ·

I. The Blue Beard and Florina.

III. The King of the Peacocks, and Rosetta.

Whereunto is added,

An excellent New S O N G, entitled,

The F A I R I E S Dance.

Printed and Sold in Aldermary Church-Yard, Bow Lane, London.

8 An eighteenth century chapbook title page

there were guide books which provided detailed information about expeditious movement from one district to another, taking in important fairs and festivals on the way. A general picture emerges, but individual histories are hard to trace because itinerant merchants were not the kind of people who left behind them records of their journeys or their transactions.

In the USA chapbooks never enjoyed the same popularity as they did in England and Scotland. Initially they were imported from London, but from quite early in the Colonial period there were printers at work in several states. The most distinctive American contribution to the contents of chapbooks was the 'Indian captivity' tale, in which a prisoner of the Indians would be brought up as one of the tribe, to be discovered in a variety of circumstances many years later. The distribution of chapbooks was exactly the same in the US as it was in the mother country, except for the fact that pedlars had very much greater distances to cover.

V. E. NEUBURG, *Chapbook Bibliography* (2nd Edition, 1972).
JOHN ASHTON, *Chap-books of the Eighteenth Century* (1882, and recent facsimile reprints).
There are substantial chapbook collections in The British Library, The Bodleian Library, The Houghton Library, Harvard, and elsewhere. There are two recent studies, both outstanding. One, in German, is R. SCHOWERLING, *Chapbooks* (1980); the other is M. SPUFFORD, *Small Books and Pleasant Histories* (1981).

See *Chapbook printing (Great Britain; Chapbook printing (USA)*.

Chapmen. See also *Yankee peddlers*. Itinerant merchants, also known as pedlars, hawkers, and in some cases as 'Scotch hawkers'. The wandering seller of goods had been a familiar figure on the roads of the British Isles from the Middle Ages, and had been the object of more or less repressive legislation which was designed to control vagabonds. A statute of Queen Elizabeth I lumped together 'juglers, pedlars, tunkers and petye chapmen' as undesirables. Nevertheless, at a period when there were few shops outside towns, the chapman fulfilled a crucial role as a travelling shopkeeper, providing a selection of wares like pins, needles, ribbon and thread which small isolated communities could not manufacture for themselves, or otherwise easily obtain.

From at least the seventeenth century, part of the chapman's stock in trade included printed matter – initially broadsides (qv), and in the eighteenth century, chapbooks. There were apparently some chapmen who specialized in printed matter, and they were often known as 'flying' or 'running stationers'. The importance of itinerant vendors in the distribution of the printed word, to say nothing of the other wares they sold, can hardly be overestimated. They provided an essential link in the economy of the inland trade of pre-industrial times;

and indeed, street sellers, their lineal descendants, are still to be found.

Literature on chapmen is fairly sparse. There are some good illustrations in SIGFRED TAUBERT, *Bibliopola* (2 vols., 1966). See also K. F. BEALL, *Cries and Itinerant Traders, a Bibliography*, (1975). In MASSIN, *Händlerrufe aus Europäischen Städten* (1978, original French edition *Les Cris de la Ville*, 1978) the illustrations speak for themselves. Other useful items include:

FELIX FOLIO, *The Hawkers and Street Dealers of the North of England* (2nd Edition, ?1860).

HENRY MAYHEW, *London Labour and the London Poor* (4 vols., 1851–64). Excellent on street sellers, including those who sold ballads.

Pedlar autobiographies are:

The Life, Adventures and Experiences of David Love (1825).

WILLIAM GREEN, *The Life and Adventures of a Cheap Jack* (New Edition, 1881).

J. STRATHESK (ed.), *Hawkie; the Autobiography of a Gangrel* (1888).

Charlie Chan. Chinese detective created by Earl Derr Biggers (qv). Chan was a Detective Sergeant, and then Inspector, of the Honolulu Police. The first book about him was *The House without a Key* (1925). This was followed by *The Chinese Parrot* (1926); *Behind that Curtain* (1928); *The Black Camel* (1929); and *Charlie Chan Carries On* (1930). The final Chan book was *Keeper of the Keys*, published in 1932, and this was the only Chan novel which was not filmed. In 1947 Dennis Lynds (pseudonym of Michael Collins, American mystery writer, 1924–) wrote an original paperback, *Charlie Chan Returns*.

Chan was an unusual detective – a student of Chinese philosophy, given to quoting aphorisms, and always affable. Early films featuring the detective were not very successful, but in 1931 Fox produced a closely adapted version of *Charlie Chan Carries On*, with Warner Oland in the title part, and this was so successful that he played the part in 15 subsequent films. After Oland's death in 1938 Chan films continued to be produced, and there were radio and television series.

CHARTERIS, Leslie (1907–). American writer, creator of one of the most popular detectives, Simon Templar, better known as 'The Saint' (qv).

Charteris was born in Singapore, son of a Chinese father and an English mother, and his original name was Leslie Charles Bowyer Yin. He received a varied education, including a year at Cambridge University during which he wrote his first novel, *X Esquire*, which was published in 1927. By that time he had left Cambridge and had several jobs; but *Meet the Tiger*, featuring Simon Templar, followed in 1928, and *The Bandit* and *Daredevil* (non-Saint novels) in 1929.

In 1932 Charteris moved to the USA, and in 1946 he became a naturalized citizen. He wrote a large number of Saint books which were endlessly reprinted, put into paperback and sold to foreign publishers.

For a time he worked as a scriptwriter for Paramount in Hollywood, where several Saint films were made. His *Lady on a Train* (1945) was another non-Saint novel.

CHASE, James Hadley (1906–). Pseudonym of René Raymond, British writer born in London. His first novel, *No Orchids for Miss Blandish*, was written while he was working for a book wholesale firm. When published in 1939 it became an instant success, selling one million copies within five years. It features David Fenner, newspaper reporter turned detective, who becomes involved in the case of a kidnapped heiress who has fallen into the hands of brutal gangsters. The blend of sex and violence with an American background proved irresistible to readers, and Chase went on to write seventy-eight more books, nearly all of them set in the USA. He has in fact visited only Florida and New Orleans, and he uses maps and a slang dictionary to provide an authentic background.

Curiously, Dave Fenner appears in only one other book, *Twelve Chinks and a Woman* (1940). Other characters created by Chase are Vic Malloy, a Californian private detective who features in *You're Lonely When You're Dead* (1949) and *Figure it Out for Yourself* (1950); and Mark Girland, a former CIA agent, who is in *This is for Real* (1965) and *You Have Yourself a Deal* (1966). Chase wrote one volume of short stories, *Get a Load of This* (1951); and he also wrote

under the names of Raymond Marshall, James L. Docherty and Ambrose Grant.

There have been film versions of *No Orchids for Miss Blandish* and other Chase novels.

GEORGE ORWELL, 'Raffles & Miss Blandish', published in *Critical Essays* (1946).

Cheap Repository Tracts. See *More, Hannah.*

Cheap reprints of literary classics. The history of this subject has never, so far as I know, been written. The search for origins takes us back to the Aldine Virgil of 1501, but in reality cheap editions of proven books designed for a popular market are a feature of the nineteenth and twentieth centuries, clearly connected with developments in education and the growth of a mass readership both in Britain and the USA.

William Milner (qv), a Yorkshireman, was the first publisher I have discovered who issued reprints of standard works of literature on a large scale. Between 1837 and 1839 an edition of Robert Burns's poetry sold about 30,000 copies. Other poets issued by Milner included Byron, Milton, Pope, Bloomfield and Longfellow. At a shilling or a little less they were, perhaps, not cheap – certainly not as cheap as reprints were to become later in the century. In 1875 Cassell's Library of English Literature was commenced. It came out originally in parts, and eventually ran to five solid volumes,

Penny Popular Novels. 50

(Edited by W. T. STEAD.)

1. CLEG KELLY.

By S. R. CROCKETT.

2. ROME.

By EMILE ZOLA.

3. NEWS FROM NOWHERE.

By WILLIAM MORRIS.

REVIEWED BY W. T. STEAD.

THE MASTERPIECE LIBRARY,
"REVIEW OF REVIEWS" OFFICE, LONDON.

9 Three novels for one penny!

illustrated throughout. The scope remains impressive after more than one hundred years. The Editor was Henry Morley, Emeritus Professor of English Literature at University College, London; and he was responsible in this undertaking for the most successful popularization of English literature for the mass market ever embarked upon before the days of cinema, radio and television. The same editor was also responsible for Morley's Universal Library, a series which covered world literature in 63 volumes costing 1/- or 1/6d. each. Very much cheaper was Cassell's National Library, founded in 1886. The 16mo weekly issues cost 3d. in paper and 6d. in cloth; and this enterprise was so successful that Routledge began a World Library with weekly volumes at the same price. Finally, Ward & Lock brought out a similar New Popular Library of Literary Treasures.

Prices were kept low for several reasons: (i) reprinting had become highly competitive; (ii) print runs were long; (iii) advertisements were carried in each volume; and (iv) no royalties had to be paid. Cheap classics were, however, to become even cheaper. Towards the end of the nineteenth century Cassell issued a Penny Shakespeare, each number, with a coloured cover, containing a complete play printed in double column. At the turn of the nineteenth and twentieth centuries The Masterpiece Library, edited by W. T. Stead, was issued by the 'Review of Reviews Office, London'. There were two series, Penny Popular Novels and Penny Poets. Novels were abridged. In one volume of 60 pages there were *Cleg Kelly* by S. R. Crockett; *Rome* by Emile Zola; *News from Nowhere* by William Morris; and an abridgement of *Jane Eyre* was available in 76 pages. The poetry ran to 48 volumes and covered most of the major figures. At about this time, too, the firm of George Newnes began issuing its own Penny Library of Famous Books. In these cheap series, standards of production were low and the paper bindings flimsy.

The year 1900 saw the beginning of more substantial reprinting. Nelson commenced the New Century Library at 2/- a volume, and in 1905 the series became Nelson's 6d. Classics. World's Classics was started by Grant Richards in 1901. The series was taken over in 1905 by Oxford University Press, and it took on a new paperback form, described by the publishers as 'an elegant mass-market format', in 1980. Collins began their Shilling Series in 1903, and Dent started Everyman's Library in 1905.

There was considerable exporting of all four series in their early decades, notably to the USA; and this probably explains why reprinting of the classics there was long delayed – The Modern Library took off in the 1930s.

Today the reprinting of standard works of literature for the mass market still goes on, although most of the reprints are paperbacks. Many firms are involved, both in Britain and the USA.

Note: The Penguin Classics series,

founded in 1945 with Homer, *The Odyssey*, has done a great deal to make foreign classics available to a wide range of readers. To take an early title at random, Sophocles, *The Theban Plays*, which was published in 1947, had been reprinted 35 times by 1980. Such popularization of the classics is a phenomenon of the second half of the twentieth century – but there was an important, if overlooked, forerunner. Henry Grey, *The Classics for the Million*, presented in 351 pages 'an epitome in English of the principal Greek and Latin authors'. A new edition noted as 'Eighteenth Thousand' was published in 1899, and the publisher, Swan Sonnenschein, was concerned with other serious books. What kind of public did they envisage? Who could have been the purchasers? Such questions underline our present lack of knowledge about the market for cheap serious books at the close of the nineteenth century.

CHEYNEY, (Reginald Evelyn) Peter (Southouse) (1896–1951). British writer. In the course of a varied career before he turned to writing, Cheyney was a lawyer, soldier, private detective and newspaper editor. Leaving the Army after service in the First World War, he began writing songs, poems and short stories under various pseudonyms. His first novel, *This Man is Dangerous*, was published in 1936. From then until his death he produced, on average, two books a year. His best-known stories, which featured detectives Lemmy Caution and Slim Callaghan, were set amongst the violence, sex, gambling and illegal drugs of London's clubland. Three films were based on Cheyney's novels.

CHRISTIE, Agatha (1890–1976). Very prolific British author of mystery novels and short stories. Creator of Hercule Poirot and Miss Jane Marple. Poirot, the Belgian detective who solves his cases through the use of reason, appeared in 43 books, the first of which was *The Mysterious Affair at Styles* (1920) and the last *Curtain* (1975), the novel in which Poirot dies, written in the 1940s. Miss Marple, an elderly spinster, was featured in 16 books, the first being *Murder at the Vicarage* (1930) and the last *Nemesis* (1971).

In addition to featuring these two detectives, Agatha Christie wrote 31 other mysteries. Most of her output consisted of novels, but she also wrote a number of short stories and plays. In some cases the titles of her books differed in Great Britain and the USA. Under the pseudonym Mary-Westmacott she wrote six romantic novels, and in *Come Tell Me How You Live* (1946) she wrote about her archaeological trips to Syria with her second husband.

One of her plays, *The Mousetrap* (1952), based upon the novel *Three Blind Mice* (1948), ran for more than two decades on the English stage. Curiously enough, the same play was a flop in New York. Many of her stories have been turned into films, and her work has been produced on radio and television.

J. FEINMAN, *The Mysterious World of Agatha Christie* (1975).

GWEN ROBYNS, *The Mystery of Agatha Christie* (1978).

R. TOYE. *The Agatha Christie Who's Who* (1980).

CHRISTOPHER, John (1922–). British writer. Pseudonym of Christopher Sam Youd. Several of his early short stories were published in *The Twenty-Second Century* (1954); and his first novel, *The Year of the Comet* (1955) was about future societies run as businesses. His novel *The Death of Grass* (1956) – US title *No Blade of Grass* – established his reputation, and he followed it with *The World in Winter* (1962) – US title *The Long Winter*. He has written several subsequent novels and a number of juvenile stories.

CLARE, John (1793–1864) British poet. Clare was born within a living ballad and chapbook tradition. His father's memory was stored with old ballads, and he used to boast that he could sing or recite over one hundred. Scattered throughout Clare's poetry and prose are many references to popular literature like this one in the poem 'Well, Honest John'

the bookman comes –
The little boy lets home-close nesting go,
And pockets tops and taws, where daisies blow,
To look at the new number just laid down,
With lots of pictures and good stories too,

And Jack the Giant Killer's high renown.

Equally interesting is the description of a contemporary who owns a small library:

John Billings was an inoffensive man he believed everything that he saw in print as true & had a cupboard full of penny books *The King & the Cobbler The Seven Sleepers* accounts of people being buried so many days and then dug up alive of bells in churches ringing in the middle of the night of spirits warning men when they were to die he had never read Thomson or Cowper or Wordsworth. . . .

This extract was taken from 'The Autobiography 1793–1824' published in *The Prose of John Clare*, edited by J. W. and A. Tibble (1951), p. 93. There are other references in the book to reading. So far as the poetry is concerned, the same editors' *John Clare Selected Poems* (1965) is fairly comprehensive. Also useful is E. Robinson and G. Summerfield, *Selected Poems and Prose of John Clare* (1967).

CLARKE, Arthur C. (1917–) British writer. Founder member of the British Science Fiction Association in 1937, and prolific author of science fiction short stories and novels. His abiding interest has been in space flight, and much of his work deals with this theme. He has also written non-fiction.

Among collections of his short stories are: *The Wind from the Sun* (1972); *Of Time and Stars: The Worlds of Arthur C. Clarke* (1972); *The Best of Arthur C. Clarke 1937–1971* (1973).

His best-known novels are probably: *The Sands of Mars* (1951); *Prelude to Space* (1951); *Islands in the Sky* (1952); *Against the Fall of Night* (1953) – later revised and published as *The City and the Stars* (1956); *2001 – A Space Odyssey* (1968); *Imperial Earth* (1975).

Classics in comic form. The presentation of classic works of literature in the form of comic strips began in the USA when the first issue of The Classics Comics, *The Three Musketeers*, was published in November 1941 by the Gilberton Company. The founder of the firm was Albert Lewis Kanter, a self-made man who never went to college and who 'merely wanted to place the original books in a form more accessible to a generation that was then beginning to recoil from the linearity of printed matter into a more immediate, less cerebral medium'. The venture was immediately successful. The first twelve issues contained 64pp and cost 10 cents. Shortage of paper in wartime soon reduced the number of pages to 56, with the price unchanged; and in the face of continuously rising prices the number of pages was eventually reduced to 48. In 1947, with No 35, the name was changed to Classics Illustrated. When *Julius Caesar* appeared, as No. 68 in February 1950, it caused some adverse comment. Kanter seemed undeterred, although with No. 70 he did add the words: 'Now that you have read the CLASSICS ILLUSTRATED edition, don't miss the added enjoyment of reading the original, obtainable at your school or public library.' *Hamlet* was No. 99. Classics Illustrated Junior was started in 1955, a series in which fairy tales were presented in comic form. In 1962 the Classics ceased publication with No. 167, although Nos. 168 and 169 were published six years later.

Kanter was the most important figure in this kind of publishing, but amongst other ventures was an Illustrated Classics Supplement published during the late 1940s and early 1950s by four American newspapers, *Newark Star-Ledger*, *New York Times*, *Chicago Sun* and *Milwaukee Journal*. The Supplement comprised 14 titles including *Silas Marner*, *A Christmas Carol* and *Tom Sawyer*, each in four instalments containing 16 pages.

In Britain D. C. Thomson (qv), the Dundee publishing firm, put out at least one classic, *Robinson Crusoe*, in hardback during the early 1950s; but for the most part classics in comic form available in Britain came from the USA.

Very little has been written on the subject. The basic article, 'The Classics: the Forgotten Comic', is tucked away in *Pittsburgh Fan Forum*, bulletin of the Pittsburgh Comix Club, No. 35, February-March 1978. It is indispensable, and I have quoted from it in the foregoing outline. See also 'Classics Illustrated' by LENNY KAYE, in *Classics Collectors Club Newsletter*, April 1972. In Britain two articles appeared in *New Statesman and Nation*: MERVYN JONES, 'Modern

Version', 3 March 1951; and MAR-GARET USBORNE, 'On First Looking into Classics Illustrated'. SHEILA LYND wrote a critical piece, 'Murder Most Foul!', published in the *Daily Worker*, 8 October 1951; and in the *Times Educational Supplement*, 21 April 1955, 'The Classics as Comics' by an anonymous contributor provoked a longish letter from R. H. SIDE two weeks later.

Also: 'Gilberton Publishing Company', in H. H. CRAWFORD, *Crawford's Encyclopedia of Comic Books* (New York 1978), pp. 205–230.

Clerihew. See *Bentley, E. C.*

Cody, W. F. Better known as **Buffalo Bill.** See *Western novels.*

Colportage. Term used to describe the hawking of religious tracts (qv) and other devotional literature. It came into use in about 1846, and is derived from the French 'colporteur', meaning hawker. Tracts were, of course, widely distributed before this term came into being.

The word is current in Britain today, where the Christian Colportage Association still offers a wide range of reading matter which goes well beyond the notion of a religious tract. Its own publication by F. H. WRINTMORE, *Two Feet for God* (ND ?1973), details its activities. For an earlier period, Rev. R. COOKE, *Colportage: Its History and Relation to Home and Foreign Evangelization*, ed. Mrs W. FISON (Margaret Fison) (1859), is invaluable. C. H. SPURGEON and others, *Booksellers*

and Bookbuyers in Byeways and Highways (1882), provides a view from 'inside', as it were.

See *Religious Tracts, Spurgeon, C. H.*

Comic books. These were initially an American phenomenon. In the USA comic strips were first published in newspapers at the turn of the nineteenth and twentieth centuries, and as early as 1911 a collection of Mutt and Jeff strips was reprinted in book form as a promotional stunt. A more recognizable beginning, however, was the appearance in May 1934 of *Famous Funnies*, containing 64 pages, price 10 cents. It contained reprints in colour of comic strips which had originally appeared in the daily or the Sunday Press, but was in fact the first venture in comic strips publishing independent of newspapers or newspaper sponsorship.

At first it was not financially successful, but by No. 7 it was making a profit. Other publishers were initially reluctant to follow the example of Eastern Color Printing Company in this enterprise; but what seems to have stimulated the market was the production of a comic book which featured an old-established favourite called 'Skippy'. The idea was that a copy should be given away free to every child who bought a tube of Phillips' Dental Magnesia. The print run was half a million copies, and the scheme was wildly successful. This was, incidentally, the first comic book printed in colour to be devoted to one character.

Now other publishers entered the market. In 1935 D-C Comics began *New Fun Comics*, in which they published comic strips which had not previously appeared in newspapers. In the following year King Features Syndicate issued *King Comics*, and United Feature Syndicate launched *Tip Top Comics*. Another innovation by D-C Comics was *Detective Comics* in 1937, the first to feature original short story detective fiction.

1938 saw the beginning of Superman (qv) in *Action Comics* (D-C Comics), and *Jumbo Comics* (Fiction House). A year later Timely Publications introduced *Marvel Comics*, and in 1940 Dell Publishing Company began *Walt Disney Comics*. By this time comic book publishing had become extremely profitable – the public in the USA alone was numbered in millions.

In Britain there was a much slower start. *Famous Funnies* was available during the mid-1930s at some branches of Woolworth's stores. The outbreak of war in 1939 meant the end of 'American comics', as they were called, in Britain; but after the war many of them, some with British imprints, became available in the United Kingdom.

For something like a quarter of a century (*c.* 1940–*c.* 1965) comic books were a dominant and pervasive element in American popular culture, and to a slightly lesser extent in British culture as well. The contrast between the American productions for adults and the British ones designed for young children is, of course, striking. Nevertheless comic book characters like Superman (qv) became part of a twentieth-century Anglo-American mythology.

Attempts were also made, with varying degrees of success, to present the Bible and many classics of literature in comic strips. (See *Comic strip Bible* and *Classics in comic form*).

The sheer volume of comic books makes generalization difficult. They represent a cultural phenomenon of considerable importance, and their influence upon readers, particularly young ones, has been the subject of some speculation. During the 1950s, for instance, the importation into Britain of the so-called 'horror comics' (comic books which specialized in violence) called forth predictable condemnation from a senior prelate and other public figures, Conservative newspapers and left-wing publications. Much of this comment was shrill and uninformed: on the other hand, the Comics Campaign Council (an ad hoc body) did attempt serious analysis in a couple of pamphlets, G. H. Pumphrey, *Comics and Your Children*, and P. M. Pickard (ed.) *Comics An Appraisal*, both undated, *c.* 1955. The most telling criticism was American. In *Seduction of the Innocent* (1953), Fredric Wertham attacked violence and sex in comic books.

The reference material on comic books is slight. HUBERT H. CRAWFORD, *Crawford's Encyclopedia of Comic Books* (1978), is essential; DICK LUPOFF and DON THOMPSON (eds.), *All in Color for a Dime* (1970), presents a sentimental view of the subject; and there is a useful chapter in COULTON WAUGH, *The Comics* (1947).

See also *Comics*.

Comics. Comics have become so much a part of our lives in the last quarter of the twentieth century that any comprehensive definition might appear unnecessary – and would, in any case, be extraordinarily difficult to formulate. Fortunately, in his pioneer study *The Comics* (1947) Coulton Waugh put forward a working definition that has stood the test of time. It is both clear and valid. Summarily put, it says that comics are a form which comprises these elements: a story told in a sequence of pictures; a group of characters who continue from one sequence to the next; dialogue and/or text that is included with the pictures.

The problem of origins is more complex. There is, of course, a need – almost a compulsion – to look for the origins of the comic in a fairly remote past. Forerunners and examples would include the Bayeux Tapestry, Hans Holbein's 'Dance of Death' drawings, and, more recognizably, John Reynolds, *The Triumph of God's Revenge Against the Crying and Execrable Sinne of Murder* (1621–1635), in which a number of murder stories are told, each of them prefaced by a pictorial summary of the ensuing narrative. Equally, ancestors of the comic include William Hogarth, *A Rake's Progress* (1735), and the James Gillray cartoons attacking republican France, and later Napoleon, which were published between 1790 and 1815. The comic magazine *Punch* was started in London in 1841. Other examples could be cited without difficulty, and a chronology of the comic strip and its antecedents could be readily established. The first modern comic, however, is generally held to be 'The Yellow Kid' (qv) created by the American artist Richard Felton Outcault in 1895.

By the early years of the twentieth century the comic was well established. 'Weary Willie and Tired Tim' (qv) had been created in 1896 by Tom Browne; 'Tiger Tim', drawn by J. S. Baker, first appeared in 1904; the first successful daily strip, 'Mr A. Mutt' (later 'Mutt and Jeff') by H. C. 'Bud' Fisher, appeared in the *San Francisco Chronicle* in 1907; in 1913 George McManus originated 'Bringing up Father' (qv), and George Herriman's 'Krazy Kat' started as a regular strip.

With the exception of the first two titles mentioned, all were American; and it was in the USA that the comic strip developed most strikingly, creating a mythology – even a folklore – for a public which, because so many comic strips were syndicated and thus appeared simultaneously in newspapers across the USA, was numbered in millions. The standard of artwork and colour reproduction was generally high, and between the two world wars in Britain the term 'comic' was sharply distinguished from 'American comic'. The reasons for this were not just a matter of higher standards of artistic and technical excellence, but rather that in Britain, Alfred Harmsworth (later Lord Harmsworth of Amalgamated Press), and later D. C. Thomson (qv) – the main firms producing comics – aimed their publications at the juvenile market. Harmsworth, in fact, had started his halfpenny weeklies *Comic Cuts* and *Illustrated Chips* as early as 1890. They were the first of many which were to appear under the imprint of Amalgamated Press (qv).

From the 1930s American comics were increasingly available in Britain. *Famous Funnies*, the first monthly magazine of comics in full colour, was published in May 1934 by Eastern Colour Printing Company. With 64 pages, priced at ten cents, it set a pattern in comic publishing in its own country, and was soon available in Britain. To an increasing extent – films and music had started the process – American popular culture was penetrating the British market. The process was intensified both during and after the second world war, when large numbers of Britons and Americans came into personal contact for the first time.

Among the famous comic strips which appeared originally in the USA were the following:

		Artist/Storyline
1907	Mutt and Jeff (qv)	Bud Fisher
1918	Gasoline Alley (qv)	Frank King
1919	Thimble Theatre (Popeye (qv) made his appearance in this strip in 1929)	E. C. Segar

1923	Felix the Cat (qv)	Pat Sullivan
1924	Little Orphan Annie	Harold Gray
	Wash Tubbs	Roy Crane
	Boots and her Buddies	Edgar Martin
1928	Tim Tyler's Luck	Lyman Young
	Joe Palooka	Ham Fisher
1929	Buck Rogers (qv)	P. Nowlan & R. Calkins
	Tarzan (qv)	Harold Foster
	(By this time the adventure strip was definitely established)	
1930	Mickey Mouse (qv)	Ub Iwerks
1931	Dick Tracy (qv)	Chester Gould
1934	Flash Gordon (qv)	Alex Raymond
	Mandrake the Magician	Lee Falk & Phil Davis
	Li'l Abner (qv)	Al Capp
	Terry and the Pirates (qv)	Milton Caniff
1938	Superman (qv)	Jerome Siegel & Joe Shuster
1939	Batman (qv)	Bob Kane & Bill Finger
1942	The Sad Sack	George Baker
	Barnaby	Crockett Johnson
1950	Peanuts (qv)	Charles Schulz
	Beatle Bailey	Mort Walker
1954	Hi and Lois	Mort Walker & Dik Browne
1964	The Wizard of Id	Johnny Hart & Brant Parker
1970	Broom Hilda	Russell Myers

British comic strip characters were fewer in number. Among the best known were:

1921	Pop (qv)	John Millar Watt
1932	Jane's Journal Later Jane (qv)	Norman Pett
1937	Buck Ryan	Jack Monk
1950	The Gambols (qv)	Barry Appleby
1957	Andy Capp (qv)	Reg Smythe.

The comic strip is one of the most important innovations in twentieth-century communications, and there can be few countries where it is entirely unfamiliar. There are numerous national comic strip characters, and international ones like Mickey Mouse demonstrate an engaging ability to transcend frontiers and speak the language of the country in which they are published. The comic strip is immensely versatile as a genre, and is widely used for amusement, for instruction and for advertising.

One development, however, is fairly recent, and this is the use of comic strip techniques to disseminate radical and Marxist ideas. In 1966 the first version of a Chinese comic book, *The Red Detachment of Women*, was published in Peking. Five years later, in 1971, a Marxist analysis of Walt Disney comic strips, *Para Leer al Pato Donald* by Ariel Dorfman and Armand Mattelart, was published in Chile. An English edition translated and introduced by David Kunzle, *How to Read Donald Duck. Imperialist Ideology in the Disney Comic*, was published in New York in 1975. In the following year a comic book entitled *Marx for Beginners* by 'Ruis' (pseudonym of Eduardo del Rio, *b*. 1934, a Mexican artist) was published in London. Although not his first attempt at popularizing radical ideas, this was Ruis's most important book. It was followed three years later by Paul Rydberg, *The History Book*, which contained 152 pages printed in three colours, and went from 'European Capital-ism to World Imperialism.' The English version – it was originally published in Danish – was by Kirsten Ribeiro, and translations in ten other languages are said to have been published.

This radicalization of the comic strip indicates an important new dimension for this twentieth-century popular art form, and almost certainly for popular literature in general.

The bibliography of the comic strip is considerable, and constantly growing. The best general survey known to me, with an excellent international bibliography, is in German: WOLFGANG J. FUCHS and REINHOLD REITBERGER, *Comics – Handbuch* (Hamburg, 1978). COULTON WAUGH's study of the American strip – the first and in some ways the most illuminating of its kind – has already been referred to. The standard work is PIERRE COUPERIE and others, *A History of the Comic Strip* (1968), translated from a French version which had appeared one year earlier.

There are two major, even indispensable, works of reference: MAURICE HORN (ed.), *The World Encyclopedia of Comics* (1976); and HUBERT H. CRAWFORD, *Crawford's Encyclopedia of Comic Books* (1978).

See also *Comic books*.

Comic strip Bible. Attempts have long been made to produce illustrated Bibles. At the turn of the

10 The original American edition of Picture Stories
from the Bible

eighteenth and nineteenth centuries, for instance, a Picture Bible was available in both English and German; but the production of a comic strip Bible designed for a mass public did not come until the 1950s. In March 1951 an advertisement appeared in the London-published *Radio Times* for *The Bible in Pictures*. Edited by the Rev. Ralph Kirby, it contained 320 pages and over 1,000 pictures. A substantial hardback, it was priced at 8/6d., or 9/6d. for a de luxe edition. 'New! First all-picture version', said the publishers. It is not easy to say whether this in fact pre-dated the better known *Picture Stories from the Bible* in two volumes, of which over three million copies had been sold in the USA before an English edition came out in September 1953; but the age of the comic strip Bible had arrived.

According to the publishers, '*Picture Stories from the Bible* was prepared in the United States by a former professor of Harvard University, the late M. C. Gaines, assisted by an editorial panel of religious leaders and teachers drawn from all denominations.' It was claimed that the work had taken 12 years and that the accuracy of the Bible text had not been sacrificed in any way. 'Many leading churchmen and teachers' encouraged the project in Britain. There was, however, some criticism, and the comic strip Bible was never so popular in Britain as it was in the USA.

Company of Stationers of London, The. Has a complex history. It was started some time during the fourteenth century as a fellowship of craftsmen who supplied the materials for documents and for books written by hand. By 1403 it had become the Guild of Stationers. Soon after the establishment of printing in England (*c.* 1475) the Guild petitioned for a Royal Charter and a virtual monopoly in printing. Such a Charter was granted in 1557. Printing was restricted to members of the Company, whose Master and Wardens were empowered to seek out illegal printers (i.e. those who were not members of the Company) and destroy both their equipment and their publications, and to prosecute them as well.

Books, pamphlets and broadsides printed by members of the Company were, upon payment of a fee, entered in a Register. The early Registers (there is an inexplicable gap between 1571 and 1576) are particularly important for early popular literature (and, indeed, more literary works) because they provide a catalogue of what was actually printed.

In 1873, Professor Edward Arber began transcribing the early Registers. After 20 years, with the aid of several assistants, five quarto volumes covering the period from 1554 to 1640 had been published. The work was continued by G. E. Briscoe, who added three further volumes covering the years between 1640 and 1708.

From these *Transcripts* – themselves a marvellous repository of varied material – Prof. H. E. Rollins (qv) compiled *An Analytical Index* to the *Ballad Entries (1557–1709) in the Registers of the Company of Stationers of London* (1924; reprinted, with a Foreword by Leslie Shepard, 1967). It lists 3081 ballads, and is an invaluable source of knowledge, particularly as the entry in the Register may be the only evidence for the existence of a particular ballad.

The standard history of the Company is C. BLAGDEN, *The Stationers' Company. A History, 1403–1959* (1960).

CONAN DOYLE, Sir Arthur (1859–1930). British creator of Sherlock Holmes (qv), the greatest detective in literature. He also wrote historical romances and a number of short stories.

COOKSON, Catherine. Contemporary British romantic novelist, born on Tyneside. The North of England provides the setting for many of her stories. She has a powerful narrative style, and her work is characterized by human warmth, pathos, comedy and tragedy.

Mary Ann, a warm-hearted heroine, appears in many of her books. *Katie Mulholland* (1967) was a best-seller, and *The Mallen Streak* (1973) became a British television series.

COOPER, James Fenimore (1789–1851). Popular American historical novelist who was accorded the distinction of being called 'the American Sir Walter Scott'.

Altogether he wrote 34 books: the earliest, *Precaution* and *The Spy* were published in 1821; the last, *The Ways of the Hour*, came out in 1850, the year before his death. Several of his stories were set in the American West. See also *Western novels and stories*.

CORELLI, Marie (1855–1924). Best-selling British writer whose most famous novel, *The Sorrows of Satan*, was published in 1895 and sold more copies than any previous English novel.

BRIAN MASTERS, *Now Barabbas was a Rotter* (1978).

Count Dracula. The most famous vampire in literature created by Bram Stoker (qv) in the novel *Dracula* (1897). Dracula is a Transylvanian nobleman who appears only between sunset and dawn, spending the rest of his time sleeping in a coffin. Deathless, he ensures his immortality by sucking blood from the throats of living people. He is never seen to eat or drink, and has no reflection in a mirror.

There have been several films of *Dracula*. The best-known starred Bela Lugosi in 1931, and the same actor had achieved fame in 1927 in the title role of a stage version. The Dracula theme is still popular.

RAYMOND T. MCNALLY and RADU FLORESCU, *In Search of Dracula* (New York, 1973; London, 1974). LEONARD WOLF, *The Annotated Dracula* (1975).

Cowboy stories. See *Western novels and stories*.

COXE, George Harmon (1901–). American writer. Worked in a lumber camp and a car factory before going into journalism in California, Florida and New York. From 1927–32 he worked for an advertising agency in Cambridge, Mass. He went on to a very successful career writing mystery stories for pulp magazines, as well as love, sports, adventure and sea stories. He also wrote more than 60 hardback works of fiction, the first of which was published in 1935. During the late 1930s he was a film script writer in Hollywood, and wrote scripts for radio and television.

COZZENS, James Gould (1903–1978). American novelist. In particular his *By Love Possessed* (1957) was a bestseller.

Craig Kennedy. Scientific detective created by Arthur B. Reeve (qv). Kennedy is a professor at Columbia University and a private detective using his specialized knowledge to solve crimes; but far from being merely a gifted theorist, he is also a man of action, often uses a gun and is a master of disguise. He was sometimes referred to as the 'American Sherlock Holmes'.

His adventures were told in 26 books, the earliest *The Silent Bullet* (1912) – short stories, British title *The Black Hand* – and the last *The Stars Scream Murder* (1936). Kennedy's exploits were first filmed in 1915 – *The Exploits of Elaine* starred Pearl White, and the detective did battle with the Clutching Hand who wanted her fortune. There were other Kennedy films, and in 1952 he was featured in a US television series of 26 episodes.

CREASEY, John (1908–1973). Prolific British author of nearly 600 books written under 28 pseudonyms. Before his first book was published in 1930 he had received 743 rejection slips. His best known character was 'The Toff' (qv).

The following is a list of other characters and series, and the pseudonyms under which their adventures were published:

George Gideon	'J. J. Marric'
Patrick Dawlish	'Gordon Ashe'
Mark Kilby	'Robert Caine Frazer'
Liberator Series ⎱ Bruce Murdoch ⎰	'Norman Deane'*
The Baron Series	'Anthony Morton'
Superintendent Folly	'Jeremy York'*
Dr Emmanuel Cellini	'Michael Halliday' (US pseudonym 'Kyle Hunt')

* Several non-series books were published under this pseudonym.

There were also the Roger West, Dr Palfrey and Department Z series (which featured Gordon Craigie and later merged with Dr Palfrey). Other pseudonyms used by Creasey were 'Ken Ranger', 'William K. Reilly', 'Tex Riley', 'Peter Manton'.

For Creasey's publications see *John Creasey, Master of Mystery* (New York, Harper and Row 1972).

Crime Club, The. Series of crime and detective novels founded by Sir William Collins, the publisher, in May 1930. Many famous British and American writers were published under its imprint.

Crockett, David. Known as Davy Crockett. See *Western novels.*

CROFTS, Freeman Wills (1879–1957). Irish engineer and prolific writer of detective stories. He turned to writing after a severe illness in 1919, and his first book, *The Cask* (1920), was an immediate success. It was translated into several languages, and sold over 100,000 copies within two decades. Thereafter he wrote a mystery novel almost every year until his death. In addition, he wrote some 50 short stories; a play, *Sudden Death* (1932); 30 radio plays for the BBC; a children's mystery story, *Young Robin Brand, Detective* (1947); and a religious work, *The Four Gospels in One Story* (1949). The most famous of Crofts's characters was Inspector French (qv) of Scotland Yard.

CRONIN, A. J. (1896–1981). Best-selling British novelist. He began studying medicine at Glasgow University, served during the Great War as a surgeon sub-lieutenant in the Royal Navy, then returned to Glasgow to complete his studies. After qualification he served for a time as a ship's doctor, went into general practice in South Wales, and in 1926 moved to London to continue his work as a doctor. In 1930 he gave himself a three-month sabbatical in order to write a novel: the result was *Hatter's Castle* (1931). It was an immediate success, and was made first choice by the newly-formed Book Society. This guaranteed it a sale of 15,000 copies; and within a few months it had sold over a million. Three further bestsellers followed: *The Stars Look Down* (1935), *The Citadel* (1937) and *The Keys of the Kingdom* (1941).

A. J. Cronin continued writing until he was in his eightieth year, although later novels were not so successful. In the 1960s, however, his name became known to a new generation with the British television series *Dr Finlay's Casebook*, based upon a collection of short stories written during the 1930s under the title *The Adventures of a Black Bag*. The series proved so popular that Cronin was persuaded to allow other scriptwriters to base further episodes upon the characters which he had created.

For the last 35 years of his life Cronin lived in Montreux, Switzerland. It was here that he died on 9 January 1981.

CROUCH, Humphrey (?–1671). British writer of popular ballads – one of them on Guy of Warwick (qv) – and pamphlets. There were several booksellers and publishers with the name of Crouch in seventeenth-century London, and it is not possible to distinguish between them. Among them was John Crouch (?–1681), a royalist verse writer who was probably Humphrey's brother.

CROWE, Catherine (née Stevens) (1799/1800–1876). British popular novelist, and author of an abridgement of *Uncle Tom's Cabin* for children. Her most famous book, often reprinted, was *The Night Side of Nature: or, Ghosts and Ghost Seers* (1848).

There was also Louisa A. Crow, another English popular novelist whose writing life spanned about 40 years. She died in 1895.

CUMMINS, Maria Susanna (1827–1866). American writer, whose best-known novel, *The Lamplighter* (1854), sold 40,000 copies within eight weeks of publication in Boston, Massachusetts. It went through numerous editions, in the USA and in Great Britain; and it was last reprinted, with a biographical and critical introduction by Donald A. Koch, in New York in 1968. She wrote other books, but this is the one for which she is remembered.

11 An English edition of The Lamplighter

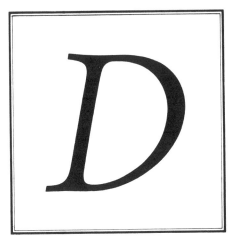

DALY, Carroll John (1889–1958). American author who, in the course of a long writing career, wrote for many pulp magazines (qv). He created Race Williams for *Black Mask* (qv). Williams – the prototype of Mike Hammer (qv) – was tough, and so popular that when he appeared on the cover of *Black Mask* sales increased by 15 per cent. Daly also created Vee Brown, whose adventures were published in a rival magazine.

DANIEL, George (1789–1864). British collector who for most of his working life was a stockbroker, but his leisure time was devoted to the pursuit of literature. In addition to being a book-collector, he was also a miscellaneous writer: his *Merrie England in the Olden Time* (2 vols., 1825) contains a series of studies on old books and customs, and was a pioneer work on popular culture – though he did not use this term.

His library, described in *Catalogue of the Most Valuable and Highly Important Library of the Late George Daniel Esq. of Canonbury* (N.D., 1864), contained many examples – some unique – of fugitive and rare early popular literature. Most important was the collection of 70 early ballads (qv), which Daniel described in *An Elizabethan Garland* (1856, 25 Copies printed for Private Circulation). At his death the ballads were bought for £750 by Henry Huth, who published the texts for members of the Philobiblon Club in 1867. In the same year Joseph Lilly published them, with nine others, in a normal commercial edition, *A Collection of Seventy-Nine Black-Letter Ballads and Broadsides*. This was reprinted in 1870, and has since appeared in an American facsimile edition. The story of Daniel's acquisition of these ballads is briefly told by V. E. Neuburg in *Popular Literature* (1977).

Amongst other items in Daniel's library were garlands (qv) and jestbooks (qv) – one of the latter a very fine copy of *The Life of Long Meg of Westminster* (1635) – see

Long Meg of Westminster. The many treasures in the library were sold to several purchasers at a sale in July 1864, and some of them are indicated in a marked copy of the *Catalogue* in Islington Public Library.

D. C. Thomson and Co. Publishers in Dundee, Scotland. The firm was founded in 1905, when three members of the Thomson family and their wives decided to regularize the publishing interests that they had acquired. They saw that there was money to be made at the lower end of the market, and within a few years their two newspapers, *Courier* and *Argus*, were well established. It was as newspaper publishers that they started out; but in the 1920s they entered the magazine market. By the time they decided to extend their interests the firm was both profitable and forward-looking, they had printing equipment which was not being fully utilized, and clearly there was a growing market for story papers. Amalgamated Press (qv) had been both active and successful in publishing popular fiction from before the outbreak of war in 1914, and were continuing to expand during the 1920s. D. C. Thomson entered the field early in this decade, and have continued to play a prominent part in it ever since. They have published (in addition to newspapers) story magazines for young readers, for teenagers and for adults, fiction series, annuals and comics, all of which were, and indeed still are,

efficiently distributed throughout Britain.

Despite the importance of the firm, and its very considerable achievement in the field of popular literature, hard facts about D. C. Thomson and Co. are difficult to come by. It seems curious that, while comics like *The Dandy* (1937–) and *The Beano* (1938–), and characters like Lord Snooty, Desperate Dan, the Broons, Dennis the Menace, Beryl the Peril, have become virtually national institutions, so little is known about the firm from which they emanated.

The fullest source known to me is GEORGE ROSIE, 'The Private Life of Lord Snooty', an article published in *The Sunday Times Magazine*, 29 July 1973. Also useful is *The D. C. Thomson Bumper Fun Book* (1977), a collection of essays about D. C. Thomson which presents a critical and informed look at both the products and the practices of the firm.

Deadwood Dick. See *Wheeler, Edward L.*

DEEPING, Warwick (1877–1950). British popular novelist, also a doctor of medicine. He wrote some 60 books, from *Love Among the Ruins* (1904) to *Exiles* (1950), and is perhaps chiefly remembered for *Sorrell and Son* (1925).

DEIGHTON, Len (1929–). British author who, after doing a variety of jobs, became a successful author of spy thrillers (qv) featuring a nameless agent who has a dislike for authority. The films made from Deighton's novels give him the name of Harry Palmer, and present him as a kind of hero.

Spy thrillers by Deighton are: *The Ipcress File* (1962), *Horse under Water* (1963), *Funeral in Berlin* (1964), *The Billion Dollar Brain* (1966), *An Expensive Place to Die* (1967), *Spy Story* (1974).

DE LA ROCHE, Mazo (1885–1961). Canadian author of 16 best-selling novels which chronicle several generations of the Whiteoaks family. The first in the series, *Jalna* (1927), carried the name of the family residence.

DELL, Ethel M. (1881–1939). British romantic novelist whose first book, *The Way of an Eagle* (1912), had been reprinted 27 times by 1915. She wrote 37 books in all, the last, *Sown Amongst Thorns*, appearing in the year of her death.

The standard biography is PENELOPE DELL, *Nettie and Sissie* (1977).

DELONEY, Thomas (1543?–1600?). British writer of ballads and popular fiction. His earliest known ballad came out in 1586 and described a disastrous fire in Beccles, Suffolk. Deloney appears to have had something of a reputation among his contemporaries, and in 1596 he had a brush with the law over the contents of 'a certain Ballad, containing a Complaint of great Want and Scarcity of Corn within the Realm.' He wrote a large number of ballads, and three novels which were extremely popular: *The Pleasant Historie of John Winchcomb, in his younger years called Jack of Newbery* (1597?) – the earliest extant edition, the 10th, is dated 1626; *The Gentle Craft* (1597?) – the earliest extant edition is dated 1626, and there is also a second part (1600?) the only extant edition of which is dated 1639; *Thomas of Reading* (1602?) – the earliest extant edition is dated 1623.

The disappearance of so many early editions of these novels, together with their frequent reprinting, point to an immediate popularity when they were published. Deloney is unique amongst Elizabethan minor popular writers in that there is a scholarly edition of his prose and verse.

F. O. MANN, *The Works of Thomas Deloney* (1912).

Dennis the Menace. British comic strip character created by the late David Law. His first appearance was on 17 March 1951 in *The Beano*. Dennis, a practical joker and mischief maker, was very popular, and his creator launched a female counterpart, Beryl the Peril. Other derivations were Minnie the Minx (Leo Baxendale) and Roger the Dodger (Ken Reid).

DERLETH, August (William) (1909–1971). Prolific American author of more than 130 books, numerous short stories, poems, reviews, essays and anthologies. He wrote all kinds of popular fiction and a number of mystery stories featuring Solar Pons (qv). There was also a series about Judge Ephraim Peck, the best known of which was *Death Stalks the Wakely Family* (1934), (American title *Murder Stalks the Wakely Family*), and a series of crime stories for which he used the pseudonym Tally Mason.

In 1940 he was a co-founder with Donald Wandrei of the publishing firm Arkham House, which specialized in horror and supernatural fiction. A subsidiary firm, Mycroft and Moran, published mysteries, most of them dealing with the adventures of Solar Pons.

Desmond Merrion. See *Rhode, John.*

Detective stories. The detective story is of considerable antiquity. Its origins may be reasonably stretched to include *The Apocrypha*, where Daniel's cross examination saves Susanna from the false witness of lecherous elders and establishes the deceitfulness of Bel's priests. Daniel, in fact, solved both the cases submitted to him, and was therefore a remote ancestor of Sherlock Holmes (qv)!

More recognizably, the detective story has its origins in the three stories that Edgar Allan Poe (qv) wrote between 1841 and 1845. Other founding fathers were Wilkie Collins (1824–1889), whose novel *The Moonstone* (1868) introduced the detective Sergeant Cuff: and Charles Dickens, whose *The Mystery of Edwin Drood* remains an unfinished masterpiece. Within two months of the appearance of the first part in 1870, Dickens was dead. His novel of murder had not advanced very far, and whilst others have attempted to complete it, the unfinished work remains a mystery in itself.

In 1887 Sir Arthur Conan Doyle published *A Study in Scarlet*, which introduced to the world the greatest fictional detective of all time, Sherlock Holmes. The story was a phenomenal success, and was followed not only by imitations but also by a growth in popularity and sophistication of the detective story as a genre.

In both Britain and the USA the 1930s were probably the golden age of the conventional detective story in which a specific crime, usually murder, was investigated and solved by the use of reason and deduction. But even before the sun had set on this golden age, things were changing. From the USA a new harshness, toughness and realism began to creep in. In the hands of Raymond Chandler (qv) and Dashiell Hammett (qv) the detective story, in a rather different form, went to new heights. Today, in both countries, the more conventional detective story co-exists with the tougher version. Evidence for this may be observed in any bookshop or bookstore.

What is striking is the emergence of books *about* the detective story. There are many of them, and the following list contains those that I have found most useful:

HOWARD HAYCRAFT, *Murder for Pleasure* (1941). Although an elderly book, this remains the standard history. A more recent general history is J. SYMONS, *Bloody Murder* (1972) – American title *Mortal Consequences* (1973).

ELLERY QUEEN, *Queen's Quorum* (1953). The comments are pertinent, and written by masters of the craft.

CHRIS STEINBRUNNER and OTTO PENZLER (eds.), *Encyclopedia of Mystery and Detection* (1976). Comprehensive and authoritative. The connections between printed versions and radio, television and cinema are well brought out.

OTTO PENZLER, CHRIS STEINBRUNNER (eds.), *The Detectionary* (1971). Reprinted in paperback in 1980, this is a full reference book, rather differently arranged from the preceding one.

DAVID MADDEN (ed.), *Tough Guy Writers of the Thirties* (1968). A useful collection of essays.

MICHELE B. SLUNG (ed.), *Crime on her Mind* (1975). Contains an Introduction and 15 stories about female detectives from the Victorian era to the 1940s.

See also: *Black Mask, Pulp magazines.*

DICEY, William (?–1756). A British printer/publisher, who with his son, Cluer (?–1775), and his grandson, Thomas (1742–?) was a leading producer of chapbooks (qv) and ballads in London and in Northampton. Very little is known about the family. William Dicey was associated with Robert Raikes in the

foundation of a weekly newspaper in St Ives, Huntingdonshire. The two men went into partnership, and in 1720 they established a printing office and a weekly newspaper in Northampton. Having launched the paper, Raikes moved on to Gloucester; and the partnership was dissolved in 1725. The name of Dicey appeared upon every issue of *The Northampton Mercury* up to 2 May 1885.

William Dicey maintained his printing establishment in Northampton and opened another in London. The relationship between the two is uncertain, but it seems that the eldest son, Cluer, ran the London end of the business. This was the period, probably from about 1730 onwards, when the Diceys, father and son, became pre-eminent in the field of popular literature. At one time or another they used over 30 different imprints on their chapbooks alone. Two of their trade catalogues exist: one dated 1754, in the Bodleian Library, is incomplete but contains manuscript additions made by Thomas Percy (qv); a complete one, dated 1764, is in the Library of the University of Glasgow.

So successful were the Diceys that by 1789 Thomas, grandson of the founder, was living on the family estate at Claybrook Hall in Leicestershire. It is also worth recording that when Cluer died in 1775, Hannah More wrote his epitaph. By the time of Cluer's death, however, the emphasis of the firm had changed. Whether or not they had given up printing is uncertain, but there was a firm called Dicey, Benyon & Co., Medicine Warehouse, 10 Bow Churchyard.

The history of this enterprising family remains to be written. In the meantime there is a fairly complete survey of their chapbook printing activities in v. e. neuburg, 'The Diceys and the Chapbook Trade' published in *Transactions of the Bibliographical Society. The Library*, 5th Series, vol. XXIV, no. 3, September 1969.

Dickens imitations. In his own lifetime and beyond, Charles Dickens was, and still is, an extraordinarily popular novelist. There is, however, some evidence to show that in the short run he was outsold by his imitators.

The most plagiarized of his novels was *The Pickwick Papers* (1836–37). The monthly parts started off badly, with only about 400 copies of the first number being sold. In Number 5, Sam Weller was introduced, and he took the reading public by storm. By the 15th number the novel was selling 40,000 copies of each number. As the novel caught on with the reading public who could afford the monthly parts at a shilling a time, so the adventures of Mr Pickwick *et al.* seemed an attractive proposition to writers and publishers at the lower end of the market. Pickwick appeared on the stage at the Adelphi Theatre, London. *The Peregrinations of Pickwick* (October 1836) was a huge success. Other stage versions, nearly all unauthorized, followed.

In about 1837 *Sam Weller's Scrap Sheet* and *Portraits of the Pickwick Characters* appeared. Various songbooks deriving from the novel or stage versions were published: *Lloyd's Pickwickian Songster* (*c.* 1837) (see *Lloyd, E.*); *Mr Pickwick's Collection of Songs* (*c.* 1838); *The Pickwick Songster* (1839). There were also joke books: *Sam Weller's Pickwick Jest Book* (1837); *The Pickwickian Treasury of Wit, or Joe Miller's Jest Book* (1837) (See *Miller, Joe*).

In a year when the popularity of *The Pickwick Papers* was clearly at its height – 1837 – Edward Lloyd published the first number of *The Posthumous Notes of the Pickwick Club*, edited by 'Bos' (this was probably T. P. Prest (qv)). He claimed that this – better known as *The Penny Pickwick* – was selling 50,000 copies a week. G. W. M. Reynolds (qv) wrote *Pickwick Abroad* (1837–38), which sold 12,000 copies a week; and he followed this up with *Pickwick in India* (1840) and *Pickwick Married* (1841), serialized in a temperance magazine called *The Teetotaller*. 'Bos' later produced *Pickwick in America* and *Master Humphries' (sic) Clock* (1840). Reynolds wrote *Master Humphrey's Clock – Master Timothy's Book-Case* (1842); and there were *Nickelas Nickelbery* and *Current American Notes* by 'Buz' (1842). There were also abridgements of *The Old Curiosity Shop* and *Barnaby Rudge*, which were by H. Hewitt and were published during 1841 in 'Parley's Penny Library'. They sold between 50,000 and 70,000 copies a week.

There were many other plagiarisms, imitations and abridgements of Dickens's work. They demonstrate not only the immense popularity of the characters which he created, but also the existence of a mass public which, unable to afford the price for the monthly parts in which his work was issued, was ready and able to pay for penny versions of inferior novels by a range of hack writers whose work derived from Dickens.

The unofficial Dickens industry remains a murky and complex field for investigation. The best account known to me is LOUIS JAMES, *Fiction for the Working Man* (1974), Chapter 4, pp. 51–82. (I am deeply indebted to it for the above details.)

Dick Tracy. American comic strip detective created by Chester Gould. The strip began as a Sunday feature on 4 August 1931, and became a daily item one week later. In the first daily episode Tracy was the impotent witness of a hold-up in the course of which his sweetheart, Tess Trueheart, was kidnapped and her father murdered. As a result, Tracy joined the police force.

Eagle-nosed, square-jawed, Tracy was relentless in his fight against crime. His adversaries included 'The Brow', 'Pruneface', 'Shaky' (who had to kill in order to steady his nerves), 'Shirtsleeves Kelton', 'Ribs Mocco', 'Borrs Arson' and others. Their ultimate fates were as horrible as their misdeeds. Some were shot, some hanged, others were scalded or frozen to death, buried alive or impaled on flagpoles.

In his fight – invariably successful – Tracy was assisted by Chief Brandon, Pat Patton, Sam Catchem and Lizz the policewoman. The strip was realistic, violent and brutal. In this it was the first of its kind, and its influence upon comic strip art has been considerable.

Tracy also appeared on film, radio and television in the USA.

DICKS, John (?–1881). During the 1850s Dicks became one of the largest publishers in London, largely through his association with the bestselling novelist G. W. M. Reynolds (qv). He was in business for over 40 years. In 1892 his 'Standard Plays' series comprised 1,200 titles; and he also published 'Dicks' English Classics', 'Dicks' English Novels' and 'Dicks' English Library of Standard Works'.

The typography of his books, often issued in paper wrappers, left much to be desired, with small print and sometimes three columns to a page; but the books were cheap. Little is known about his life, but his achievement as a publisher was considerable.

'John Dicks', an article in *The Bookseller*, March 1881.

Dick Turpin. Highwayman born in Hempstead, Essex, in 1705, hanged at York in 1739 and buried in the churchyard of St George's, Fishergate Postern, where his gravestone can still be seen.

Turpin was little more than a ruffian who, after his death on the gallows, developed into a popular hero and a legendary figure. A mythical ride to York on his horse Black Bess is described in W. Harrison Ainsworth's novel *Rookwood* (1834). He was the hero of 33 toy theatre plays, and there is at least one nineteenth-century street ballad about him. Later he became the hero of several adventure stories for boys, and in the 1930s he lent his name to a 'Dick Turpin Library' of boys' stories.

He appeared in at least one film, and had something of a vogue on British television in the late 1970s and early 1980s.

CHARLES HARPER, *Half Hours With the Highwaymen* (2 vols., 1908). The chapter on Turpin was reprinted, with additional illustrations, as a pamphlet entitled *Dick Turpin – Highwayman* in 1964 (F. Graham, Newcastle upon Tyne).

Dick Whittington. A poor, ill-treated orphan boy who ultimately made good and became Lord Mayor of London. As he sat on Highgate Hill he was inspired by hearing Bow bells ring out a peal which seemed to say:

Turn again Whittington,
Lord Mayor of London.

The story was told in ballads, chapbooks, puppet plays and pantomimes. In 1605 a licence was granted for the publication of a ballad called 'The vertuous Lyfe and memorable Death of Sir Richard Whittington'. No copy of it is known to survive, but it marked the beginning of Whittington's popularity as a fictional and exemplary character.

In fact the real Sir Richard Whittington (*d.* 1423) was Mayor of London three times, and the story of his life has eight columns devoted to it in DNB. He was never a poor boy, as legend has it; but he did marry Alice Fitzwarren, as popular versions of his career tell us. The latter part of his life, after the death of Alice, was devoted to pious and charitable activities.

The Model Merchants of the Middle Ages, exemplified in the Story of Whittington and his Cat, by the Rev. SAMUEL LYSONS (1860) and *Sir Richard Whittington*, by WALTER BESANT and JAMES RICE (1881), are both useful, if rather uncritical in accepting legend as fact.
Different in scope and strikingly interesting is an article by HARRY B. WEISS, 'American Editions of Sir Richard Whittington and his Cat', which first appeared in *The Bulletin of New York Public Library*, June 1938, and was later reprinted as a 12-page pamphlet with a useful bibliography.
Whittington is also mentioned in W. A. CLOUSTON, *Popular Tales and Fictions* (2 vols., 1887, facsimile reprint 1968).

Dime novels. Paper-bound novels sold, usually at ten cents a time, during the second half of the nineteenth century.

In the 1830s the population of America was approaching 20 million, many of whom were literate; but because of the high price of clothbound books, and because there were few libraries, the majority of readers were denied access to reading matter. Thus there was a potential market for cheap fiction, and this gained tremendous impetus from the introduction of the steam rotary press and subsequent developments in both production and marketing techniques. Several firms began to tap this potential, and amongst story papers dating from this period were: *New York Mercury* (1838) from Southworth and Whitney; *Brother Jonathan* (1839) from Wilson and Company of Boston; *Flag of our Union* (1845) from Ballou; *Waverley Magazine* (1846) from Moses and Dow; *New York Ledger* (1855) from Robert Bonner; *New York Weekly* (1855) from Street and Smith; and *Stars and Stripes* (1859) from Frank Leslie.

Competition amongst publishers of story papers was intense, and firms came and went. One, though, was very successful indeed – the publishing firm Beadle and Adams, founded in 1856 by the brothers Erastus and Irwin Beadle, together with Robert Adams. For several years after its foundation the business teetered on the brink of insolvency, until almost by chance – but tempered by a sense of shrewdness! – they published in 1860 a novel by Ann Sophia Stephens, *Malaeska, the Indian Wife of the White Hunter*. Measuring 4½ inches by 6½ inches, with 128 pages of text in a salmon covered wrapper which bore the legend 'Books for the million! Beadle's dime novels', it sold for ten cents. Such was its success that within a few months 65,000 copies had been sold. The firm never looked back.

As a leading publisher of dime novels, Beadle and Adams made a special contribution to publishing which was not a literary, but rather, an organizational one. The product was a standard one, but it was marketed with consummate skill. For many years the name of this firm was synonymous with dime novels, and at one time or another it employed nearly 200 authors to turn out the stories for which there was an insatiable demand.

In 1863 George Munro, Beadle and Adams's printing foreman, left to found his own firm. It lasted for about 30 years. Robert de Will began publishing dime novels in 1867, and during the following ten years issued 1,118 separate titles. George Munro's brother, Norman, began his own firm in 1870, and Frank Tousey started a similar venture in 1878. The most successful publishing house of all in the field of popular fiction, Street and Smith (qv), started their dime novel series in 1889.

These were the leading firms until the 1890s, when Beadle sold out, Munro's went out of business, and Street and Smith turned dime novels into pulp magazines (qv), absorbing Tousey's firm in the process. The last dime novels of all were probably published by Street and Smith in about 1912. During the 40 or so years which saw the rise and decline of dime novels, millions of titles were produced. Although usually ten cents, prices could be a nickel, and occasionally they were as much as a quarter. Editions were between 60,000 and 70,000 copies, and some novels would go through ten or 12 editions in a year. Authors were paid from $50 to $250 for a complete novel, the precise sum depending upon length and the reputation of the writer.

The Wild West was a favourite theme in dime novels – Buffalo Bill (qv), Daniel Boone, Kit Carson and others were ready-made homespun heroes. Other subjects included the American Revolution, the War of 1812, the Mexican War, the Civil War, pirates, city tales of high life and low life, crime, secret service. . . . The style of the writing was undistinguished. The public knew what it wanted, and clearly found its pleasure in knowing exactly what it would find in the pages of these novels. Literary or artistic innovation was not favoured, and 'the mixture as before' proved an irresistible attraction for something over four decades. Attitudes to women were simple: no sex, nor any suggestion of it; a villain, facing the heroine, might 'gaze into her white, lovely face with fiendish triumph', but that was as far as it went. Blood and bullets were the things that mattered – it was action all the way in these stories. It was not any lack of moral sense in dime novels, but rather the continuous sensationalism and violence that some critics, often the parents of young readers, objected to.

In the dime novel everything was possible. One hero, Rocky Mountain Sam, from a distance of half a mile, shot out of the Red Indian's hand the flint and steel being used to light the torture fire! The best known of all heroes was Buffalo Bill, a name and character created by the writer E. Z. C. Judson (qv) in a novel called *Buffalo Bill, King of the Border Men* (1869). Judson had met and chatted with a little known man named William F. Cody, who afterwards adopted the dress and style of the story's hero.

Pulp magazines (qv), which had almost taken over from the dime novel by 1910, specialized in similar fiction and took the name from the coarse paper upon which they were printed in order to make them eligible for second class postal rates. In its heyday the dime novel had been read all over the US, and in the 1860s Beadle and Adams had a London office called 'Beadle's American Sixpenny Publishing House'.

ALBERT JOHANNSEN, *The House of Beadle and Adams and its Dime and Nickel Novels. The Story of a Vanished Literature* (2 vols., Norman, Oklahoma, 1950). Supplementary vol. (1962).
DARYL JONES, *The Dime Novel Western*, Bowling Green, Ohio, (1978).
RUSSELL B. NYE, *The Unembarrassed Muse*, New York, (1970).

Donald Duck. Cartoon duck created by Walt Disney in 1934, following the success of Mickey Mouse (qv) who had made his first appearance in 1928.

MARCIA BLITZ, *Donald Duck*, 1979.

A. DORFMAN and A. MATTELART, *How to Read Donald Duck. Imperialist Ideology in the Disney Comic* (1975). As the title suggests, this is an attack upon Walt Disney's characters and their world.

Dracula. See *Count Dracula.*

(Dr) Fu Manchu. Chinese master criminal created by Sax Rohmer (qv). Following the Boxer Rebellion in China at the turn of the century there were fears that a 'yellow peril' might engulf Western civilization; and thus the oriental villain was an immediate success. Ruthless, fiendish, brilliant (he had degrees from three European universities), possessor of intimate and extensive knowledge of the occult and several esoteric sciences, Fu Manchu – believed to be a Chinese noble – was indeed the Devil Doctor of sensational fiction. His chief adversary was Sir Denis Nayland Smith, vaguely connected with Scotland Yard and knighted for his efforts to thwart the schemes of Fu Manchu. He had an assistant, Dr Petrie.

There are 16 Fu Manchu books, 14 of them novels. The first was *The Mystery of Dr Fu Manchu* (1913) – US title *The Insidious Dr Fu-Manchu*; and *Emperor Fu Manchu* (1959) appeared during the year in which his creator died. After Rohmer's death two volumes of his short stories were published, *The Secret of Holm Peel and Other Strange Stories* (1970) – this contains 'The Eyes of Fu Manchu' – and *The Wrath of Fu Manchu* (1973).

Many films were made, the earliest in 1923 starring Henry Agar Lyons in a series of British short films. These were followed by a full-length *The Mysterious Dr Fu Manchu*, Paramount 1929, which starred Warner Oland and was based upon the first of the novels. Of subsequent film versions *The Castle of Fu Manchu*, made in Britain in 1972, was the last.

During the 1930s there were radio series in Britain and in the USA; and in the early 1950s American television ran a series of 13 half-hour Fu Manchu episodes with Glen Gordon in the title role.

Dr Gideon Fell. See *Carr, John Dickson.*

Dr Lancelot Priestley. See *Rhode, John.*

Dr Thorndyke. Created by R. Austin Freeman (qv). With his highly technical and specialized methods of solving crimes, Dr John Evelyn Thorndyke is the most famous of medico-legal detectives. His adventures are chronicled by his assistant, Christopher Jervis, and he has a butler-cum-jack-of-all-trades named Nathaniel Polton.

Dr Thorndyke's exploits, in novels and in short stories, were published in 27 books. The first of these was *The Red Thumb Mark* (1907) and the last *The Jacob Street Mystery* (1942) – US title *The Unconscious Witness.*

There is also an anthology, *The Best Dr Thorndyke Stories* (1973), which contains the first book publication of *31 New Inn*, a story which had first appeared in an expanded version in 1912 as *The Mystery of 31 New Inn.*

Dr Watson, (John H.). Created by Sir Arthur Conan Doyle. Friend of Sherlock Holmes (qv) and narrator of the detective's adventures. Born in 1852, he studied medicine in London and later saw active service with the 5th Northumberland Fusiliers in India. He was wounded at the Battle of Maiwand, returned to England, left the Army and shared rooms with the detective.

On the 31 January 1941 Rex Stout addressed the New York Chapter of the 'Baker Street Irregulars', one of the many clubs and societies founded to honour and perpetuate the memory of the great detective. His talk was entitled 'Watson was a woman', and was supported by a good deal of textual 'evidence'. Faithful Sherlockians, however, are outraged by the suggestion.

Dr Who. Created by Terry Nation, this time traveller first appeared on British television in the mid-1960s, often in conflict with a group of curious beings called Daleks. Several books chronicling the Dr's adventures were published after his television popularity had been established.

Drury Lane. See *Ellery Queen.*

DUGDALE, William (1800–1868). Leading publisher of erotica in nineteenth-century London. Born in Stockport, he was implicated in the Cato Street Conspiracy in 1820. He published under his own name and those of a number of aliases – Turner, Smith, Young and Brown – from several addresses in Holywell Street, Wych Street and Russell Court, Drury Lane. The nature of his business compelled him to change his address fairly frequently, but despite this precaution he had several brushes with the law, and was often imprisoned. He was, indeed, serving a sentence in the House of Correction when he died.

There is an account of Dugdale and a shop that he occupied in Holywell Street in Michael Sadleir's novel *Forlorn Sunset* (1947), pp. 410–422. Dugdale appears as the publisher, J. Bernstein, for whom Paul Gladwin, a leading character in the story, works as a hack writer.

He had a younger brother, John, who was engaged in the same kind of publishing. John worked from addresses in Holywell Street and Rupert Court, using the pseudonyms W. Johns and J. Turner.

No bibliography of Dugdale publications exists, though many of them are recorded in 'Pisanus Fraxi', *Index Librorum Prohibitorum* (1877); *Centuria Librorium Absconditorum* (1879); and *Catena Librorum Tacendorum* (1885). Pisanus Fraxi was the pseudonym of Henry Spencer Ashbee (1834–1900), whose three-volume bibliography of erotica mentioned above ran to more than 1,600 pages. For Ashbee, see PETER FRYER, *Forbidden Books of the Victorians* (1970), pp. 1–55; and

G. LEGMAN, *The Horn Book* (1970), pp. 9–45.

DU MAURIER, Daphne (1907–). British author of romantic fiction. Her best known novel, *Rebecca* (1938), is one of the most popular ever written and has sold several million copies. It was filmed by Alfred Hitchcock in 1940. Amongst her other books are *Jamaica Inn* (1936), *My Cousin Rachel* (1951), *The Scapegoat* (1957), and *The House on the Strand* (1969).

DURBRIDGE, Francis (1912–). British author of mystery novels, radio, film and television scripts. His best known character was the detective Paul Temple, who has appeared in several radio serials, films and novels. The first such novel was *Send for Paul Temple* (1938).

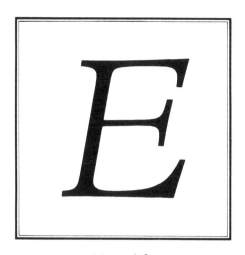

EDSON, J. T. Prolific contemporary British author, mostly of Western and cowboy stories. Born in a Derbyshire village, he was first encouraged to write by a local schoolmaster. When he left school at 15 he became a labourer in a stone quarry. In 1946 he was called up for National Service, and he remained in the Army until 1953, when he opened a fish and chip shop in Melton Mowbray, Leicestershire. A bad fire caused him to sell out, and he went to work in a local factory. He gave this up to embark upon full-time writing, but despite having won a prize for a novel entitled *Trail Boss*, and despite his contributions of stories and scripts to the Scottish publishers D. C. Thomson (qv), he could not make enough to live on; and so he became a postman. However, he continued writing, and in 1972 turned once more, this time very successfully, to full-time authorship.

Altogether J. T. Edson has written more than 112 books, and many have been translated into other languages. All are issued first in paperback, though some are later resold for republication in hard covers. A J. T. Edson Appreciation Society exists, and published the first number of its *Newsletter* in April 1981. (I am indebted to the secretary of the Society for the foregoing details.)

See *Western novels*, *Grey, Z.*, *Mulford, C. E.*

EGAN, Pierce (1772(?) – 1849). British author whose *Life in London* (1821) was a bestseller (see *Tom and Jerry II*). He also wrote *Boxiana*, 2 vols. (1812, 1818); and these sketches of prizefighting and prizefighters show him to have been the earliest popular sporting writer. He produced other books, including some fiction; but he is chiefly remembered for the two titles mentioned.

J. C. REID, *Bucks and Bruisers* (1971).

EGAN, Pierce, The Younger (1814–1880). Son of the above, artist

87

and popular British novelist. He produced a great deal of fiction, much of which was published in penny parts and then in book form. His best known work was probably *Robin Hood and Little John; or, The Merry Men of Sherwood Forest* (1840) in 41 numbers. It was often reprinted. Most of his 50 or more novels had an historical setting.

ELDERTON, William (?–1592?). The leading British ballad writer of his time. According to John Stow, Elderton was at one time an attorney. He was writing from about 1559 to 1584, and over 20 of his ballads have survived. The earlier ones are rather stiff, while the later ones go with a swing. He had a reputation as a drunkard – Gabriel Harvey, a contemporary, refers to his 'ale-crammed nose' and the fact that he 'armed himself with ale' when he wrote ballads.

The late Sir CHARLES FIRTH wrote about Elderton in an article, 'Ballads and Broadsides', which was reprinted in his *Essays Historical and Literary* (1968 (1938)). See also H. E. ROLLINS, 'William Elderton: Elizabethan Actor and Ballad Writer', *Studies in Philology* XVII (1920) pp. 199–245.

ELLERY QUEEN. Pseudonym of two Brooklyn-born cousins, Frederick Dannay (1905–   ) and Manfred B(arrington) Lee (1905–1971), who created Ellery Queen and made him world famous as an author, as a detective and as an editor. Another of their

pseudonyms was 'Barnaby Ross', author of four mystery novels featuring as the detective a retired Shakespearian actor called Drury Lane.

Ellery Queen (Detective) appeared in 40 books, the first of which was *The Roman Hat Mystery* (1929). Queen assists his father, Inspector Richard Queen of the New York City Police, in solving difficult cases. By profession a writer, he is also a collector of rare books. He has featured in a number of films, on radio and on television. Ellery Queen's methods are intellectual. He is skilled in the assessment of character and evidence, able to juggle clues, times, motives, personalities, and arrive with logical and articulate precision at the only solution possible.

Ellery Queen (Editor). Besides *Ellery Queen's Mystery Magazine* (qv), he has edited over 70 anthologies of detective stories. These include *101 Years' Entertainment* (1941), published to celebrate the 100th anniversary of Edgar Allan Poe's first detective story, 'The Murders in the Rue Morgue'; *The Detective Short Story; a Bibliography* (1942); and *Queen's Quorum* (1951). Some critical writing about the detective story which originally appeared in *Ellery Queen's Mystery Magazine* was collected in *In the Queen's Parlor* (1957).

There is a full-length study by FRANCIS M. NEVINS, *Royal Bloodline: Ellery Queen. Author and Detective* (1974). For a checklist of book titles, dates and details of film, radio and television presentations, see C. STEINBRUNNER and O. PENZLER, *Encyclopedia of Mystery and Detection* (1976), pp. 329–331.

Ellery Queen's Mystery Magazine was founded by Ellery Queen (qv) in 1941. In its early days it reprinted scarce detective stories, not otherwise readily available to readers, for Frederic Dannay had amassed a library of mystery short stories (now at the University of Texas). Another function of this publication was to encourage new authors, and many mystery writers had their first stories published in its pages. There were also 13 annual competitions (1946–1957; 1962) in which established writers submitted stories. The critic and author Anthony Boucher (1911–1968) said: 'Ellery Queen's Mystery Magazine has published every important crime writer who every wrote a short story.'

ELLIS, Edward Sylvester (1840–1916). Prolific American writer of about 400 dime novels (qv), many of which were published by Beadle and Adams (qv). His best-known book was *Seth Jones; or the Captives of the Frontier* (1860), which sold around 60,000 copies soon after publication, and eventually something like 600,000. It was translated into several languages.

Ellis followed this success with other novels of a Western or frontier interest. He used several pen names: James Fenimore Cooper Adams, Captain Bruin Adams, J. G. Bethune, Captain Latham C. Carleton, Frank Faulkner, Capt. R. M. Hawthorne, Lieut. Ned Hunter, Charles E. Lasalle, H. R. Millbank, Billex Muller, Lieut. J. H. Randolph, Emerson Rodman, E. A. St. Mox, Seelin Robins. In private life he was a schoolmaster, and he wrote a number of school textbooks.

Épinal. Town in N.E. France famous for its popular prints, some in colour, produced by the Pellerin family during the last three centuries.

JEAN MISTLER, F. BLAUDEZ and A. JACQUEMAIN, *Épinal et l'Imagerie Populaire* (1961).

ERRYM, Malcolm J. See *Rymer, James Malcolm.*

Fairies. Fairies crop up in early popular literature. The best collections of traditional tales about them and their kindred are to be found in oldish books like Thomas Keightley (qv), *Fairy Mythology* (2 vols., 1828), and Wirt Sikes, *British Goblins* (1880).

Family magazines (British). See *Titbits.*

FARNOL, Jeffery (1878–1952). British writer of many swashbuckling romantic historical novels. *The Broad Highway* (1910) was the first, and the final one, *Glass Summer*, came out in 1951, a year before his death. A memorable character of his was Jasper Shrig, a Bow Street Runner who, although successfully fighting crime in early nineteenth-century England, was essentially a modern detective. See *The High Adventure* (1926).

Farthing novelette. At the turn of the nineteenth century in Britain, most drapers' shops priced their wares with three farthings (¾d., i.e. three-quarters of one old style penny) in addition to the round numbers of pounds, shillings and pence. In some establishments a farthing novelette was given in lieu of change. See Frederick Willis, *A Book of London Yesterdays* (1960). The practice of 'three farthing' pricing lingered on into the 1930s – but by then novelettes were not given as change!

Faust/Faustus. German student who is striving after esoteric knowledge beyond his reach. When he is weary and discouraged, the devil appears to him and they strike a bargain. In return for Faust's soul, the devil will grant him several years during which he may give himself up to sensual pleasures and self-indulgence. After the agreed length of time, the devil reappears and carries off Faust as a condemned soul.

The legend, based possibly upon a remote historical figure, came into existence around 1540. A printed version, in German, was published in Frankfurt in 1587, and Johann Spies, the original publisher, issued a number of reprints. There were pirated versions as well; and Dutch and French translations soon appeared. The earliest surviving English version is dated 1592. In the seventeenth and eighteenth centuries Faust cropped up in English ballads and chapbooks; but he did not belong exclusively to popular literature, for he was immortalized by Marlowe, Lessing and Goethe.

P. M. PALMER and R. P. MORE, *The Sources of the Faust Tradition* (1936).
C. H. HERFORD, *Studies in the Literary Relations of England and Germany in the Sixteenth Century* (1886), Chapter IV, pp. 165–241. A much older book, but very helpful.

Felix the Cat. Created in the USA by Pat Sullivan, appearing first in an animated cartoon made in 1917. Before his death in 1933 Sullivan made over 100 Felix cartoons. On 14 August 1923, in an American Sunday newspaper, Felix became a comic strip character, and a daily strip began on 9 May 1927. In Britain, too, Felix was extremely popular, and seven issues of a *Felix Annual* were published.

Felix outlived his creator. In the USA during the 1940s and 1950s a comic book was named after him and he continued to appear in cartoons on American television. He still appears in a few US newspapers, but he is very much more popular in Europe now, where his adventures are presented in comic strip form.

Flash Gordon. American comic strip character created by Alex Raymond in 1934. Flash Gordon, 'renowned polo player and Yale graduate', his girl companion Dale Arden, and a scientist, Dr Hans Zarkov, set out in the doctor's spaceship for Mongo, an alien planet whose rulers have threatened to destroy the earth. Soon they are locked in combat with Ming the Merciless, emperor of Mongo.

Flash Gordon was enormously successful, and became more popular in the USA than Buck Rogers (qv). There have been comic books, radio programmes and a television series. More recently there has been a film.

Flashgun Casey. Tough photographer working for the 'Boston Express', created by G. H. Coxe (qv). His first appearance was in the story 'Return Engagement', published in *Black Mask*, March 1934. Altogether there are six books about Casey, published between 1942 and 1964. He has also been featured on radio and in films.

FLEMING, Ian (Lancaster) (1908–1964). British journalist, secret service agent, and author whose most famous creation was James Bond (qv).

Because he spent some years with British Intelligence, Fleming's novels are said to have a more authentic basis than most spy thrillers. As he wrote in the Introduction to *From Russia With Love* (1957): '. . . a great deal of the background to this story is accurate.' In the end, though, Fleming became disenchanted with superhero Bond, and described the books about him as 'trivial piffle'. The Bond novels, whose villains are always foreign and usually Russian, are in reality fairy tales about the triumph of Good – superhuman moral and physical strength – over Evil which is utterly ruthless and vicious.

See J. PEARSON, *The Life of Ian Fleming* (1966).

Fools. See *Simple Simon.*

FORESTER, C(ecil) S(cott). (1899–1966). Creator of Horatio Hornblower, a naval officer in Nelson's time whose career is followed through a number of novels. He also wrote other popular novels and several thrillers.

FORSYTH, Frederick (1938–). British author of bestselling spy stories: *The Day of the Jackal* (1971), which is said to have been written in 35 days; *The Odessa File* (1972); *Dogs of War* (1974); *The Devil's Alternative* (1979).

Fortunatus. Hero of a popular fifteenth-century German romance. After Dutch and French translations his adventures appeared in English in 1676 – and there may possibly have been an earlier version in 1650. Fortunatus survived into the eighteenth century as a chapbook hero, and featured in fairy tale collections during the succeeding one.

Fotonovel. A comic book version of a romantic novel in which photographs take the place of drawings. This form originated in Europe in the early 1950s. Sophia Loren was featured in a fotonovel (or photonovel) when she was 'discovered' by a film producer.

Fotonovels made their appearance in the USA in 1978, when Frederick A. Klein issued *Lips Like a Geranium* and *Darling*. They cost 75 cents each and contained 64 pages of four-colour photographs with captions which told a complete story. There is neither violence nor blatant sex: plots have the simple complexity of soap opera. In Italy fotonovels sell 30 million copies per month. Klein aims at a readership of women aged between 15 and 70 and he took an option on 21 Italian productions.

Another American firm based in Los Angeles, Fotonovel Publications, specializes in versions of successful films and television shows. Illustrations are taken from the original and dialogue is inserted in balloons. On the frontispiece the books say: 'I'm the film at your fingertips, in a room alone with the stars. . .'. *Grease* has sold over two million copies. There seems no reason to doubt that this kind of publishing will continue to be successful.

FRANCIS, Dick (1920–). Welsh jockey who became a journalist and then author of mystery stories. The first of these, *Dead Cert*, appeared in 1962. Francis's stories have various sporting backgrounds, but are usually written from the point of view of a jockey or an airline pilot. He has produced over a dozen novels and one autobiographical work, *The Sport of Queens* (1957).

Frank Merriwell. See *Street and Smith*.

Frankenstein. The novel *Frankenstein: or, the Modern Prometheus* by Mary Shelley (qv) was first published in three volumes in 1818, and has not been out of print since. It is the story of a brilliant scientist, Dr Victor Frankenstein, who discovers the secret of life and creates an eight-foot giant. The monster is gentle but has a grotesque appearance, terrifying all who come into contact with him. It is a bizarre and sometimes poignant story which has attracted film-makers since 1910. Boris Karloff (1887–1969), who played the monster in a 1930s version, became a major star as a result of his performance.

FRASER, George Macdonald (1920–   ). British author of several successful, bawdy and readable novels dealing with the adventures of Flashman, the school bully who made his first appearance in Thomas Hughes, *Tom Brown's Schooldays* (1857). The first was *Flashman* (1969).

FREEMAN, Richard Austin (1862–1943). British author and creator of Dr Thorndyke (qv), probably the world's most famous scientific detective. Freeman was a doctor whose first book, *Travels and Life in Ashanti and Jaman* (1898), was based upon his experiences as a colonial surgeon in West Africa. *The Adventures of Romney Pringle* (1902) was his first crime book. It was a collaborative effort, and appeared under the name of Clifford Ashdown.

Freeman wrote novels and short stories. Apart from his creation of Dr Thorndyke, he made a great contribution to the technique of mystery novels by his invention of the 'inverted' detective story, in which interest centres not upon the identity of the criminal and whether he will be caught, but upon *how* he is brought to justice. The reader is in fact a witness to the crime.

FURNIVALL, Frederick James (1825–1910). One of the most enthusiastic and able of nineteenth-century British scholars who was able to communicate his delight in English literature to students and to contemporaries. He founded a number of literary and text societies, among them the Ballad Society (1868–1899), which began an impressive programme of publishing the texts of the larger collections of ballad literature in Britain. The most notable achievement was the reprinting of the Roxburghe Ballads in eight volumes between 1871 and 1899 (see *Ballad* – Sources). The other main publication was J. W. Ebsworth (Editor), *Bagford Ballads* (2 vols. and Supplement, 1876–1880). The Society also published in 1871 Furnivall's study of Elizabethan popular literature, *Captain Cox, his Ballads and Books*. This was based upon *A Letter . . .* by Robert Laneham (1575), a pamphlet describing Queen Elizabeth's visit to Kenilworth Castle. On p. 34 Captain Cox, a mason, is mentioned, and a list of titles in his library is given. Furnivall follows up each one and provides a good deal of further information. His study was reprinted in 1907 as *Robert Laneham's Letter . . .*

Frederick James Furnivall. A Volume of Personal Record (1911) contains a biography by JOHN MUNRO, together with memories of Furnivall by some people who had known him.

See *Percy, Thomas.*

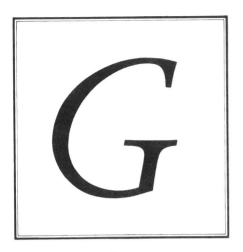

GABORIAU, Émile (1832–1873). French author whose detective novel *L'Affaire Lerouge* (1866) – US title *The Widow Lerouge* (1873), British title *The Lerouge Case* (1881) – introduced the detective Lecoq, who became popular in several subsequent novels.

The importance of Gaboriau's work is that in the 'roman policier', which he invented, attention was focused upon the gathering and interpretation of evidence. The standard plot, as it was exploited by numerous French hack writers, involved a brutally murdered victim and a police officer who showed his skill in piecing together the evidence and solving the crime. Usually, too, there were old family scandals, and often a criminal of noble birth.

GALLICO, Paul (1897–1976). Sports writer and war correspondent who turned to fiction. He wrote thrillers of which *The Poseidon Adventure* (1969) is the best known. His sentimental tale *The Snow Goose* (1941) was enormously popular.

Gambols, The. British comic strip featuring domestic comedy, created by Barry Appleby. It first appeared in the *Daily Express* on 16 March 1950. The first paperback collection came out in 1952, and since then many volumes have been published.

GARDNER, Erle Stanley (1889–1970). American author and creator of the lawyer, Perry Mason (qv), and his secretary, Della Street. After working as a boxer, a lawyer, a tyre salesman and then as a lawyer again, Gardner began writing in 1921 and two years later sold his first mystery story to a pulp magazine. Between 1923 and 1932 he sold hundreds of stories which were published in various magazines under a variety of pseudonyms: Charles M. Green; Robert Parr; Kyle Corning; Les Tillray; Charles J. Kenny; Carleton Kendrake. Sometimes one issue of a magazine would carry several of his stories, each published under a different name. In 1932 he earned $20,525 from his magazine sales.

After several rejections his first novel, *The Case of the Velvet Claws*, was published in 1933 by William Morrow & Company. It featured Perry Mason who, at the suggestion of Thayer Hobson, president of Morrow, became a series character. The series was an immediate success, and Gardner gave up the practice of law to devote himself to writing. He bought a thousand-acre estate in California, and it was here that the 'fiction factory' was situated. Six secretaries were employed full-time. Under the pseudonym A. A. Fair, Gardner wrote 29 novels published between 1939 and 1970 which told the adventures of a private detective team of Bertha Cool – fat, sixtyish – and Donald Lam – a slightly-built disbarred lawyer.

He was a man of wide interests, including natural history, archaeology, geology, photography and hunting – the latter a pastime which he gave up in 1950 because he felt that the odds were stacked too heavily against the animals hunted.

Gardner wrote several works of non-fiction, but it is as a writer of detective stories that he must be rated as one of the most popular and bestselling authors of all time. Over 200 million Mason books have been sold in the US, and some of the titles have been translated into 30 languages. There were six Perry Mason films in the 1930s, and the attorney also appeared in radio and television series. 'I write', Gardner said, 'to make money and to give the reader sheer fun'.

The standard biography is DOROTHY B. HUGHES, *Erle Stanley Gardner. The Case of the Real Perry Mason* (1978).

Garland. A collection of traditional ballads published in a chapbook (qv).

GASKIN, Catherine (1929–   ). Irish Australian best selling romantic historical novelist. Her books include *The Other Eden* (1946), which was written when she was 14, *Sarah Dane* (1955); *Fiona* (1970); *A Falcon for the Queen* (1972).

Gasoline Alley. American comic strip created by Frank King in 1918. Initially it featured a group of motor car enthusiasts, and achieved a modest popularity. Then on 14 February 1921 Walt Wallet, bachelor, found a baby boy in a basket left on his doorstep. The boy, named Skeezix, became the hero of the strip, and from the time of his appearance it achieved enormous popularity. The spectacle of ordinary American children growing up proved iresistible to more than 50 million readers. The original adult characters – Walt, together with Doc, Avery, Bill and their wives – remained fairly static, but Skeezix and his friends developed into adulthood as the strip went along. In this, King's creation was unique. When he died in 1969 the strip was continued by Bill Perry and Richard Moores, and still appears today, with the emphasis upon a new batch of individuals who have appeared in the story.

George A. Greene. See *Pinder of Wakefield, The.*

GERNSBACK, Hugo (1884–1967). Gernsback was editor of the first US magazine to specialize in science fiction, *Amazing Stories* which appeared in April 1926. (The first magazine to use the term science fiction and to devote its contents entirely to this genre had been *Hugin*, launched by Otto Witt in Sweden in 1916.) He took a limited view of science fiction, seeing little value in it other than technical mastery of the future. In fact he was an inventor, and began publishing fiction in 1911 to fill the pages in a magazine called *Modern Electrics.* The material was so popular that he eventually launched *Amazing Stories* – a title which survived his own bankruptcy in 1929.

Giants. Giants turn up in early popular literature from time to time. There is no large number of books about them, but F. W. FAIRHOLT, *Gog and Magog* (1859) is charming and authentic. So too is H. J. MASSINGHAM, *Fee, Fi, Fo, Fum. The Giants in England* (1926).

GILBERT, Anthony (1899–1973). Pseudonym of Lucy Beatrice Malleson, British author whose first mystery novel, *The Tragedy at Freyne*, was published in 1927, although earlier in her career she had written non-mystery fiction. Early novels, like *The Body on the Beam* (1932), usually featured Scott Egerton, a rising young politician, as the detective; but in *Murder by Experts* (1936) he was replaced by Arthur Crook (qv), who was enormously popular. Her autobiography *Three-a-Penny* was published in 1940.

Girly magazines. Copiously illustrated pornographic periodicals widely sold in Great Britain and in the USA. Readily identifiable by their revealing covers, they have such titles as *Playbirds*; *Big Girls*; *The Journal of Sex*; *Bounce*; *Romp*; *Fiesta*; *Exposure*, and the like.

The field is a constantly changing one, especially in Britain where the obscenity laws tend to be more uncertain than they are in the USA. In the latter country, in addition to girly magazines, there are also sex tabloids (closely resembling newspapers in appearance) which are on sale at news-stands. Their titles include, or have included, *Voyeur*; *Pussycat*; *Hump* and *Pleasure*. The extent to which such publications are popular literature is uncertain. What is beyond doubt is that there are many of them, and their number is increasing.

Details about the trade are hard to come by, and consequently there seems to have been little of substance written about it. GILLIAN FREEMAN, *The Undergrowth of Literature* (1968), was a pioneer study, and there has, so far as I know, been nothing comparable since. HUGH HERBERT wrote a fairly substantial article on the subject, 'Porn of a Dilemma', which was published in *The Guardian* of 15 November 1978 and provoked two letters of comment which appeared on the 23 and 27 November. For the USA, DICK MILES, *The Dirtiest Dozen* (1971) tells the story of the sex tabloids.

GLYN, Elinor (1864–1943). British novelist, author of the bestseller *Three Weeks* (1907) which, in the nine years before the appearance of a cheap edition, sold very nearly two million copies in Great Britain, the British Empire and the USA. It was also translated into most European languages, and was particularly popular in Scandinavia, Spain and South America. Cheap editions in English began in 1916, brought out by three separate publishers in Britain. Altogether, total world sales of the novel were said to be five million copies. The novel had a reputation for immorality and provoked a good deal of adverse comment. In the USA, for example, it was not allowed to be sent through the post; and in Ohio in 1932 a Mickey Mouse film cartoon was banned because of a scene showing a cow reclining in a field and reading *Three Weeks*.

Elinor Glyn was a prolific writer, producing at least 36 books between 1900 and 1940. She published an autobiography, *Romantic Adventure* (1936), and there is the standard biography by ANTHONY GLYN, *Elinor Glyn A Biography* (1955), which has on page eight a complete list of her books.

GORDON, Richard (1921–   ). British surgeon and writer of comic novels about medical life. *Doctor in*

the House (1952) began a whole 'Doctor' series, and led also to films.

Gothic novels. Romantic and sensational popular fiction of the late eighteenth and early nineteenth centuries. The genre was closely connected with the mood of the Romantic Movement.

Literally hundreds of such novels were published, most of them by women authors. The world they created bore little relation to reality – the air was thick with the smell of putrefying corpses on lonely gibbets, and picturesquely ruined castles on the mainland of Europe were inhabited by bats and deranged nuns; generations of virtuous but sadly insipid heroines languished in dark and dreary dungeons from which they were rescued by a hero, as a fitful moon shone through a break in the clouds after the storm with which these novels invariably began. It was almost a convention that the said hero should have been cheated out of his inheritance by a scheming relative who had murdered the young man's parents. Often ghosts of the murdered ones shocked the villain into a confession; and the rightful heir was restored to his estates after rescuing his beloved from the unwelcome attentions of the villain. With variations, this was very much the model for gothic novels. The best example of this kind of fiction is probably Ann Radcliffe (qv), *The Mysteries of Udolpho* (4 vols., 1794). Other successful practitioners were Elizabeth Helme (qv), Regina M. Roche (qv) and Jane Porter (qv). In *Northanger Abbey*,

Jane Austen satirizes novels of this kind. The importance of the gothic novel lies in the fact that it provided the roots from which so much modern romantic fiction has sprung.

The literature is considerable. MONTAGUE SUMMERS, *A Gothic Bibliography* (N.D., 1940), remains a monument to its compiler's wealth of esoteric learning, J. M. S. TOMPKINS, *The Popular Novel in England 1770–1800* (1932), is judicious and widely-ranging. D. P. VARMA, *The Gothic Flame* is also recommended.

See *Minerva Press, The.*

GOULD, Nat (1857–1919). Prolific British author of novels with a horse-racing theme.

GRAEME, Bruce. (1900–   ). Pseudonym of Graham Montague Jeffries, British author and creator of Blackshirt (qv). After a first novel was rejected Graeme wrote a 10,000-word Blackshirt story, and this was bought by a magazine editor who commissioned seven more. In 1925 T. Fisher Unwin, the London publisher, used the eight stories to launch a new series of cheap novelettes. More than one million copies of *Blackshirt* were sold over 15 years, and a successor, *The Return of Blackshirt* (1927), proved equally popular.

Other pseudonyms used by Graeme are Peter Bourne and David Graeme.

GREY, Zane (1872–1939). American bestselling author of novels about cowboys and the American West. In all of them noble heroes fought and won a stereotyped battle against ruthless villains. His start as a writer, however, was slow. While attempting – unsuccessfully – to establish himself as a dentist in New York between 1898 and 1904, he wrote his first book, an historical romance called *Betty Zane*. Several publishers turned it down, and in 1904 he issued it himself. He went on writing and in 1912, after much hesitation, Harpers, the publishing firm, brought out *Riders of the Purple Sage*. It sold one million copies, and 800,000 more in reprints.

Grey was an extremely prolific writer. By 1947 he had written 63 novels with a total sale of more than 19 million copies. His publishers had to ration his enormous output – when he died he left a number of manuscripts, and the publishers generally brought out a book a year, his last, *Lost Pueblo*, appearing in 1954.

FRANK GRUBER, *Zane Grey: a Biography* (1969).

GRUBER, Frank (1904–1969). American author of mystery and detective stories and film scripts. He was a prolific writer for pulp magazines, and eventually became one of the highest paid writers in the United States. The story of his ups and downs is told by him in *The Pulp Jungle*, 1967. More than 300 of his short stories appeared in some 50 magazines. In addition, he wrote 60 novels, 70 film scripts and 150 television scripts. His books were

99

translated into 24 languages, and combined sales exceed 90 million copies. Gruber used the following pseudonyms: Stephen Acre; Charles K. Boston; John K. Vedder; C. K. M. Scanlon; Tom Gunn.

Guide books. A specialized and readily identifiable kind of popular literature whose origins go back at least to Pausanias. His *Guide to Greece* in the second century A.D. is readily available in an English version published by Penguin Classics (2 vols., 1979). More recognizably, the modern guide book dates from the last decades of the eighteenth century, when English men and women were beginning to discover for themselves the pleasures – or otherwise – of travel in their own country and holidays by the sea.

Guide books come in all shapes, sizes and lengths. The coming of the railway gave a great stimulus to their publishing. (Railway companies in Britain were to become heavily involved in the genre themselves during the twentieth century.) The bicycle, as the first personal transport available to masses of people, and later the arrival of the motor car, together with a general increase in leisure time and the beginning of paid holidays from work, all helped in the growing popularity of the guide book. It is no accident that one large oil company is active in publications of this kind today. The earliest guide books tended to be formal in their approach; but informality, notwithstanding a high regard for accuracy, began to creep in rather tentatively round about the middle of the nineteenth century. In 1866 Abel Heywood, the Manchester publisher, began issuing a series of *Penny Guides* which represented the first attempt to reach a working class public which was beginning to use trains for purposes other than travel to work. These guides covered places as far apart as Buxton, Southport, Bath and the Isle of Wight, and there were more than 20 titles in the series.

The growth of leisure and a steady increase in the travelling public, together perhaps with the success of Heywood's guides, prompted other publishers to enter this field. Among them were Ward Lock, who brought out the first of their 'Red Guides' in 1896 priced at one shilling. The series is still in existence, the volumes being constantly revised. At the turn of the century Methuen began their 'Little Guides', some of which were being reprinted in the 1920s. Between the two world wars the production of guide books multiplied (there was even a *London for Heretics*, by William Kent, published in 1932!). In the years following the Second World War the widening stream of guide books became a flood. In the USA, too, people's increasing interest both in travel and in their own past has prompted a proliferation of guides.

For those who ventured abroad, John Murray's 'Handbooks for Travellers' were essential. The first of these, covering Holland, Belgium and North Germany, was published in 1836. (The first of his British guides, dealing with Devon and Cornwall, appeared in 1851. This series was completed in 1899 with the 60th volume, which was on Warwickshire.) The great name in foreign guides in the second half of the last century was Karl Baedeker. His guide to Holland and Belgium had been first published in 1839, and it was followed by many others. Guides to foreign places, however, were never as popular with British readers as those to their own country. In the nineteenth century foreign travel was very much more restricted than it is today, so that there existed no mass market to be tapped with guides to Europe and beyond.

In general, guide books have been neglected by scholars, though less so, perhaps, by collectors. This is a pity. They are popular literature of a didactic kind, and they have much to tell us about tastes and values of the past and the present.

The literature of the subject is scattered, but often high in quality. JOHN VAUGHAN, *The English Guide Book c. 1780–1870* (1974) covers its period reasonably well; and a pamphlet by K. M. CLARKE, *150 Years of Town Guides* (1965), is an admirable comparative study dealing with the town of Rye in Southern England. In *Murray's Magazine* (November 1889) there is an article by JOHN MURRAY on 'The Origins and History of Murray's Handbooks for Travellers' (pp. 623–629). It was written in response to an article, 'How Guide-Books are Made. An Interview with the English Editor of "Baedeker" ', which had been published anonymously in *The Pall Mall Gazette* of 23 August 1889. JACK SIMMONS, 'West Country Guide Books' published in *Parish and Empire* (1952), pp. 97–106, is brief but very perceptive. E. S. DE BEER, 'The Development of the Guide-Book until the Early Nineteenth Century' published in *Journal of the Archaeological Association*, 3rd Series, vol. 15, 1952, pp. 35–46, is both readable and magisterial.

Apart from Sunday newspaper and periodical articles, the twentieth-century guide is rarely discussed. See V. E. NEUBURG, 'A Guide to Guide Books for the Visitor to Britain' published in *British Book News*, July 1979, pp. 547–550; and 'J.T.', 'Maps and Guides' published in *The Bookseller*, 21 February 1981, pp. 594–599.

Finally, a catalogue issued by the antiquarian booksellers Kohler and Coombes in December 1973 is entitled *Two Centuries of Travel 1768–1968*. It lists a large number of relevant items.

Guy of Warwick. Sir Guy, Earl of Warwick, was one of the most popular of legendary English heroes. The story of his life would include his love for Felice and his adventures during a pilgrimage to the Holy Land. Upon his return to England, the King entreated him to fight Collorand, the Danish champion; and his victory saved the country from the Danes. Subsequently Guy withdrew to a hermitage where he spent the remainder of his days.

Printed versions began to appear

before 1500. Elizabethan chroniclers treated the story as serious history. Samuel Rowlands (qv), *Famous History of Guy Earl of Warwick* (1608), gave the story a new lease of life as fiction; and popular versions were issued in prose and in ballad form. In the eighteenth century Guy was a chapbook hero, and by the nineteenth century his adventures were retold as a fairy tale for children.

R. S. CRANE, 'The Vogue of "Guy of Warwick" from the Close of the Middle Ages to the Romantic Revival', *Publications of the Modern Language Association of America*, vol. XXX, 2; New Series vol. XXIII, 2 (1915).

L. A. HIBBARD, *Mediaeval Romance in England* (1963 (1924)).

V. B. RICHMOND, *The Popularity of Middle English Romance* (1975). Chapter VI is a very good account of Guy's early popularity.

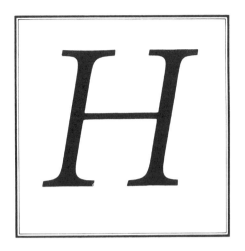

HAILEY, Arthur (1920–). Bestselling American novelist whose work is based upon rigorous research. In his stories he explores the inner workings of politics, an hotel, an airport, high finance, an electrical breakdown – respectively *In High Places* (1962), *Hotel* (1965), *Airport* (1968), *The Money Changers* (1975), *Overload* (1979).

HALL, Sam S. (1838–1886). American writer of Western novels (qv). A friend of Buffalo Bill (see *Western novels*) and Prentiss Ingraham (qv), Hall took up authorship after military service in the American Civil War and an abortive venture into the hotel business. He was often known as 'Buckskin Sam'; and altogether he wrote some 70 novels.

HALLIDAY, Brett (1904–). Pseudonym of Davis Dresser, American writer who began writing, after a chequered career, in 1927, and contributed mystery, Western, love, adventure and sex stories to pulp magazines (qv) under various pseudonyms – Matthew Blood, Peter Shelley, Anthony Scott, Sylvia Carson, Kathryn Culver. Under the name Asa Baker his first mystery novel, *Mum's the Word for Murder*, was published in 1938. His most successful character was the private detective Michael Shayne (qv).

HALLIWELL (later **HALLIWELL-PHILLIPPS**), **James Orchard** (1820–1889). British writer and editor best known as a biographer of Shakespeare – and for the bitterness with which he was pursued by Sir Thomas Phillipps, whose daughter he married. Halliwell made a useful contribution to the study of popular literature. He belonged to a tradition of dilettante men of letters who loved 'old books', and was accused – rightly, one supposes – by Richard Garnett in *The Philological Essays* (1859, p. 120) of 'shallowness and irrelevancy' in his editing of early texts. What he did extraordinarily well was to preserve, and more important, to record, ephemeral publications which might otherwise have been lost, or remained unknown. His *A Catalogue of Chapbooks, Garlands, and Penny Histories in the Possession of J. O. Halliwell* (1849) demonstrates clearly that he knew a great deal about the subject, and that he was one of the earliest commentators to realize its significance. Unfortunately, his catalogue was issued, like so many of his works, in a tiny 'privately printed' edition. Many of his publications are, to this day, hard to trace, even in libraries. This method of publishing was, however, quite intentional, as he explained in a pamphlet, *On the Means Adopted to ensure the Rarity of Privately Printed Works* (London: For Private Circulation Only. 1854)!!

Notwithstanding such a quirk, everything that James Orchard Halliwell wrote about popular literature is worth looking at. Most of it is recorded in JUSTIN WINSOR, *Halliwelliana: a Bibliography of the Publications of James Orchard Halliwell-Phillipps* (1881). A more personal view of Halliwell will be found in A. N. L. MUNBY, *The Family Affairs of Sir Thomas Phillipps* (1952).

HAMILTON, Charles (Harold St. John) (1876–1961). Prolific British author of school stories and some adventure tales, mainly for Amalgamated Press (qv) and other publishers, for over 60 years. His earliest efforts were published under his own name in 1895; but he used altogether 25 pseudonyms, of which the best known were 'Frank Richards', 'Martin Clifford', 'Owen Conquest' and 'Hilda Richards'. Under the first of these names he wrote about the fat boy of Greyfriars School, Billy Bunter (qv).

Throughout his long working life Hamilton remained a bachelor. In 1952 he published *The Autobiography of Frank Richards*, a curiously evasive piece of writing which was reissued a year after his death in a 'Memorial Edition'. This had an appreciation of Hamilton by Eric Fayne, containing some details of his career as an author. *The World of Frank Richards* by W. O. G. Lofts and D. J. Adley (1975) is not very satisfactory as a biography, though it does include some useful material – including a complete list of pseudonyms. A biography by a relative, Mrs Una Hamilton Wright, has remained unpublished.

One of the most interesting critical pieces on Hamilton, 'Boys' Weeklies' by GEORGE ORWELL, was published in a London literary magazine, *Horizon* (March 1940), and there was a riposte by Hamilton in the May issue. Orwell's piece has subsequently been reprinted in *Critical Essays* (1946) and elsewhere.

HAMILTON, Donald (1916–). American author and creator of Matt Helm (qv), the American equivalent of James Bond. Hamilton has also written a series of Western novels. One of these, *Ambush at Blanco Canyon*, was serialized in *The Saturday Evening Post* and then published as *The Big Country* (1957); and it was later made into a film starring Charlton Heston and Gregory Peck. Most of Hamilton's novels first appeared as paperbacks. They have received much critical praise, and *Date with Darkness* (1947), a tale of counterespionage, is a good example of his work.

HAMMETT, Dashiell (1894–1961). American author. As a young man he worked as a newsboy, freight clerk, labourer, messenger, stevedore, advertising manager and, for eight years, as an operative on the Pinkerton detective agency in Baltimore and in San Francisco. His first short story appeared in the magazine *Black Mask* (qv) of 1 October 1923, and his fiction writing career ended in 1934. He contracted tuberculosis during the First World War, and for much of his life suffered from ill health and alcoholism, though he did serve for three years with the US Army in World War II. In 1951 he went to prison for five months rather than testify at the trial of four communists accused of conspiracy.

Hammett published five novels: *Red Harvest* (1929), *The Dain Curse* (1929), *The Maltese Falcon* (1930), *The Glass Key* (1931), *The Thin Man* (1934). The first two featured the 'Continental Op', a nameless agency detective, and the third, Sam Spade (qv). *The Thin Man* featured Nick and Nora Charles.

Nearly all of Hammett's 62 short stories were originally published in *Black Mask*, but most of them have been reprinted in the following volumes which are more accessible: *Blood Money* (1943), *The Adventures of Sam Spade and Other Stories*

(1945), *The Continental Op* (1945), *Hammett Homicides* (1946), *Dead Yellow Women* (1947), *Nightmare Town* (1948), *The Creeping Siamese* (1950), *Woman in the Dark* (1952), *A Man Named Thin* (1962), *The Big Knockover* (1966), *The Continental Op* (1974).

The best of Hammett's work is characterized by a startling originality. Like so many innovators, he has suffered considerably at the hands of his imitators; but his deft characterization and compact style, together with the pervasive realism of his work, have ensured his enduring reputation as one of the original founders of the American detective story.

See H. HAYCRAFT, *Murder for Pleasure* (1941); R. LAYMAN, *Shadow Man* (1981); best of all is LILLIAN HELLMAN's Introduction to *The Big Knockover* (1969). When first published in 1966, the British title was *The Dashiell Hammett Omnibus*.

HARBAUGH, Thomas C. (1849–1924). Prolific American writer of over 300 dime novels (qv), poetry and children's books. He wrote for a number of publishers, and used many pen names: Captain Howard Holmes, Howard Lincoln, Charles Howard, Major S. S. Scott, Major Walter Brisbane, George B. Lee, Capt. Dick Steadman, Major Walt Wilmot, Capt. Walt Winton, Harry Winton, Major G. W. Alcalaw, Col. T. B. Bostwick, Captain J. L. Kennedy. This is probably an incomplete list.

Hardboiled school. See *Black Mask; Pulp magazines.*

The Hardy Boys. Created by Edward L. Stratemeyer (see *Keene, Carolyn*) as Franklin W. Dixon. They are teenage brothers who solve mysteries on their own or with their detective father, own a car and a boat and have access to their father's private plane. Stratemeyer's name appears on the first nine Hardy Boys books; in fact they were produced by a 'ghost writer', Leslie McFarlane, who tells the story of his connection with Stratemeyer in an autobiography, *Ghost of the Hardy Boys* (1976). The remainder – well over 50 – were written by other members of the Stratemeyer Syndicate. Sales exceed 50 million copies, and Walt Disney has featured the brothers on television.

Harlequin. Harlequin Enterprises, Toronto, Canadian publisher of romantic fiction. The firm was founded in 1949 by Richard Bonnycastle. He was part-owner of a printing plant, and the other partner published a wide range of cookery books, craft books, Westerns and mysteries under the name Harlequin. Bonnycastle bought him out, and his wife Mary, offended by some of the more lurid books on the list, initiated a series of 'Harlequin Romances' with titles purchased from Mills and Boon (qv), London. Such was the success of this venture that in the early 1970s the two firms amalgamated, and their respective names have become synonymous with romantic fiction.

For details of the Harlequin enterprise see SHERI CRAIG, 'Harlequin took a page from P & G's marketing book to sell "romance" ', published in the Canadian journal *Marketing*, 13 October 1975.

HAZLITT, William Carew (1834–1913). British editor and man of letters, he was grandson of William Hazlitt, and wrote, compiled or edited many books, several of which reflected his long-standing interest in popular literature. Amongst the most important of these are *Old English Jest-Books* (3 vols., 1863–64). 15 titles are reprinted, but the texts cannot always be relied upon as Hazlitt – unlike W. J. Furnivall (qv) – deleted and altered lines which he felt might offend the sensibilities of his reader. Nonetheless, these three handsome volumes remain the most available versions of most of the early jestbooks – a fact which underlines the need for scholarly editing of such material. E. A. Horsman (ed.), *Dobsons Drie Bobs* (1955), is a good example of jestbook editing. It is the only one known to me.

Other relevant books by W. C. Hazlitt are: *Remains of the Early Popular Poetry of England*, 4 vols (1864–66); *The New London Jest-Book* (1871); *Studies in Jocular Literature* (1890); *Early Popular Poetry of Scotland and the Northern Border* (1895); *Tales and Legends of National Origin* (1899); *Some Prose Writings* (1906). This book contains an essay entitled 'Some Deeper Uses of Popular Literature', which is one of the earliest general discussions of the subject.

HEDDLE, Ethel F(orster) (no dates). Popular British novelist of the late nineteenth and early twentieth centuries. Her best-known work was *Three girls in a Flat* (1896). Very little is known about her life, but she was the subject of an article signed 'P' and entitled 'The author of our New Serial. A Talk with Miss Ethel F. Heddle', published in *The Young Woman*, vol. V, 1896–97, pp. 464–466. Her married name was Marshall.

HEINLEIN, Robert A. (1907–). Prolific and influential American writer of science fiction, both novels and short stories. He used the pseudonyms Anson MacDonald and Lyle Monroe. He has been writing since 1939, when 'Life-Line' was published in *Astounding Stories* (see *Campbell, J. W.*, Junior). His reputation was quickly established and has endured, many of his stories appearing in the same magazine. The best of his fiction is characterized by the convincing backgrounds against which it is set.

J. D. OLANDER and M. H. GREENBERG, *Robert A. Heinlein* (1977).
ALEXEI PANSHIN, *Heinlein in Dimension* (1968). This is the most detailed study of any science fiction writer yet attempted.

HELME, Elizabeth (?–1813). British author of a number of gothic novels (qv). *The Farmer of Inglewood Forest* (4 vols., 1796) was originally published by the Minerva Press (qv). It remained in print for something over one hundred years,

being reissued again and again in cheap one-volume editions.

HEMYNG, (Samuel) Bracebridge (1841–1901). Prolific British writer of popular novels and creator of Jack Harkaway, a hero of boys' stories in Britain and the USA. Hemyng went to America in 1874, writing there for *The Police Gazette* and producing a number of the American Harkaway tales. Eventually he returned to England, where he continued writing until his death.

Hercule Poirot. See *Christie, Agatha.*

Heroes – Heroines. See *Jack the Giant Killer.*

HEYER, Georgette (1902–1974). British author of some 40 historical novels set in Regency England. She also wrote a number of mystery novels, and of these, *Death in the Stocks* brought her great acclaim when it was published in the USA. It is, however, for her Regency romances that she is best remembered and still read. Amongst the best known are *The Devil's Club* (1932), *The Spanish Bride* (1940), *The Reluctant Widow* (1947), *Arabella* (1949), *The Quiet Gentleman* (1951), and *Cotillion* (1953).

HIBBERT, Eleanor (1906–). Bestselling British novelist specializing in historical novels and using several pseudonyms.

As Jean Plaidy she uses backgrounds which range from the Middle Ages to the Victorian era. Set in England, Spain, Italy and France, they are based upon meticulous research and portray many historical characters who are brought to life convincingly.

As Victoria Holt she writes 'Gothic' novels featuring dark brooding houses and menacing terror. As Philippa Cary she produces light historical romances.

Other pseudonyms are Eleanor Burford, Ellalice Tate, Elbur Ford and Kathleen Kellow.

HIGHSMITH, Patricia (1921–). American author of mysteries and short stories. Her first novel, *Strangers on a Train* (1950), brought her immediate success, and subsequent books have been very popular. She often explores, at a sophisticated level, the relationships of people brought together by crime.

HILTON, James (1900–1954). British author of several novels. *Catherine Herself* (1920) was the first; and, as Glen Trevor, he wrote some detective stories during the 1930s. His bestselling *Lost Horizon* (1933) introduced 'Shangri-la' into the English language; while *Goodbye, Mr Chips* (1934) was written in four days and first published in the Christmas 1933 issue of *British Weekly*. Both were made into successful films.

HINDLEY, Charles (1821–1893). British editor and writer, he has about 16 books to his name. Some confusion may exist because his son, a bookseller and publisher, was also named Charles. He wrote in a rather ponderous style, but his books are valuable because he preserves in them a great deal of popular literature which might otherwise have been lost. Furthermore, he knew and talked to people connected with the street ballad trade.

Amongst his most important books are: *The Catnach Press* (1869); *Curiosities of Street Literature* (1871. Reprinted 1966 with a life of Charles Hindley by Leslie Shepard; reprinted 1969 with a perceptive Foreword by Michael Hughes); *The Life and Times of James Catnach* (1878); *A History of the Cries of London* (1881, 1884); *A History of the Catnach Press* (1886, 1887); *The True History of Tom and Jerry* (1892).

HOLT, Victoria. See *Hibbert, Eleanor.*

Hopalong Cassidy. Cowboy hero created by Clarence E. Mulford (qv).

HOPE, Anthony (1863–1933). Pseudonym used by Sir Anthony Hope Hawkins, British author of *The Prisoner of Zenda* (1894), which was enormously popular as a book, and later as a film. Set in an imaginary kingdom in Central Europe called Ruritania, it was a story of court intrigue and romance. The words 'Ruritania' and 'Ruritanian' have passed into the English language, and are to be found in *The Oxford English Dictionary*.

A sequel, *Rupert of Hentzau* (1898), was not so popular; and his other books, *The Dolly Dialogues*

(1894) and *Tristram of Blent* (1901), are now hardly remembered at all.

HORLER, Sydney (1888–1954). British author who started as a journalist, and went on to write sports fiction for magazines. His first novel was *Goal* (1920). *The Mystery of No. 1* (1925) was his initial venture into thriller writing, and it was so successful that he turned to this activity full-time. He was a prolific author, and wrote altogether more than 150 books. The advertising slogan 'Horler for Excitement' appeared on the jackets of his books published by Hodder and Stoughton of London.

Horler's most famous character was the Honourable Timothy Overbury 'Tiger' Standish, who was similar to Bulldog Drummond (qv). Other characters were Ian Heath, British secret agent, and Gerald Frost, the Nighthawk, who steals from society ladies of questionable reputation. He wrote about his life and working methods in *Writing for Money* (1932) and *Excitement: an Impudent Autobiography* (1933).

Horler also wrote under the names of Peter Cavendish and Martin Heritage.

Horner, W. B., and Son. Late nineteenth-century publishers of wholesome rather than sensational cheap fiction. Originally based in Dublin, the firm later moved to London. New titles in 'Horner's Penny Stories for the People' were published on the first and third Tuesdays of each month, and by 1889 147 novels were being adver-

tized. Popular ones were reprinted, and sales might range from 150,000 to 450,000 copies.

'As forceful, fresh, and fascinating as they are wholesome', said a reviewer of Horner stories in the *Congregational Magazine*, quoted by the publishers. Occasionally one of the novels would be used in a 'service of song' – a popular event in nonconformist chapels, when the reading of an edifying story would be interspersed with the singing of appropriate hymns and solos. On 11 November 1912 the 1,000th novel was published – and the firm was still active in 1927. By then, however, it had been taken over by Amalgamated Press (qv). One of the writers who contributed many novels to the Horner series was Grace Pettman (qv).

HORNUNG, Ernest William (1866–1921). British author and creator of Raffles, the gentleman crook (qv). When he was 18 Hornung emigrated to Australia because his health was poor, and he wrote several romantic crime and adventure stories set in that country. Upon his return to England he married Constance Doyle, sister of Sir Arthur Conan Doyle, and served in France during the Great War with the YMCA. His only son was killed in action. Apart from the Raffles novels and short stories, Hornung's best known book was *The Crime Doctor* (1914), a series of tales in which Dr John Dollar uses psychological means to solve crimes.

Hot historicals. See *Bodice rippers.*

HOUSEHOLD, Geoffrey (1900–). British author of novels dealing with suspense, mystery, and often international intrigue. Born in England, he went to Romania, to Spain, then to the USA during the Depression. After two years hack writing there he returned to England. He wrote some short stories, but his reputation was made with *The Third Hour* (1937) and *Rogue Male* (1939) – his first thriller. His other books include *The High Place* (1950), *A Rough Shoot* (1951), *A Time to Kill* (1951), *Watcher in the Shadows* (1960), *Olura* (1965), and *Dance of the Dwarfs* (1968).

HUME, Fergus(on) (Wright) (1859–1932). British author who wrote over 130 novels, but is remembered for only one, *The Mystery of a Hansom Cab* (1886), published in Melbourne, Australia. The first edition (only two copies are known to exist) was published at the author's expense. He did not do very well out of it, and sold all rights to an English group called the Hansom Cab Publishing Company for £50. The book quickly became the best-selling detective novel of the nineteenth century.

Hymns as popular literature. Hymns represent a genuine and deep-seated tradition in popular literature, and reflect some at least of the values and ideas of society. This is particularly true of the nineteenth century, when attendance at church or chapel was very much more widespread than it is today. To some extent, then, hymns were part of the experience of most people.

Before he published the first edition of the *Dictionary of Hymnology* (1891), Dr John Julian, the Editor, examined some 400,000 hymns in several languages. Collections of hymns sold in large numbers. John Keble, *The Christian Year* (1827), went through 43 editions; and Cecil Francis Alexander, *Hymns for Little Children* (1848), sold more than 100 editions by the end of the century. Between 1800 and 1820, when clerical opposition to hymn singing was still strong, nearly 50 different hymnbooks were being used in Anglican churches: by 1872, about 200 were in circulation. *Hymns Ancient and Modern* was a bestseller, with four and a half million copies sold within seven years of publication; and more than 90 million copies of the Sankey hymnbook were sold.

Victorian hymn writers tended to stress the denial of physical pleasure and the virtues of hard work, deference and sobriety. Later in the century a sense of responsibility towards the poor and the subject peoples of the British Empire became apparent in hymns.

SUSAN S. TAMKE, *Make a Joyful Noise unto the Lord* (1978), is an excellent study of Victorian hymns and the values and attitudes implicit in them. It contains a good bibliography. EUGENE D. GENOVESE, *Roll, Jordan, Roll* (1975), has some pertinent things to say about black slave religion, including hymn singing, in the USA.

HYNE, (Charles John) Cutliffe (Wright) (1866–1944). British author and creator of Captain Kettle, a bearded and fiery sailor. Hyne travelled extensively throughout the world, and used his experiences as authentic background for his stories. Captain Kettle first appeared in a magazine serial, 'The Great Sea Swindle', reprinted in book form as *Honour of Thieves* (1895). Another of Hyne's characters was the detective Mr Horrocks, whose exploits were told in a series of short stories the first five of which were published in *The Derelict* (1901).

INGRAHAM, Colonel Prentiss (1843–1904). Prolific American author of dime novels (qv). After a successful military career in the USA, Mexico, Egypt and Europe, he spent some time in the West with Buffalo Bill (see *Western novels*), about whom he wrote many stories. Indeed, he is credited with actually writing some of the novels credited to Buffalo Bill. As a writer he worked quickly and turned out two 35,000 or one 70,000 word novels a month, over a considerable period. Most of his fiction was published by Beadle and Adams (qv). Under his own name he wrote more than 500 novels. Amongst the pseudonyms he used were: Major Dangerfield Burr, Fifth Cavalry, USA; Dr Noel Dunbar; Midshipman T. W. King; Lieut Harry Dennies Perry; Major H. B. Stoddard and Captain Alfred Taylor.

INNES, Michael (1906–   ). Pseudonym of John Innes Mackintosh Stewart, British scholar and author of detective novels. His first novel was *Death at the President's Lodging* (1936); but when published in the USA it was retitled *Seven Suspects*, so that it would not be thought to be a book about the chief executive. The detective featured in this and 28 subsequent books is John Appleby.

Inspector Bucket. Character in *Bleak House* (1852–1853), by Charles Dickens. Probably the first important detective in English literature. Dull, solid, hard-working, competent, successful, he typified most of the official detectives who were later to appear in crime fiction both in Britain and in the USA.

Inspector French. Scotland Yard detective created by Freeman Wills Crofts (qv). He first made his appearance in *Inspector French's Greatest Case* (1924).

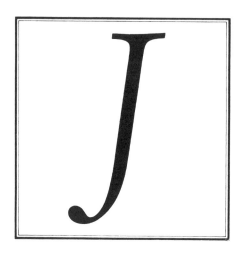

Jack the Giant Killer. In his essay 'Raffles and Miss Blandish' (*Critical Essays*, 1946, p. 153), George Orwell puts forward the view that Jack is a typical hero – Robin Hood and Popeye are others – who fights against all odds, and that he represents 'the basic myth of the Western World.' This is almost certainly true, and Jack seems to have descended from those legendary Teutonic or Indo-European heroes whose exploits were widely enjoyed long before the advent of printing. His adventures were told in eighteenth-century chapbooks, and the appearance of a traditional tale in such a popular medium is an indication of the way in which legendary material could be preserved – even petrified – in print.

The problems involved in tracking down the transformations, metamorphoses, even the adaptability of traditional heroes – and equally, of course, heroines – from early, oral times to their appearances in print are almost insuperable, and the search for origins of 'popular', and to some extent archetypal, characters is endless. The figure of Jack the Giant Killer exemplifies both the difficulties and the inevitable ambiguities involved.

From a fairly considerable, if occasionally oblique, literature which bears to some extent upon the subject, the following may be found useful.

W. A. CLOUSTON, *Popular Tales and Fictions*, 2 vols. (1887. Reprint Detroit, 1968). An old book, but it contains a wealth of knowledge and cannot be ignored.

LORD RAGLAN, *The Hero* (1935). Always stimulating, even when one disagrees. Although an oldish book, it has been twice reprinted.

W. B. STANFORD, *The Ulysses Theme* (2nd ed., 1968). Subtitled 'A Study in the Adaptability of a Traditional Hero', this is an admirable and unusual book.

Of an equally high quality is T. P. COFFIN, *The Female Hero in Folklore and Legend* (1975).

JACOBS, W(illiam) W(hymark) (1863–1943). British author. The son of a wharf overseer in Wapping, London, Jacobs wrote many short stories about the River Thames and dockside life. His best known tale, 'The Monkey's Paw' was published in *The Lady of the Barge* (1902). He also wrote several plays.

James Bond. Fictional secret agent created by Ian Fleming (qv). His service number '007' indicates with its two noughts that he is 'licensed to kill'. Bond is intensely patriotic, fearless, and pursues the enemies of his country with enthusiasm. He loves good living, women and gambling.

His adventures were recounted in the following novels: *Casino Royale* (1953); *Live and Let Die* (1954); *Moonraker* (1955); *Diamonds Are Forever* (1956); *From Russia With Love* (1957); *Dr No* (1958); *Goldfinger* (1959); *For Your Eyes Only* (1960); *Thunderball* (1961); *The Spy Who Loved Me* (1962); *On Her Majesty's Secret Service*; (1963); *You Only Live Twice* (1964); *The Man With the Golden Gun* (1965); *Octopussy and the Living Daylights* (1966), (US title *Octopussy*).

Bond has been featured in a number of highly successful films. A comic strip based upon him has been drawn by an artist called Horak; and he has been the subject of several burlesques and parodies, of which the best is probably *Colonel Sun* (1968) by Robert Markham (pseudonym used by Kingsley Amis).

ORESTE DEL BUONO and UMBERTO ECO, *The Bond Affair* (1966).
O. F. SNELLING, *007 James Bond. A report* (1964).

Jane. British comic strip character created by Norman Pett. She first appeared in the *Daily Mirror*, 5 December 1932, with the title 'Jane's Journal, the Diary of a Bright Young Thing'. Immediately popular, Jane became a national figure during the war, renowned for her readiness to strip and show off her shapely limbs. The strip lasted until 10 October 1959, when Jane and her beloved Georgie Porgie sailed off together into the sunset; and her disappearance from the pages of the *Daily Mirror* brought obituaries and articles in other papers. She was replaced by a teenager called 'Patti', who lasted from 1959 to 1961; then by 'Jane, daughter of Jane' – but she lasted for only two years. Jane, it seemed, was irreplaceable.

Various reprints of her adventures were published in book form. There was a film, *The Adventures of Jane*, in 1949; and a strip-tease show featuring Jane toured British music halls during the war.

Jeeves. See *Wodehouse, P. G.*

Jestbooks. Collections of prose tales or anecdotes designed for entertainment. The earliest collection was made in Renaissance Italy by Poggio, whose *Facetiae* was widely known and enjoyed before his death in 1459. The first English version was a series of 12 'Fables of Poge the

Florentyn', which William Caxton appended to his *Fables of Esope* (1484).

Jestbooks flourished throughout the sixteenth and seventeenth centuries in England. They were of three main types:
(a) collections of single jests, e.g. *Hundred Merry Tales* (1526)
(b) comic biographies, e.g. *Merry Tales of John Skelton* (N.D. ?1566/ 67)
(c) collections of humorous tales. e.g. Tarlton's *News Out of Purgatory* (1590).
Most of the material in such books was far from original – old jokes were capable of constant renovation, and so far as England was concerned they could always be given a Protestant twist. Foreign names, if very outlandish, could easily be anglicized.

The problem with jestbooks is their survival. Given the fact that they were designed to be read and read again, their mortality rate was very high. In some cases only fragments remain: the only perfect copy, for instance, of *Hundred Merry Tales* is in the University Library at Göttingen. Literary antiquaries of the nineteenth century reprinted a number of jestbooks, and some have been reissued in this century. It has to be said, however, that the task of editing and publishing popular prose texts has not yet, with a few notable exceptions, been approached with the kind of critical care that the late Professor H. E. Rollins (qv) brought to the study of the seventeenth-century ballad.

A useful range of jestbook material is to be found in two books by P. M. ZALL, *A Hundred Merry Tales and Other Jestbooks of the Fifteenth and Sixteenth Centuries* and *A Nest of Ninnies and Other English Jestbooks of the Seventeenth Century*, both published at Lincoln, Nebraska (1963 and 1970 respectively). W. C. HAZLITT, *Shakespeare Jest-books* (3 vols., 1864), has been reprinted in its entirety. It can be recommended with reservations.

Two essential studies are: F. P. WILSON, 'The English Jestbooks of the Sixteenth and Seventeenth Centuries', reprinted in F. P. WILSON, *Shakespearean and Other Studies* (1969); and E. SCHULZ, 'Die Englischen Schwankbücher' in *Palaestra* CXVII (1912). An admirable – even unique – piece of jestbook editing is E. A. HORSMAN, *Dobsons Drie Bobbes* (1955).

J. G. Reeder. Character created by Edgar Wallace (qv). Reeder was once connected with Scotland Yard, then employed by Banker's Trust, and was finally on the staff of the public prosecutor. He is presented as a successful private investigator with a mild manner and an extraordinary memory for faces. Conventionally dressed with a bowler hat and pince-nez, he always carries a rolled umbrella in the handle of which a knife blade is concealed. He also carries a gun.

His adventures were featured in: *The Mind of J. G. Reeder* (1925 – US title *The Murder Book of J. G. Reeder*, 1929); *Red Aces* (1929); *The Guv'nor and Other Stories* (1932 –

US title *Mr Reeder Returns*, 1932). The above were all collections of short stories. Reeder was also the central character in two novels: *Room 13* (1924); *Terror Keep* (1927).

There were several films featuring Reeder's adventures.

Joe Miller's Jests; Or, the Wit's Vade-Mecum. Title of a famous joke book first published in 1739 at the price of one shilling. Very little is known about the original Joe Miller who gave his name to a collection which immediately became popular, and was reprinted until quite late in the nineteenth century with altered contents but still with his name on the title-page.

The best edition, called *The New London Jest Book* (1871), has a very useful Introduction by w. c. HAZLITT. The same author's *Studies in Jocular Literature* (Popular edition, 1904) has several references to Joe Miller, and provides essential background for any understanding of this very homely kind of popular literature. Also helpful is JOHN WARDROPER, *Jest upon Jest* (1970), which is an anthology of printed jokes from the reign of Richard III to George III, with a longish Introduction and notes.

See also *Jestbooks*.

JOHNSON, Richard (1573–1659?). British writer of popular fiction whose best-known book was the *Famous Historie of the Seaven Champions of Christendom*. The oldest surviving edition is dated 1597, but this may be the second edition, as it was entered at Stationers' Hall in 1596. Johnson also wrote a jestbook, *Pleasant Conceites of Old Hobson the Merry Londoner* (1607), which went through several editions.

JONES, Hannah Maria (married name Lowndes) (*d.* 1858/59?). British author of some 24 novels, many of them so popular that they were often reissued in unauthorized editions. A number of her books bore no date, but the first was probably *Gretna Green* (1820) and the last *Katherine Beresford; or, the Shade and Sunshine of a Woman's Life* (1850).

She was one of the writers whose work was reprinted by William Milner (qv), and also by other publishers like J. S. Pratt of Stokesley, Yorkshire, and W. Nicholson of Halifax (and later Wakefield), Yorkshire. Both these firms ran cheap series which resembled Milner's 'Cottage Library'.

JUDSON, Edward Zane Carroll (1821–1886). American writer. The life and adventures of 'Colonel' Judson, who was better known as 'Ned Buntline', were as lurid and various as the characters he wrote about in his fiction. As a boy he ran away to sea and served with the United States Navy. He resigned in 1842, and after roaming the prairie he started a magazine called *Ned Buntline's Own* in 1844, while he was in Kentucky. Four years later he revived it in New York. At this period of his life he was writing stories – besides capturing, single-handed, two men wanted for murder and being involved in a duel in which

115

he shot his adversary dead. During the Civil War he served in the Federal Army, and was discharged in 1864 as a private! He was married six times. Despite such an active life, he found time to write – or was credited with writing – 65 sensational novels, most of which were published by Beadle and Adams (qv).

JAY MONAGHAN, *The Great Rascal* (1951).

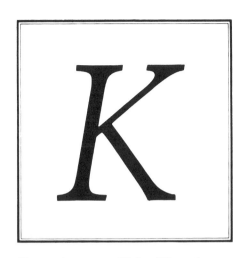

Katzenjammer Kids, The. American comic strip created by Rudolph Dirks in 1897. It told the story of the twins, Hans and Fritz, and their perpetual war against authority. Their usual targets were Mama, der Captain (a former ship-wrecked sailor who acts as their stepfather) and der Inspector. All the characters spoke a kind of English-German, with an effect both unusual and effective.

In 1912 Dirks wanted to change his publisher and a court action ensued. The upshot was that W. R. Hearst, the publisher, kept a legal right to the title of the strip, while Dirks retained rights to the characters. The Katzenjammer Kids reappeared in 1914, drawn by Harold Knerr. He continued until his death in 1949, and was followed by other artists; but quality and appeal dwindled considerably. It is the oldest comic strip in existence. There was a stage version in 1903, and many film cartoons have been based upon it. Rudolph Dirks meanwhile created *The Captain and the Kids*. He died in 1968, and the strip was taken over officially by his son John, who had been assisting his father since 1946. Although it survives, the strip is not widely circulated throughout the USA.

KEENE, Carolyn (1862–1930). Pseudonym of Edward L. Stratemeyer – and later his daughter Harriet S. Adams – American author of children's books who created Nancy Drew (qv). Stratemeyer wrote three novels about this young detective, and his daughter the remainder. He began his career early, writing dime novels; and in 1906 he founded the Stratemeyer Syndicate which published over 1,200 children's books. He supplied plot outlines and edited some 700 of these before his death. He was succeeded by his two daughters, and one of them, Harriet S. Adams, still runs the firm. Amongst the successful series published were those featuring: Tom Swift; the Rover Boys; the Bobbsey Twins; the Hardy Boys (qv); Ted Scott;

Bomba the Jungle Boy; the Pioneer Boys; Dave Porter; the Dana Girls; Kay Tracy; and of course Nancy Drew. It is said that, under 46 pseudonyms, Stratemeyer Syndicate books have so far sold over 100 million copies.

KEIGHTLEY, Thomas (1789–1842). British antiquary and historian who spent his life in literary and journalistic work in London. Among his publications are two of especial value to the study of popular literature, *Fairy Mythology* (2 vols., 1828), which appeared anonymously; and *Tales and Popular Fictions; their Resemblance, and Transmission from Country to Country* (1834).

KEMP, William (*fl.* 1600). British comic actor who was very popular with audiences during his lifetime. In 1599 he attracted a great deal of attention by dancing a jig from London to Norwich. The event was celebrated in a jestbook (qv), *Kemps Nine Daies Wonder* (1600), which was reprinted under the same title, with an Introduction and Notes, by the Rev. Alexander Dyce in 1840.

There is an entry on Kemp in the *Dictionary of National Biography*.

Kent Murdock. Photographer and detective created by G. H. Coxe (qv). His adventures were told in 21 novels published between 1935 and 1969.

KNIGHT, Charles (1791–1873). British publisher, author and editor.

Knight became publisher to the Society for the Diffusion of Useful Knowledge, and involved in a number of educational enterprises of which the most notable was *The Penny Magazine*. It ran from 1832 to 1845, and by the end of its first year there was a sale of 200,000 copies weekly; but by the mid-forties the circulation had fallen to 40,000 and costs of production were barely covered. The magazine had been founded to provide working-class readers with wholesome and didactic matter. In the event, it was not altogether successful in this aim, and it did not reach the public for whom it was intended.

Knight published several instructional works, including a series of 'Weekly Volumes for All Readers'; but although many of these were good, and the series paid its way, he did not succeed in reaching the mass market in the way that, for example, James Catnach (qv) did. Knight's importance for popular literature lies in the fact that he was concerned to persuade people to buy books for themselves, and his advocacy of self-help book clubs – for which he provided instructions and free book labels – was both practical and successful.

Knight's three-volume autobiography, *Passages of a Working Life* (1864–65) is the best source for his life and achievements.

R. K. WEBB, *The British Working Class Reader 1790–1848* (1955).

HAROLD SMITH, *The Society for the Diffusion of Useful Knowledge 1826–1846. A Social and Bibliog-*

raphical Evaluation, Dalhousie University, School of Library Service, Occasional Paper No. 8, (1974). Knight himself wrote an essay, 'The Beginnings of Popular Literature', published in *Once upon a Time* (New and Enlarged Edition, 1865).

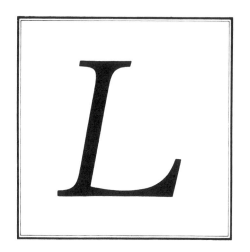

LACKINGTON, James (1746–1815). British bookseller born in the West Country, who started in business at the age of ten selling pies in the street. He then became an almanac seller. In 1773 he went with his wife to London, where he ran a bookstall and a shoemaker's shop. In six months, having borrowed £5 from 'Mr Wesley's people', the value of his stock had increased so much that he was able to give up shoemaking and devote himself entirely to books. By 1779 his shop called 'The Temple of the Muses', situated at one corner of Finsbury Square, contained over 12,000 volumes. (The ornate doorway of Lackington's premises was the last part to survive – it disappeared in 1970). The books were arranged in a series of ascending galleries – the dearest were on the ground floor, and the higher one went, the cheaper – and shabbier – the books became.

He was one of the first booksellers to realize the importance of the remainder trade. All his business was done for cash, and no credit was allowed. His undoubted success as a bookseller (and as a publisher) was due to the fact that he met the very real need of his times for cheap books.

J. LACKINGTON, *Memoirs* (1791 and reprints) – his own account of his career.
V. E. NEUBURG, *Popular Literature* (1977).

LEBLANC, Maurice (1864–1941). French playwright, novelist, short story writer, and creator of Arsène Lupin (qv). In 1906 the first Arsène Lupin adventure appeared in a magazine; from then on, Maurice Leblanc was an extraordinarily successful author, and eventually became a member of the French Legion of Honour.

LE CARRÉ, John (1931–   ). Pseudonym of David John Moore Cornwell, British author of spy thrillers. His characters lack the glamour of James Bond (qv), and are often shown as social misfits.

Amongst his best known novels are *Call for the Dead* (1960), *A Murder of Quality* (1962), *The Spy Who Came in from the Cold* (1963), *The Looking Glass War* (1965), and *Tinker, Tailor, Soldier, Spy* (1974). Several of le Carré's books have been made into successful films.

LE QUEUX, William (Tufnell) (1864–1927). British author of mysteries and spy thrillers. A career which started in journalism continued with the writing of more than 100 books, including several volumes of short stories. His first book, *Guilty Bonds* (1890), is about political conspiracy in Russia (where the book was banned). For the next 20 years or so le Queux wrote a succession of stories in which France, and later Germany, are seen as the enemy. In *The Great War in England in 1897* (1894) Russian and French forces invade Britain; in *England's Peril* (1899) a Member of Parliament is betrayed and murdered by his wife, who is in love with the head of the French Secret Service. *The Invasion of 1910* (1905) and *Spies of the Kaiser* (1909) contain episodes which, it has been claimed, demonstrate that le Queux accurately predicted some of the events of the Great War of 1914–1918.

LEVIN, Ira (1929–   ). Versatile American author whose output includes song lyrics, television scripts and Broadway shows. His

12 James Lackington's bookshop c. 1795

121

best known novels are *A Kiss Before Dying* (1953), *Rosemary's Baby* (1967), and *The Stepford Wives* (1972) – a horrifying story of life in the suburbs. These three books have all been successfully filmed.

LEWIS, Matthew Gregory (1775–1818). Prolific British author in prose and verse, playwright, Member of Parliament. Lewis became known as 'Monk' Lewis because of his novel *The Monk* (3 vols., 1796). It was enormously popular and is one of the most famous of gothic novels (qv).

Li'l Abner. American comic strip created by Al Capp (Alfred G. Caplin), starting as a daily feature on 20 August 1934. The setting was a mythical hillbilly community where Li'l Abner was pursued by Daisy Mae, who eventually became his wife. Other characters included Pansy Yokum, Li'l Abner's 'mammy', Hairless Joe, Lonesome Polecat and Moonbeam Mr Swine. It was a brilliantly drawn satirical strip which became popular amongst millions of readers. There was something of a latterday noble savage about him. In time, however, Capp's views became increasingly disenchanted, and he had little sympathy with events such as the student protest of the 1960s and early 1970s. As the strip became more and more a vehicle for its creator's conservative views, and less vigorously funny, its popularity seemed to diminish, until Capp gave it up some time before his death in 1979.

Limerick. A five-line humorous verse.

The limerick's an art form complex
Whose contents run chiefly to sex;
It's famous for virgins
And masculine urgin's
And vulgar erotic effects.

Both origins of the form and derivation of the name are uncertain. It became popular in Britain during the 1860s. Edward Lear, painter and poet, wrote a number which were distinguished by their final rhyme being identical with that of the first two lines. This was a convention which gradually lost favour.

There was a limerick craze in Britain in 1906 and 1907. In the latter year, in a competition organized by a cigarette company, £3 a week for life was offered to the competitor who submitted the best last line of a limerick. For the most part, however, the limerick has led a clandestine, though vigorous, life as part of a bawdy oral tradition, known to everyone but admitted to by comparatively few. The so-called 'clean' limerick has also maintained popularity, and is still featured in anthologies of light verse.

The bibliography of the limerick is more extensive than one might suppose.

W. S. BARING GOULD, *The Lure of the Limerick* (1968), is the best introduction to the subject and contains a very full list of sources.

In GERSHON LEGMAN, *The Horn Book* (1964), there is a brilliantly idiosyncratic and informative essay entitled 'The Limerick. A History in 'Brief'. The earliest history of the subject, LANGFORD REED, *The Complete Limerick Book* (1924), is still worth reading, though it is of course confined to 'clean' limericks.

Literacy. Within the context of the present book the term 'literacy' is taken to mean the ability to read. In the last quarter of the twentieth century the existence of a mass reading public in Britain and the USA is taken for granted. The origins of such readership go back for several hundred years, and its growth, with the parallel growth over the last five or so centuries of a considerable popular literature, is not in doubt.

The educational experiences of the two countries were not identical during the whole of that period, but they did share the seventeenth and eighteenth century Puritan impulse to teach poor children to read God's word for themselves. It is only fair to say that the philanthropists and reformers who initiated and supported charitable educational endeavours believed that, when people had been taught to read, they would remain content with the Bible and devotional literature. Those who objected to elementary education for the poor rejected this argument – and events were to prove them right. In fact, the ability to read opened up new dimensions to human experience, and novel, radical and heterodox ideas became readily accessible. Once there was a mass reading public, things were never to be the same again.

The foundations of mass literacy, then, were laid by those who sought to provide a basic education from charitable motives, and by the time of the Education Act of 1870, the problem of inability to read was not the fundamental one in educational reform. The USA experienced some difference in that it had a special compulsion. With the influx of immigrants whose native tongue was not English, mastery of that tongue was essential if one was to survive and to succeed in terms of the Puritan work ethic in a new country.

With literacy established, mass readership was in a position to develop – and it did so as a consequence of the invention and exploitation of the printing press. What is important here is not altogether the way in which literacy is achieved, or still less the way in which its historical levels should be measured (this, incidentally, is a matter of some disagreement amongst a few British historians). The crucial issue is the impact that literacy makes upon society; and this particular theme has only recently become the subject of detailed analysis. This relationship between people and what they read, not least at a popular level, is a complex one, and future discussion must involve questions about what being able to read does to individuals and to the society in which they live.

The printed word has been a means of both social control and the spread of heterodox ideas – and both issues are live ones today. Social movements of all kinds have spawned a mass of popular publications. Nineteenth-century evangelists, for example, attached great importance to the distribution of religious tracts; and the secular movement of the nineteenth century also produced a considerable literature. The common factor was that each believed that the ability to read would help its cause – that power lay in the printed word. In a wider context, we should be asking how perceptions of the world were reshaped in the light of literacy, and what modifications to men's and women's experience were made by the printed word.

Apart from current UNESCO publications dealing with literacy in the modern world, the following are valuable:

CARLO M. CIPOLLA, *Literacy and Development in the West* (1969).
L. FEBVRE and H. J. MARTIN, *The Coming of the Book* (1975).
E. L. EISENSTEIN, *The Printing Press as an Agent of Change*, 2 vols. (1979).
From an historical point of view, see:
R. D. ALTICK, *The English Common Reader. A Social History of the Mass Reading Public 1800–1900* (1957).
V. E. NEUBURG, *Popular Education in Eighteenth Century England* (1971). The central argument of the book rests upon the assumption that the skills of reading and writing were regarded in the past as separate activities, and that the ability to read was seen by contemporaries as the more important of the two. There are details of how reading was taught in eighteenth century schools and of the range of textbooks and teaching material available. There is also a section on individual readers. See Chapters 1, 2, 3 and *passim*.
V. E. NEUBURG, *Popular Literature* (1977), pp. 293–295, contains bibliographical references to reading and readers.
DAVID CRESSY, *Literacy and the Social Order. Reading and Writing in Tudor and Stuart England* (1980).
H. S. BENNETT, *English Books and Readers* (3 vols., 1952, 1965, 1970). Comprehensive but uncritical; covering the period 1475–1640.
For the implications of literacy, see N. Z. DAVIS, 'Printing and the People' published in her *Society and Culture in Early Modern France* (1975) pp. 189–226; H. J. GRAFF, *Literacy and Social Development in the West* (1981).

See *Bunyan, John*; *Clare, John*.

'Literature on a string'. Spanish sellers of chapbooks and ballads often displayed the wares they offered for sale on lengths of string, rather like clothing hung on a line. Hence Spanish popular literature was sometimes known as 'La literatura de cordel'. Ballad sellers in Victorian London, and probably elsewhere, sometimes exhibited their sheets by attaching them to a convenient wall, cf. William Wordsworth: 'Here files of ballads dangle from dead walls' (*The Prelude* VII).

There is a model study of Spanish popular literature: JULIO CARO BAROJA, *Ensayo Sobre la Literatura de Cordel*, Madrid (1969).

LLOYD, Edward (1815–1890). British publisher, who at a very early age started a shop in Shoreditch, London, where he sold papers and magazines. In 1836 he began publishing cheap sensational fiction for boys, and soon moved into adult popular fiction, specializing in gothic horrors, historical romances and domestic tales. He also published a number of titles in which Charles Dickens's characters were shamelessly plagiarized (see *Dickens imitations*). By about 1856 he had issued more than 200 stories of various lengths, usually appearing in penny weekly parts, some of them in one or another of the magazines which he founded (*Penny Weekly Miscellany, Entertaining Journal* and *Lloyd's Penny Miscellany* are three of them: there may be others). The most famous of his stories, *The String of Pearls; or, The Barber of Fleet Street*, commenced publication in 92 numbers in 1850. It was written by Thomas Peckett Prest (qv), and the villain was Sweeney Todd (qv). Prest and Malcolm J. Merry (qv) were the most prolific and lurid of all Lloyd's authors.

He published from the following London addresses: 44 Wych Street, Strand; 62 Broad Street, Bloomsbury; 31 Curtain Road, Shoreditch; 231 Shoreditch; 12 Salisbury Square, Fleet Street.

It was from this last address that most of his stories came, and it gave rise to the term 'Salisbury Square Fiction' to describe cheap sensational novels, also known as 'penny dreadfuls' or 'penny bloods' (qv), but in later life Lloyd made strenuous efforts to live down and disown his early ventures in publishing fiction. He became a respectable newspaper proprietor and the owner of a paper mill in Kent; and indeed, so successful were his attempts to obscure his early days that in the *Dictionary of National Biography* (vol. XI, p. 1298) there is no mention of penny fiction in the account of his career!

Material on Lloyd as a publisher of fiction is sparse in the extreme. JOHN MEDCRAFT, *A Bibliography of the Penny Bloods of Edward Lloyd*, was privately published in an edition of 200 copies in 1945; there is an unpublished bibliography, 'Salisbury Square Fiction' by STEPHEN ROBERTS, in possession of the present writer, whose *Popular Literature* (1977, pp. 170–174) summarises most of what is known about Lloyd.

LOCK, William John (1863–1930). British author of over 30 novels, the first *At the Gate of Samaria* (1895) and the last *The Town of Tombarel* (1930). His most famous work was *The Beloved Vagabond* (1906), which he rewrote as a play in 1908. Lock wrote to entertain his readers, and did not see himself as having any other function. His favourite character was the vagabond whose behaviour and way of life could not be understood by dull, pompous and pretentious people.

Long Meg of Westminster. Roistering heroine (and early example of women's liberation!) whose adventures were first – and anonymously – related in *The Life and Pranks of Long Meg of Westminster* (1582). It contains 15 chapters, after each of which she emerges triumphantly from encounters with such characters as the Bailiff of Westminster, a Spanish Knight, assorted Frenchmen at Boulogne, sundry clergymen and others. The book is very much in the tradition of jest books (qv), and was enormously popular and often reprinted. It survived in a rather shortened form as an eighteenth-century chapbook.

Many early English writers, Thomas Middleton and Ben Jonson among them, make references to her; but little or nothing of substance is known, not even whether she was an entirely fictional character or based originally upon a real person.

During the nineteenth century, in the earlier volumes of *Notes and Queries*, there was some correspondence regarding the burial place of Long Meg. Fascinatingly erudite and inconclusive, the exchange of letters, with some introductory matter and two versions of Long Meg's adventures, were edited by Charles Hindley and published by Reeves and Turner in 1871. It was later included in *The Old Book Collector's Miscellany*, which was available in both three- and six-volume sets during the 1870s.

Lord Peter Wimsey. Private detective and bibliophile created by Dorothy L. Sayers (qv). His full name was Peter Death Bredon Wimsey, he was born in 1890, educated at Eton and Oxford, and took to detection after distinguished service in the 1914–18 war. His Sergeant, Bunter, later became his manservant and figures in many of the stories. Wimsey married Harriet Vane in 1935 (in *Busman's Honeymoon*).

His adventures are told in the following books: *Whose Body?* (1923); *Clouds of Witness* (1926); *The Dawson Pedigree* (1927) (US title *Unnatural Death*); *The Unpleasantness at the Bellona Club* (1928); *Lord Peter Views the Body* (1928) (Short stories); *Strong Poison* (1930); *The Five Red Herrings* (1931) (US title *Suspicious Characters*); *Have His Carcase* (1932); *Murder Must Advertise* (1933); *Hangman's Holiday* (1933) (Short stories – four are about Wimsey); *The Nine Tailors* (1934); *Gaudy Night* (1935); *Busman's Honeymoon* (1937); *In the Teeth of the Evidence* (1939) (Short stories – two are about Wimsey); *Lord Peter* (1972) (Short stories); *Talboys* (1972) (First appearance in a limited edition pamphlet, then published in the 2nd Edition of *Lord Peter*).

Wimsey has also featured in films, on the stage, on radio and on television.

LOVECRAFT, H. P. (1890–1937). American author of horror and fantasy stories. The best of his work has a nightmarish quality, although some of it is repetitive. He is remembered, however, less for his fiction than for the influence he has had upon subsequent science fiction writers.

L. SPRAGUE DE CAMP, *Lovecraft: a Biography* (1975).

Lubok. Russian broadside with woodcut and copper engravings. Dating from the early seventeenth century to the beginning of the twentieth, this was a popular form of street literature. The subject matter was varied and the illustrations were often in colour.

Y. OVSYANNIKOV, *The Lubok*, Moscow (1969). This contains an English text by Arthur Shkarovsky-Raffé and is extremely well illustrated.

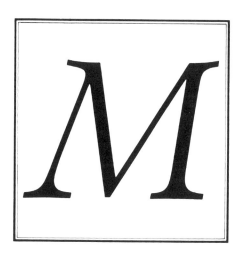

Maigret. French detective created by Georges Simenon (qv). Although he has a first name, Jules, he is always know as Maigret. After an unsuccessful attempt to study medicine he joined the Paris police, pounded the beat for two years, became a detective, and eventually a commissaire (commissioner). Between 1931 and 1972 there were 76 books about him, not all of which have been translated into English. Maigret's methods are intuitive. In his investigations he is both patient and compassionate, and invariably successful.

MANNING, William Henry (1852–1929). American writer of popular fiction, most of it published by Beadle and Adams (qv). Altogether he produced over 200 novels, using his own name and a variety of pseudonyms which included: Captain Mark Wilton, Major E. L. St. Vrain, Ben Halliday, Jo Pierce, Hugh Warren, U. S. Warren, J. T. Warren, Warren Walters, Warren F. Kent, Ned Warren, Barry De Forest, W. M. Hoyt.

Martin Hewitt. Detective created by Arthur Morrison (qv), and the first popular sleuth whose methods were modelled upon those of Sherlock Holmes (qv). Like the master's, Hewitt's exploits – recounted by his journalist friend, Brett – were first published in *The Strand Magazine* and illustrated by Sidney Paget.

Four volumes of short stories contain all the Hewitt adventures: *Martin Hewitt, Investigator* (1894); *The Chronicles of Martin Hewitt* (1895); *The Adventures of Martin Hewitt* (1896); *The Red Triangle* (1903).

Matt Helm. Created by Donald Hamilton (qv). After war service Helm went back to his peacetime job; but in the early 1960s was called back to the secret military organization in which he had previously served. The chief is known as 'Mac' (cf. 'M' in the James Bond series), and Helm is sent on a number of special assignments. The fact that the break-up of his marriage follows is accepted without demur. The stories are harsh and realistic, and do not present spying in a glamorous light.

There have been several Matt Helm films which, like the Bond films, have featured global menace, fantasy and pretty girls. Up until 1975 there were 16 Helm novels: *Death of a Citizen* (1960); *The Wrecking Crew* (1960); *The Removers* (1961); *The Silencers* (1962); *Murderers' Row* (1962); *The Ambushers* (1963); *The Shadowers* (1964); *The Ravagers* (1964); *The Devastators* (1965); *The Betrayers* (1966); *The Menacers* (1968); *The Interlopers* (1969); *The Poisoners* (1971); *The Intriguers* (1973); *The Intimidators* (1974); *The Terminators* (1975).

MAY WYNNE (1875–1949). Pseudonym of Mabel Winifred Knowles, prolific British author of popular fiction published between 1904 and 1927, some of it by Amalgamated Press (qv). An extensive list of her books appears in *Who's Who in Literature* (1933 edition). (I have been unable to discover any biographical details.)

McBAIN, Ed (1926–   ). American author. Born Salvatore A. Lombino, he changed his name to Evan Hunter; and under this name he wrote probably his most famous book, *The Blackboard Jungle* (1954), about violence in New York schools.

As Ed McBain he writes the very popular series of books abut the 87th Precinct (qv), which are characterized by realism, terror, brutality and slapstick humour. Two McBain novels, *The Sentries* (1965) and *Where There's Smoke* (1975) are not about the 87th Precinct.

He has also used the pseudonyms Richard Marsten, Hunt Collins and Curt Cannon.

Hunter has written scripts for films and for television.

McCULLOUGH, Colleen. Contemporary Australian born author of a best selling novel, *The Thorn Birds*. She started writing this at night, after a day's work, in June 1975: it was finished a year later, and published in the USA in May 1977. Within twelve months it had sold more copies than any other novel of the preceding decade, and the rights had been sold all over the world for more money than had previously been paid for a book.

The story begins in 1915 and closes after the Second World War. Its heroine is Meggie, only daughter amongst the seven children of a New Zealand farm labourer who moves to Australia. Her passionate, forbidden love for the priest Ralph de Brissicart spans more than half a century. This was the author's third novel.

McNEILE, Herman Cyril (1888–1937). British writer of crime and adventure stories, and creator of Bulldog Drummond (qv). Many of McNeile's tales were published under the pseudonym 'Sapper', British Army slang for an engineer, and

129

he did in fact serve in the Army from 1907 to 1919.

McNeile's stories were fast and full of action, featuring a blend of violence and romance, with villains who were usually foreigners with no redeeming virtues. Besides Bulldog Drummond, a similar character named Jim Maitland was featured in some of the tales, the first of them *The Island of Terror*, 1930 (US title *Guardians of the Treasure*). Another of McNeile's creations was Ronald Standish, who appeared in a novel of that name in 1933, and a second, *Ask for Ronald Standish*, came out a year before the author's death. Further stories featured other detectives, agents and adventurers, but Bulldog Drummond remains this writer's most famous character.

Mediaeval romance. Some eighteenth-century chapbooks were descended from mediaeval romance. Guy of Warwick, Sir Bevis of Southampton, Valentine and Orson, for example, had all been known in the middle ages; and eventually, after a long period of literary and social change, they had become the popular heroes of a humbler and less sophisticated literature characterized by the chapbook.

Unravelling and tracing the tangled thread of chapbook origins, however fascinating, obscures an important question: to what extent can we consider mediaeval romance itself as the popular literature of earlier times? A recent book by V. B. Richmond, *The Popularity of Middle English Romance* (Ohio, 1975), argues persuasively that printed versions of romances were indeed popular amongst fifteenth-century readers. If this argument is correct and becomes generally accepted, then discussions concerning the development of popular taste, no less than fiction, will inevitably be enriched.

MEEKE, Mary. (*fl.* 1795–1823). British writer. Under her own name and that of Gabrielli she wrote about 50 novels which were publishd between 1795 and 1823. She also translated several romances from the French.

MERRY, Malcolm J. See *Rymer, James Malcolm*.

METALIOUS, Grace (1924–1964). Bestselling American author whose *Peyton Place* (1956) formed the basis of a television soap opera which was popular both in the USA and in Britain. She also wrote *Tight White Collar* (1960) and *No Adam in Eden* (1963).

Michael Shayne. Private detective created by Brett Halliday (qv). His adventures have been chronicled in 67 books published between 1939 and 1974. Tall, tough, rugged, Shayne is intensely loyal to his friends, who include his secretary, Lucy Hamilton, a reporter on the Miami Daily News, Timothy Rourke, and chief of detectives in Miami, Will Gentry.

During the 1940s there were 12 Shayne films, the first seven starring Lloyd Nolan as the detective and the remaining five, Hugh Beaumont.

There was a short-lived radio series with Jeff Chandler playing Shayne; and in 1960 Richard Denning took the part in a 30-programme series on American television.

Mickey Mouse. Comic character who began life in Walt Disney cartoon films in 1929. He started to appear in comic strip form in January 1930, when Disney himself wrote some of the original story lines and two artists, Ub Iwerks and Win Smith, did the drawings. At this stage the strip was undistinguished, and remained at this level until Disney appointed Floyd Gottfredson to draw Mickey Mouse. Almost immediately it achieved outstanding success, and was syndicated in an increasingly large number of newspapers. By 1931 a whole Sunday page was being devoted to Mickey Mouse and to a host of supporting characters which included Minnie Mouse, Horace Horsecollar, Clarabelle Cow and Pluto. In 1938 Gottfredson found the weekly page too burdensome, and it was dropped.

The strip, however, continued – with Mickey Mouse fighting pirates, flying aeroplanes and rescuing friends from the clutches of mad scientists with hypnotic rays. Film cartoons, which continued to be popular as well, bore no relation to the newspaper strip which maintained its appearance throughout the war and into the early 1950s. It was then that a King Features edict eliminated action and adventure from humorous strips. This was the end of Gottfredson's Mickey Mouse.

Today Mickey, Minnie, and others including Donald Duck, still lead a vigorous life as comic characters, and are household names throughout the world.

DAVID BAIN and BRUCE HARRIS (eds.), *Mickey Mouse. Fifty Happy Years* (1977).

Mike Hammer. Tough – the toughest? – private detective in fiction, created by Mickey Spillane (qv). In the pursuit of justice Hammer kicks, gouges, breaks limbs and shoots in the stomach. There are no doubts. There is no self-questioning. Justice for Hammer is a matter of vengeance, and the villain deserves what he gets. Inevitably, perhaps, Hammer has been called a fascist – a charge that is meaningless but easy to sustain. His assistant, confidante, secretary, is the dark-haired Velda, the most sparkling of all the voluptuous women in the stories.

Hammer first appeared in *I, the Jury* (1947), and there were ten subsequent novels. In one of them, *Kiss me Deadly* (1952), he burns the villain to death and watches the body being consumed by the flames. *I, the Jury* was filmed in 1953, and film versions of other Hammer novels followed. In the 1950s he was featured on American radio and television.

Novels in which Hammer featured are as follows: *I, the Jury* (1947); *Vengeance is Mine!* (1950); *My Gun is Quick* (1950); *The Big Kill* (1951); *One Lonely Night* (1951); *Kiss me Deadly* (1952); *The Girl Hunters* (1962); *The Twisted*

Thing (1966) – written in 1947, previously unpublished); *The Body Lovers* (1967); *Survival . . . Zero!* (1970).

Mills and Boon. British publishing firm specializing in romantic fiction, founded in 1908 by Gerald Mills and Charles Boon. Authors published in those early days included Robert Lynd, Hugh Walpole, Jack London and P. G. Wodehouse; and there were also a number of educational titles. The outbreak of the Great War in 1914, followed by the difficult years of the 1920s and the death of Gerald Mills in 1929, brought a need for new capital.

Charles Boon was a great theatregoer, and had always published novels in the style of the Haymarket Theatre shows, free from violence, sadism and sex. The development of commercial lending libraries throughout Britain in the 1930s brought a tremendous demand for fiction of this kind, and Mills and Boon supplied it to such good effect that by 1936 sales and profits were double what they had been in 1929. As sales of romantic novels rose, the general and educational side of the business lapsed until by 1939 it was virtually non-existent, and the firm had become one of the most specialized houses in British publishing.

After the war, with the increasing appeal of television, commercial libraries declined. A major outlet was thus lost, and the firm began to feel its way back into general publishing. *Discovering Embroidery* (1955) was an instant success, and still sells well. Other titles were readily accepted by school libraries and, with a bias towards women's interests, the general list expanded. In the early 1960s school textbooks in craft and technical subjects, together with titles on home economics, were published.

The year 1958 marked a turning point. Harlequin (qv), a Canadian publishing firm based in Winnipeg, asked for the North American rights of some Mills and Boon romances. The result was a fruitful association which led to an amalgamation of the two firms in 1972. Since then Mills and Boon (Harlequin in the North American continent) have gone from strength to strength, and produce one of the fastest-selling paperback lines in the world. There are subsidiary companies in Australia, New Zealand and Holland, and translations have appeared in Finnish, Swedish, Norwegian, Danish, German, Italian, Spanish, Portuguese and Hebrew. In 1975 the firm was issuing over 150 hardback and 120 paperback titles a year, and sales throughout the world are counted in millions.

Note: No published history of the firm exists, and I am grateful to Mills and Boon for these details.

MILNER, William (1803–1850). British publisher. After setting up in his teens as a general dealer, William Milner became a jobbing printer in Halifax, Yorkshire, and then went into publishing. He specialized in cheap books, and his firm issued the novels of many popular nineteenth-century British and American authors (See *Arthur, T. S.*). The

'Cottage Library' which he founded consisted of dumpy little books measuring about three inches by five inches (Royal 32mo), and cost one shilling each in cloth bindings. The series ran for about 50 years, and outlived its founder.

Milner started publishing in 1834 with *English Bards and Scotch Reviewers* by Lord Byron, which cost one shilling and sixpence. He was soon joined by Francis R. Sowerby and the imprint became Milner and Sowerby. In 1866 the firm opened a distribution centre in London, and in 1883 the name changed to Milner and Co. Ltd. The firm finally went into liquidation in 1910.

Milner's firm was one of the most important in the provision of cheap books for the mass market. There were imitators – William Nicholson of Wakefield, Yorkshire, and later of London, for example – but the Milner publishing house stands supreme as the forerunner of notable twentieth-century paperback enterprises. The publishing history of the firm is hard to trace, because after 1867 no books appearing under its imprint were dated!

Note: For most of this information I am indebted to Miss M. B. Halstead, who drew my attention to an account of William Milner written by D. Bridge and printed in the Halifax local newspaper, *The Courier*, 24 and 31 January, 7 and 14 February, 1970.

Minerva Press, The. Publishing house and subscription circulating library founded by William Lane (?1745/6–1814), which specialized in gothic novels (qv).

DOROTHY BLAKEY, *The Minerva Press 1790–1820* (1939).
D. P. VARMA, *The Evergreen Tree of Diabolical Knowledge* (1972). Despite its somewhat idiosyncratic title, this is a thorough survey of early nineteenth-century circulating libraries.

Miss Jane Marple. See *Christie, Agatha.*

MITCHELL, Margaret (1900–1949). American author of the blockbusting bestseller, *Gone With the Wind* (1936), which she began writing in 1926. The passions and the tragedy of the heroine, Scarlett O'Hara, took the world by storm, and the story was made into an equally successful film. It was the only book that Margaret Mitchell wrote.

MORE, Hannah (1744–1833). British writer, philanthropist, evangelist and educationalist. In 1792 she wrote a tract called *Village Politics*, which was an attack upon the radical views of Thomas Paine designed for the popular market. Its success was such that the author was prevailed upon by the Bishop of London, Beilby Porteus, to initiate a series of similar publications which would provide, at a very low price, a corrective to atheism and radicalism, besides offering a challenge to the continuing popularity of the 'godless' chapbook.

The result was the series of 'Cheap Repository Tracts'. 114 of them were published between 1795 and 1798, and Hannah More herself wrote at least 50 of them. In appearance they greatly resembled chapbooks, even to the woodcut illustration on the cover; but the contents – stories, ballads and Sunday readings – were essentially evangelistic and moral in tone. Many of them – at least those written by Hannah More – were relieved from the bleakness of so much tract literature by the simple fact that she was a skilful writer, deft in her characterization and narrative, and the language she used was simple and clear. Some of her longer stories were serials. 'Next month you may expect a full account of the many tricks and frolics of idle Jack Brown. . . .'; and more forbiddingly, 'Do not forget to inquire for Jack Brown in prison.' Different titles appeared monthly, and prices were low – one halfpenny, one penny, or sometimes three halfpence. They were widely circulated, but their influence is difficult to assess. Hannah More was absolutely clear about the aim of Cheap Repository Tracts: 'Vulgar and indecent books', she wrote, 'were always common, but speculative infidelity brought down to the pockets and capacity of the poor form a new era in our history. This requires strong counteraction.' (W. Roberts, *Memoirs . . . of Mrs Hannah More*, 1834, vol. 2, p. 456). Amongst the best-known of her tracts were *The Shepherd of Salisbury Plain*; *Parley the Porter*; *The History of Mr Fantom*; *The Two Wealthy Farmers*; and *The Sunday School*.

M. G. JONES, *Hannah More* (1952). This supersedes all preceding biographies.

G. H. SPINNEY, 'Cheap Repository Tracts: Hazard and Marshall Edition' published in *Transactions of the Bibliographical Society. The Library*, 4th Series, vol. 20, 1939, pp. 295–340.

HARRY B. WEISS, *Hannah More's Cheap Repository Tracts in America* (1946, reprinted from *The Bulletin of the New York Public Library*, July and August 1946).

MORRIS, Charles (1833–1922). American author of more than 145 dime novels (qv) under a variety of pen names which included: C. E. Tripp, R. R. Inman, George S. Kaine, Paul Preston, William Murry, E. L. Vincent, J. H. Southard, Roland Dare, S. M. Frazier, Hugh Allen, J. D. Ballard, Paul Pastnor.

MORRISON, Arthur (1863–1945). British author and creator of Martin Hewitt (qv). In addition to these stories, Morrison wrote about the London slums: *Tales of Mean Streets* (1894), *A Child of the Jago* (1896), *To London Town* (1899). He also wrote several mystery stories, including *The Green Eye of Goona* (1903 – American title *The Green Diamond*) – an adventure ending in a murder.

Mother Shipton. Legendary Yorkshire prophetess who has been well-known since the seventeenth

THE HISTORY OF
MR. FANTOM,

THE
New fashioned PHILOSOPHER *and his Man*

WILLIAM.

Sold by J. MARSHALL,

(PRINTER to the CHEAP REPOSITORY for Religious and
Moral Tracts) No. 17, Queen-Street, Cheapside, and No, 4,
Aldermary Church-Yard, LONDON.

By S. HAZARD, at Bath; J. ELDER, at Edinburgh; and
by all Bookfellers, Newfmen, and Hawkers, in Town and
Country.

Great Allowance will be made to Shopkeepers and Hawkers.

PRICE THREE HALFPENCE.

Or, 6s. 9d. per 100.—50 for 2s. 9d.—2s. 3d. for 25,
A cheaper Edition for Hawkers.

[Entered at Stationers Hall.]

*13 One of Hannah More's Cheap Repository
Tracts*

century. Any traditions concerning her birth, life and death are contradictory. Her earliest appearance in print was *The Prophesie of Mother Shipton* (1641), a pamphlet of four leaves. It was followed by many others, some published as chapbooks (qv).

Mother Shipton's Prophecies (ANON., 1979 (1881), facsimile of a book first published in 1881. Besides an introduction and a useful bibliography it contains reprints of three seventeenth-century Mother Shipton publications.

See *Popular prophecy.*

MULFORD, Clarence Edward (1883–1956). American author and creator of the Western hero Hopalong Cassidy, whose adventures appeared in books published between 1907 and 1941. By 1949 66 Hopalong Cassidy films had been made, and there was a successful and long-running television series.

MUNSEY, Frank Andrew (1854–1925). American publisher, son of a Maine farmer and builder, Munsey suffered from ill health as a child and had little formal schooling. At the age of 15 he worked for the local postmaster in Mercer, Maine; and from here he went to the Western Union Telegraph Company in Portland as an operator, soon becoming manager of the office in Augusta. It was at a boarding house in this town that he met a mail order publisher and was inspired to go into publishing himself. With $40 of his own money and $260 that he borrowed, he arrived in New York on 23 September 1882 to begin a career in publishing. His first venture, *Golden Argosy*, was a magazine for boys and girls. For ten years he was not successful; but between 1894 and 1907 his magazines earned him $8,780,905.70 in net profits.

Munsey was always ready to kill off a magazine which did not sell well, and this same readiness earned him a good deal of ill will from journalists in the newspaper world, because he invariably closed down, sold or merged newspapers which he did not deem successful in terms of circulation. He was in fact less successful as a newspaper publisher, failing in his attempt to create a tabloid daily in New York; but he diversified his interests, becoming the owner of a chain of grocery stores and at least one hotel, and also founding the Munsey Trust Company of Washington, D.C. In his early days Munsey wrote fiction and sporting news for his publications. He never married, and throughout his career he kept the control of his enterprises firmly within his own hands.

For his early days in journalism see his own booklet, *The Founding of the Munsey Publishing House* (1907). See also E. J. RIDGWAY, *Frank A. Munsey: an Appreciation* (1926).

Mutt and Jeff. American comic strip created by Bud Fisher in 1907. It began as 'A. Mutt'; Jeff appeared a year later; and the strip was retitled Mutt and Jeff on 16 September 1916.

It was the first comic strip to be published on six days a week, and was at the height of its popularity during the 1920s, when there were Mutt and Jeff books and musicals. Excellent drawings (by Billy Liverpool at this period) and witty dialogue presented Mutt's constant search for big money. Its popularity declined during the 1930s and 1940s.

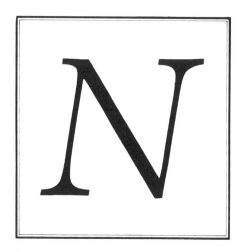

Nancy Drew. Teenage detective heroine created by Carolyn Keene (qv). Her first appearance was in *Secret of the Old Clock* (1930); since then 60 million copies of books featuring her adventures have been published. She has also starred in a number of film mysteries.

Ned Buntline. See *Judson, Edward Zane Carroll.*

Nero Wolfe. Private investigator and recluse created by Rex Stout (qv). He appeared in 47 books, the first *Fer-de-Lance* (1934) which came out initially as a serial in *The Saturday Evening Post*, and the last *A Family Affair*, which was published in 1975, the year of the author's death.

Wolfe, who is extremely fat, lives in New York and rarely leaves his brownstone house. All aspects of a private detective's job requiring travel or absence from home are carried out by a confidential assistant, Archie Goodwin, who relates his employer's stories. Something of a gourmand, Wolfe has a Swiss chef to prepare his meals. He speaks seven languages, finds work distasteful and grows a fine collection of orchids. Details of his life (some of them conjectural!) are to be found in S. Baring-Gould's biography, *Nero Wolfe of West Thirty-fifth Street* (1969).

Some years ago Wolfe was honoured by having his picture on a Nicaraguan commemorative postage stamp. He has appeared in films and on radio in the USA.

Newgate Calendar. Collection of criminal narratives drawn from real life. The title is taken from the London prison of Newgate which has long since disappeared, though there is still a Newgate Street near its site. Later editions drew upon a much wider range of criminal exploits, while the title remained unchanged. Crime has always been a major element in popular literature (see, for example, J. H. Marshburn, *Murder and Witchraft in England 1550–1640* (1971)).

The chief forerunner of the Newgate Calendar was John Reynolds, *The Triumphs of Gods Revenge Against the Crying and Execrable Sinne of Murther* (1621–35). It was very popular, and went into several editions. Reynolds cast his net widely and gave accounts of many lurid European murders. What is chiefly interesting about his work, however, is the illustrations, which are in effect comic-strip summaries of the prose accounts, complete with 'speech bubbles' coming out of the mouths of characters.

Then there was *The Prisoners of Newgate's Condemnation* (1642); *News from Newgate* (1677); *A True Relation of the Names and Suspected Crimes of Prisoners now in Newgate* (1679) – all of them anticipating *The Newgate Callendar* (sic), which was published in 1728. This is the earliest edition I have been able to trace. There is no reason to doubt its popularity – by 1773 it had grown to five volumes! It was reprinted again and again, in various forms, and its printing history is extremely obscure. The four-volume edition (nearly 2,000 pages, printed in double column) edited by Andrew Knapp and William Baldwin at the beginning of the nineteenth century is probably the best, and certainly the most fully illustrated. The most accessible edition is the most recent: Rayner Heppenstall, *Tales from the Newgate Calendar* (1981).

NEWMAN, Andrea (1938–   ). Bestselling British author whose novels *A Bouquet of Barbed Wire* (1969) and *Mackenzie* (1980) were adapted for television. Other novels include *A Share of the World* (1964) and *An Evil Streak* (1977). Her work is characterized by an obsessive pursuit of sexual themes which are often disturbing.

Nick and **Nora Charles.** Husband and wife team created by Dashiell Hammett (qv). They featured in *The Thin Man* (1934), which is narrated by Nick Charles (his real name is Charalambides), ex-private detective, married to a millionairess. The story was filmed in 1934, and was so successful that other films, together with radio and television series, followed. The original stars were William Powell and Myrna Loy, who appeared in six 'Thin Man' films. Although Powell, as Nick Charles, personified the 'Thin Man', the reference in the title was not in fact to him, but to a missing corpse in the first novel.

Nick Carter. Young American detective who has appeared in more detective stories than any other character in American literature. Only Sexton Blake (qv) has in fact solved more cases.

Carter's first appearance was in *New York Weekly*, 18 September 1886. His creator was Ormond G. Smith (1860–1933), son of one of the founders of the New York publishing firm Street and Smith. He gave the outline of this first tale to John Russell Coryell (1848–1924), who wrote it and followed it with two sequels. Thereafter Nick Carter was taken over by a number of writers who used such pseudonyms as 'The author of Nick Carter', 'Sergeant Ryan' and 'Nicholas Carter'. More than 1000 Nick Carter stories were written by Frederic Rensselaer Day (1861–1922); and other authors who made Carter popular in dime novels (qv) and pulp magazines (qv) for more than 50 years were: Thomas C. Harbaugh (1849–1924); Eugene T. Sawyer (1846–1924); George C. Jenks (1850–1929); Frederick W. Davis (1853–1933); W. Bert Foster (1869–1929); William Wallace Cook (1867–1933); Johnston McCulley (1883–1958); John H. Whitson (1854–1936); and Thomas W. Hanshew (1857–1914).

Nick Carter started off as the 'all-American detective'. He was handsome, and his grey eyes were trained to take in all kinds of detail to be used in solving mysteries. He was a master of disguise, and his voice covered the entire range of human sound. He was as strong as an ox and always in the peak of condition; and he had two assistants, Chick and Patsy. Today his adventures are still told in paperbacks, although he himself has changed. He is no longer the rather naive, clean-limbed young man that he once was – he is now a sophisticated secret agent.

Nick Carter has been featured in films and on radio and television. The earliest films to use his exploits were four serials made in France between 1909 and 1912, with André Liabel starring as Nick. On American radio the half-hour series *Nick Carter, Master Detective* began in 1943 and ran for years. In 1972 there was a television feature film, *The Adventures of Nick Carter*, with the plot set at the turn of the century, and in which Robert Conrad played the detective.

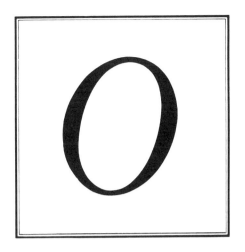

Old Man in the Corner, The. See *Orczy, Baroness Emmuska.*

ONLEY, William (*fl.* 1689). Prominent British printer/publisher of street ballads and chapbooks at the end of the seventeenth century. Nothing seems to be known about him except that his premises were at The Angel, Duck Lane, London (somewhere in West Smithfield). In about 1689 William Onley issued a list of his productions as a broadside measuring 15¼in × 19¼in. It is reproduced in a somewhat reduced form in Leslie Shepard, *John Pitts Ballad Printer of Seven Dials* (1969) between pp. 20 and 21. From a study of its contents it is evident that a great deal of cheap popular literature was being produced at this time, and that William Onley must have been one of the leading men in this branch of the book trade.

There were, however, other printers contemporary with Onley who were active in this field. They include: W. Thackeray, T. Passinger, F. Coles and W. Gilbertson. For a more complete list and an account of the ballad market in general, see Cyprian Blagden, 'Notes on the Ballad Market in the Second Half of the Seventeenth Century' published in *Papers of the Bibliographical Society of the University of Virginia,* vol. 6 1953–54, pp. 161–180.

'007'. See *James Bond.*

OPPENHEIM, E(dward) Phillips (1866–1946). British author of novels and short stories about crime, mystery and international intrigue. Born in Leicester, he worked in his father's leather business after leaving school; and while still working full time he began writing at night and had 30 books published. He sold his father's business when he was 40 and continued writing. Altogether he published 116 novels and 39 collections of short stories. Five of his novels were published under the pseudonym of Anthony Partridge. His most famous novel was *The Great Impersonation* (1920); and others included *A Maker of History*

(1905), *The Double Traitor* (1915), *The Evil Shepherd* (1922); *The Treasure House of Martin Hews* (1928), and *Envoy Extraordinary* (1937).

Oppenheim wrote an autobiography, *The Pool of Memory* (1939). He was known as 'The Prince of Storytellers', a description which was used as the title of a biography written by Robert Standish, published in 1957. Many of Oppenheim's novels were filmed.

Oral tradition. Despite the overwhelming presence of a printed popular literature in the modern industrial world, something of an older oral tradition still survives. Its forms are diverse: the dwindling number of folklore observances, the persistence of old customs and even older beliefs and superstitions, ballads, traditional tales, nursery rhymes, catch phrases, jokes, proverbs, riddles. All lead a transient and precarious life in the margins of a culture increasingly dominated by television.

The relationship between this continuing oral tradition and popular literature – or popular culture generally in the twentieth century – grows tenuous; but there are two areas where it seems relatively secure. As Iona and Peter Opie have shown, an oral popular literature still maintains a vigorous life on the school playground, at least among younger children. In the realm of popular music, too, some facets bear a striking resemblance to the lost world of the ballad singer. On the other hand, one can never be certain about the genuineness of the folk revival. Folk song was too securely rooted in the daily life of people to transplant itself naturally to a hostile, or at least a different, cultural environment. To what extent can it adapt?

IONA and PETER OPIE, *The Lore and Language of Schoolchildren* (1959). A. L. LLOYD *Folksong in England* (1967). DAVE HARKER, *One for the Money. Politics and Popular Song* (1980). T. P. COFFIN and H. COHEN, *Folklore from the Working Folk of America* (1973).

ORCZY, Baroness Emmuska (1865–1947). Hungarian/British playwright, author of romantic novels and detective short stories. She wrote a series of tales about 'The Old Man in the Corner', a nameless sleuth who solved crimes without leaving his chair in a London teashop, which began in magazines in 1901. It was the second series of these which was first published in book form as *The Case of Miss Elliot* (1905). The first series was published as *The Old Man in the Corner* (1909 – US title *The Man in the Corner*); and the third and last volume of the series was *Unravelled Knots* (1925). 12 short films based on this character were made in Britain in 1924.

Baroness Orczy's most famous character was The Scarlet Pimpernel (qv), who appeared in a number of novels about the French Revolution.

OUIDA (1839–1908). British writer. Pseudonym used by Marie

Louise de la Ramé, daugher of a French political refugee and an English mother, born at Bury St Edmunds, Suffolk. She was a popular novelist whose stories, with a background of high life in society, featured wealthy, handsome, strong and gifted men, and heroines for whom beauty and passion counted for more than considerations of shame or virtue. Her best known book, *Under Two Flags* (1868), is about a rich, aristocratic young officer in a crack British cavalry regiment who, in order to prevent a scandal, serves as a soldier in the French Foreign Legion. There he is befriended by Cigarette, who runs the regimental canteen. . . . Among her other novels were *Puck* (1869), *Ariadne: the Story of a Dream* (1877) and *Friendship* (1878).

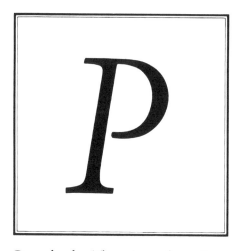

Paperbacks. There is, so far as I am aware, no general history of the paperback book. Certainly paperbacks have been around for a very long time indeed. Their origins can be traced, plausibly enough, back to chapbooks (qv), and possibly even earlier. They were readily available in Victorian times, and in the last quarter of the twentieth century they are offered for sale not only in bookshops but also in department stores, supermarkets, drugstores, newsagents' shops, news-stands and bookstalls. With its bright, visually attractive and occasionally startling cover, the paperback has become an essential part of our background.

The term 'paperback', however, has become ambiguous, and while a definition in terms of a book with paper covers is accurate so far as it goes, the very simplicity is misleading. Certainly all paperbacks have in common this format with soft covers; but while they were originally intended for the mass market, they now embrace an extraordinarily wide spread of titles ranging from a popular novel to an esoteric study of some literary figure. The rise of the academic paperback over the last 30 years or so has tended, perhaps, to obscure the connotation of mass readership that is implied in the term. Nevertheless, a consideration of the paperback as an element in popular literature must be concerned with the widely-selling kind.

Large numbers of paperbacks are on sale in Great Britain and in the USA, and many firms are involved. Two of the large firms, Penguin Books (British in origin) and Bantam (American), have published histories of their activities: Sir W. E. Williams, *The Penguin Story* (1956) and Clarence Petersen, *The Bantam Story* (2nd ed., 1975) respectively.

Penguin Books was founded in 1935 by Allen Lane (later Sir Allen Lane). He persuaded a number of publishers to lease him rights to publish sixpenny editions of recent saleable books, mainly fiction, when the cost of a new novel was 7/6d. The first title was Andre Maurois, *Ariel*; the second was Ernest

Hemingway, *A Farewell to Arms*, and the third Eric Linklater, *Poet's Pub*. Booksellers in Britain were slow, even perverse, and certainly wrong in seeing the development of good books at such a low price as a threat to their hardback sales, and the first Penguins were sold by Woolworth's. The venture was successful, and in 1937 Penguin Specials and Pelican Books followed. The publication in January 1946 of Homer, *The Odyssey*, launched Penguin Classics, and altogether Penguin Books have used something over 30 imprints. The great achievement of Penguin Books was to produce paperbacks of all kinds which their readers could regard as shelvable rather than merely as expendable.

The tremendous success of Penguin Books was noticed in the USA where, with $500 borrowed from his father, Ian Ballantine opened their first American office in July 1939. There had been paperbacks in the US before this – many publishers had cashed in upon the fact that there was a virtually unlimited supply of British authors whose works could be published without the necessity of paying royalties; but all this was ended by the international copyright law of 1891, and the paperback did not come to life again until the 1930s when Robert de Graff founded Pocket Books. 'My idea', he said, 'was to put out 25-cent books which could fit easily into a pocket or purse, and to provide them with attractive picture covers.' De Graff had been impressed by the success of Penguin Books, but his

pictorial covers (he chose, by the way, a kangaroo as his trade mark) were in sharp contrast with the austere typographical covers in the early Penguins with their distinctive but discreet colour coding. Amongst the ten titles with which Pocket Books were launched in 1939 were James Hilton, *Lost Horizon*; William Shakespeare, *Five Tragedies*; and Agatha Christie, *The Murder of Roger Ackroyd*.

In 1945 Ballantine began his own firm, Bantam Books. 20 titles went on sale on 3 January 1946, including Mark Twain, *Life on the Mississippi*; Frank Gruber, *The Gift Horse*; Zane Grey, *Nevada*; and John Steinbeck, *The Grapes of Wrath*. They sold for 25 cents apiece – including the last-named title which ran to 576 pages! Bantam went on to publish authors as diverse as Barbara Cartland, Winston Churchill and Bertrand Russell. After the first 20 books they produced four additional titles each month. Printing runs averaged about 200,000. There were reprints of popular titles, and some first printings of popular novels or Westerns might be 600,000 copies. The books were not offered on a sale or return basis – if a title did not sell, the retailer was offered another one in its place.

What is referred to as the 'paperback revolution' consisted less in the form or matter of the books than in their marketing. Special racks were supplied for Bantam books, and titles were displayed 'face on' to facilitate identification and choice; but it is *distribution* which has been one important characteristic of the paperback as popular literature. In Britain, Penguin had started in Woolworth's and moved fairly soon into bookshops, while it took rather longer for paperbacks to reach department stores and other places as points of sale. In America, sales were by no means confined to bookshops – notably, of course, the 'drugstore', where books could be bought, had no counterpart on this side of the Atlantic. So far, then, as there was a 'paperback revolution' it lay in the new and aggressive methods of salesmanship which were pioneered in the US and only then, rather more tentatively, developed in Great Britain. The rapidly increasing use of strikingly pictorial covers by publishers in Britain is an indication, too, that the American lessons have been learned and are to an ever greater extent being put into practice.

Penguin Books, as has been mentioned, moved into America in 1939. Bantam set up a London subsidiary, Transworld Publishers Ltd, which has published Corgi books, its own paperbacks, since 1951. This internationalization of mass publishing is another distinguishing feature of paperbacks as popular literature. 'We sell in every country in the world except behind the Iron Curtain, and even there we sometimes manage to get some books in . . .', said Alun Davies, a Bantam sometime Vice-President and international division manager.

Today there are more and more paperbacks being issued by a variety of publishers. The one constant in the scene was neatly put by Bantam's historian: 'What never changes is the search – for new authors, new ideas, new readers – because that, after all, is what paperback publishing is about.'

Bibliographical Note: The two books mentioned earlier, *The Penguin Story* and *The Bantam Story*, are rather different. Both are publishing histories, but the former is a straightforward account of Penguin while the latter includes some supporting information about marketing methods. In the absence of the general history which I deplored at the outset, these two books – both inevitably in paperback! – serve as background which is authentic if selective.

In 1951 Penguin Books published an 18 page pamphlet, *Penguins. A Retrospect 1935–1951.* Six years later *The Times Literary Supplement*, dated 12 July 1957, ran a 4 page 'Paperback Section' which contained, amongst several perceptive articles, an elegant piece by John Carter entitled 'Paperback Revolution'. Although the author was, I believe, wrong about some aspects of what he called 'the educative series of the 1830s and 1840s', it is a very good, if brief, survey and deserves reprinting.

J. E. MORPURGO, *Allen Lane King Penguin* (1979).
H. SCHMOLLER, 'The Paperback Revolution' in Briggs, A. (ed.) *Essays in the History of Publishing* (1974).
See also P. SCHREUDERS, *Paperbacks USA*, which was published in Am-

sterdam in 1981. Later in the same year, it appeared in Britain as *The Book of Paperbacks*. As the title of the Dutch edition suggests, it deals mainly with American paperbacks. It is a lively, well illustrated book with a good bibliography, but it lacks any serious historical dimension.

PARKER, Martin (?–1656?). British author, ballad monger and royalist. The most famous of his many ballads was 'When the King enjoyes his owne again' (1643); and amongst his prose writings was *A True Tale of Robin Hood* (1632).

PATIENCE STRONG (? d. of birth). (Pseudonym). Inspirational poet. Her work has been published in numerous books, magazines and newspapers. One of her best known enterprises was commenced in 1935, when she was in her twenties: under the heading 'The Quiet Corner' she wrote for many years, six days a week, a rhymed message of hope for readers of the *Daily Mirror*. Selections from these were published in book form in 1937 and 1940. She also wrote the words for the songs 'Jealousy', 'The Dream of Olwyn' and 'The Haunted Ballroom'.

Her publishers, Frederick Muller, produce a list of all her titles in print – there are currently over 50 of them. They include *Windows of Hope* (1940); *Blessings of the Years* (1944); *Wayside Glory* (1948); *Magic Casements* (1950); *Harbours of Happiness* (1954); *The Windows of Heaven* (1963); *The Harvest of a Quiet Eye* (1969); *Give me a Quiet Corner* (1972).

Patience Strong's poetry reaches a very wide range of readers, many of whom write to her. For this reason her publishers will not reveal her identity, and act as a 'filter' for the correspondence addressed to her at their office. She was born in 'the period between the end of the Edwardian sunset and the accession to the Imperial Throne of the King-Emperor George V in 1911.' She can, as she says, remember two world wars. Whatever critics or posterity may say about her work, two points must be made. First, her verses have given a great deal of pleasure to many people over a long period of time. Secondly, she is probably the only poet since Tennyson who has made a comfortable living out of published verse.

Her autobiography, *With a Poem in my Pocket* (1981), reveals her as a thoroughly professional writer. In other respects it is curiously, but understandably, opaque.

Paul Temple. See *Durbridge, Francis*.

Payments to authors. The authors of bestsellers, almost without exception, do very well now out of their work. Those who write run-of-the-mill cheap fiction do better now than they did in the past, and can sometimes make a comfortable living. In the nineteenth century, however, payments in this field were generally niggardly. The term 'penny-a-liner' speaks for itself. There is also the fact that, so far as writers for the popular market (workers in what might be termed the fiction factory) are concerned, details of their lives, let alone their dealings with publishers, remain extremely obscure. I have come across only one contract made by a publisher with a writer of penny novels. See *Pettman, Grace* for details.

Peanuts. American comic strip started by Charles Monroe Schulz. The original title was to be 'Li'l Folks', and Schulz had considerable difficulty in selling his idea. When finally accepted by United Features Syndicate it was re-christened 'Peanuts', and made its debut as a daily strip in October 1950.

The theme is *non*-success. Charlie Brown, the hero, is teased by Lucy van Pett; she has a brother Linus who goes to pieces without his security blanket; Schroeder plays Beethoven continually on his toy piano; and there are Peppermint Patty, Pigpen Franklin and others. The major character, however, is Snoopy, Charlie Brown's dog. No adult ever appears, although all the children act like adults. The ambiguities of sadness, cruelty and laughter have made this the most successful American strip of all time.

See J. H. LORIA, *What's It All About, Charlie Brown?* (1968).

Penny-a-liner. Victorian term which was used, often with derisive overtones, to describe a hack writer of popular fiction whose work was paid for on the basis of one penny for every line published.

Penny bloods (or 'penny dreadfuls'). Cheap, sensational, lurid novels sold in penny parts during the nineteenth century. The term 'bloods' or 'twopenny bloods' was current until about 1939. For publishers of such material see *Lloyd, Edward*; *Amalgamated Press.*

Penny readings. The Penny Reading Movement was started in Suffolk in the 1850s by Charles Sulley, Editor of the *Ipswich Express*. It represented a conscious effort on the part of the middle class to woo working men and women away from public houses and musical saloons by providing a more wholesome kind of entertainment. In suitable premises, there were readings of extracts from a wide range of English literature, often interspersed with music.

At one such meeting in Liverpool a member of the audience suggested that one penny should be charged for admission. The suggestion was eagerly followed up, and the Penny Reading Movement became popular throughout Britain. The decline of the movement towards the end of the nineteenth century is not altogether easy to explain. Possibly there was a feeling of resentment on the part of working-class audiences at the element of patronage implied; but whatever the reason, the impetus dwindled, leaving behind a legacy of recitation at Band of Hope meetings or within the family. As Winifred Peck put it: 'That ghastly habit of recitation, the last backwash I suppose of the Penny Readings of the sixties, lingered on in the provinces into this century.' (*Home for the Holidays*, 1955, p. 170).

The literature on penny readings is sparse. The best contemporary account I have come across is J. E. CARPENTER, 'The Penny Reading Movement' in *Penny Readings in Prose and Verse*, New Edition 1865, pp. 1–8. SAMUEL TAYLOR read a paper on the subject to the Annual Meeting of the Social Science Association in 1858, and there is a reference in the *Annual Report. Yorkshire Union of Mechanics' Institutes* for 1862 and 1864. Amongst later writers J. F. C. HARRISON, *Learning and Living 1790–1860* (1961), is useful, though brief; and there is H. P. SMITH, *Literature and Adult Education a Century Ago: Pantopragmatics and Penny Readings*, Documentary No. 3, Oxford 1960. OLIVER EDWARDS published an article on the subject, 'All for a Penny', in *The Times*, 24 November 1966. See also V. E. NEUBURG, *Popular Literature* (1977) pp. 242–246.

PEPYS, Samuel (1633–1703). British collector. Chiefly known as a diarist (*the* diarist) and perhaps as a civil servant, Pepys was also a lifelong collector of ballads (qv) and of chapbooks (qv). Both collections are at Magdalene College, Cambridge.

The ballads are well-known. Many of them were printed in H. E. ROLLINS (qv), *A Pepysian Garland* (1922, 1971); and there is an admirable profile of the collection by LEBA

M. GOLDSTEIN in 'The Pepys Ballads' published in *Transactions of the Bibliographical Society. The Library*, 5th Series, vol. XXI, no. 4, December 1966, pp. 282–292. So far as the chapbooks are concerned, see ROGER THOMPSON, *Samuel Pepys' Penny Merriments* (1976), which offers a selection but is poorly edited. The same writer's 'Samuel Pepys' Penny Merriments: A Checklist' is published in *Transactions of the Bibliographical Society. The Library*, 5th Series, vol. XXXI, no. 3, September 1976, pp. 223–234.

PERCY, Thomas (1729–1811). British ballad editor, Church of England divine; Dean of Carlisle in 1778; and from 1782 until his death Bishop of Dromore. His main interest in life was literature. When he was about 30 years old, he discovered in the house of his friend Humphrey Pitt 'lying dirty on the floor under a Bureau in ye Parlour' a manuscript which was 'being used by the maids to light the fire.' It turned out to be a collection of transcripts, made about the middle of the seventeenth century, of poems, ballads, songs and metrical tales. The texts ranged from the fourteenth to the seventeenth century. Percy realized its importance, and decided to publish a selection from it. The result was *Reliques of Ancient English Poetry* (3 vols., 1765), a series of 'improvements' made by him upon the text of the original manuscript, together with material from ballad collections and from the stock of William Dicey (qv) – to whom Percy behaved with ingratitude and snobbishness. The *Reliques*, however, were popular – the poetry was soothing, pleasant, and did not 'plainly contradict Antiquity', all qualities designed to appeal to the eighteenth-century reader. There was a 4th edition in 1794, and several editions after that. The best one, in three volumes edited by Henry B. Wheatley, was published in 1886.

The manuscript from which Percy worked was not published in its entirety until the end of the nineteenth century, in four volumes edited by J. W. Hales and F. J. Furnivall (qv). The first three volumes (1867–68), comprising over 1700 pages of text, presented only editorial problems which, given the experience, staying power and knowledge of the editors, were not insoluble. The fourth volume (1867), subtitled 'Loose and Humorous Songs', presented moral as well as textual problems. A slender volume of viii + 128 pages, it is prefaced with a 'Notice' and a 'Second Notice'. In the former the editors say 'We make no excuse for putting forth these Loose and Humorous Songs. . .'. In the latter the tone is a shade more hesitant: 'Some of these songs the Editors would have been glad had it not fallen to their lot to put forth.' They go on to justify their decision to print and publish the manuscript entire by pointing out that such songs are a part of it, and the themes are equally a part of Elizabethan and Jacobite times.

Despite the rather sad fact of Percy's 'improving' the text, the *Reliques* did have an importance for what one historian, Peter Burke in *Popular Culture in Early Modern Europe* (1978), has called 'the discovery of the people'. It was one of the earliest examples of 'popular poetry' to be published in Europe, and as such probably had a greater influence than Percy's editorial methods deserved.

For Thomas Percy see ARTHUR JOHNSTON, *Enchanted Ground* (1964), Chapter III and *passim*.

PEROWNE, Barry (1908–   ). British author. Pseudonym of Philip Atkey, who wrote crime, adventure and mystery stories. He also wrote a long series of adventures about Raffles (qv), whom he revived by arrangement with the estate of E. W. Hornung (qv). He converted the sophisticated cracksman into a tough adventurer whose exploits appeared in *The Thriller*, a weekly paper published between the wars in London by Amalgamated Press (qv). In 1950 he wrote another series of Raffles stories with a turn-of-the-century background. 14 of them were published in *Raffles Revisited* (1974), and many appeared in *Ellery Queen's Mystery Magazine* (qv).

Apart from the Raffles series, Perowne wrote paperbacks featuring Dick Turpin the Highwayman, Red Jim the first air detective, and many others. Some books appeared under his own name, and he also used the pseudonym of Pat Merriman.

Perry Mason. The most famous attorney in fiction, created by Erle Stanley Gardner (qv), whose adventures were recounted in over 80 novels published between 1933 and 1973. The highest number of titles published in any one year was four, in 1959.

Mason was assisted by a secretary, Della Street, who refused his offers of marriage on five occasions – she wanted to go on working and knew that Mason would never allow his wife to work. Investigations were carried out for Mason by Paul Drake, a private detective; the District Attorney was Hamilton Burger, whose office was never successful in any prosecution of Mason's clients; and Lieutenant Arthur Tragg was usually the arresting officer, bearing his continual defeats at Mason's hands with near equanimity.

PETTMAN, Grace (1870–1952). Prolific British author of wholesome cheap fiction. She contributed 158 stories to the series published by W. B. Horner (qv), and wrote also for other firms such as William Nicholson of Wakefield, Yorkshire (and later London), who had long specialized in publishing cheap books. Periodicals for which she wrote included *The Girl's Own Paper*; *Railway Mission Magazine*; *The Quiver*; *Sunday Companion*; *Sunday Circle*; *The Boy's Own Paper*; and in addition she was the author of several religious tracts.

Amongst the pseudonyms which Grace Pettman used were: C. E. C. Sutherland; Spencer Dean; Nigel Strong; 'A Daughter of the Manse'; '. . . the Stewardess'; 'The Curate's Wife' and Helen Kent.

She had her first article published in 1888. Three years later, when she was 21 her first story *Helen*, 20,000 words long, was published by Horner. She remained a professional writer for the rest of her life. Despite her undoubted dedication, and despite her ability to write to a deadline and to conform to fairly strict publishers' requirements, the financial rewards for Grace Pettman and for writers like her were not high. A contract dated 7 July 1900 offered her the following terms: '£10 for a novel which sold 50,000 copies – £15 for a circulation of 100,000 copies, and £5 extra for each additional 25,000 circulation attained.' The novel referred to would almost certainly have been sold retail at one penny! If these figures represent standard practice of the time – and one can only suppose that they do – then authors of cheap fiction were hard done by. Grace Pettman certainly resented the fact that she was exploited by publishers, but there was little she could do about it. She had a family to support.

For all these details I am grateful to Muriel Pettman, daughter of Grace. Because of her unstinting assistance, her mother emerges as the one writer of penny fiction about whom some concrete facts are known. Of course she is not typical, but her prolific output and her experiences at the hands of publishers may be. There is a collection of her work, with other material, in the Library of the University of

Kent. The present writer has a small Pettman collection which includes an autobiographical fragment, together with informative letters from Muriel Pettman.

Philip Marlowe. Private detective created by Raymond Chandler (qv). Marlowe epitomises the fictional private eye, tough, wry, cynical, romantic and totally uncorruptible. The detective agency he runs doesn't make much money, for Marlowe sees himself as a righter of wrongs rather than as becoming wealthy in the fight against crime.

He appeared in the following seven novels: *The Big Sleep* (1939); *Farewell, my Lovely* (1940); *The High Window* (1942); *The Lady in the Lake* (1943); *The Little Sister* (1949); *The Long Goodbye* (1953); *Playback* (1958).

Marlowe fell in love with a 36-year-old millionairess, Linda Loring, and their marriage was described at the beginning of *The Poodle Springs Mystery*, a novel which Chandler left unfinished at his death.

Philo Vance. Detective created by S. S. van Dine (qv). Young, aristocratic, successful, Vance helps to solve murder cases in which his best friend District Attorney Markham is involved. After initial dislike, Sergeant Heath of the New York Police Department becomes a friend of Vance and welcomes his assistance. There are 12 Vance cases, and the titles follow the same pattern: *The Benson Murder Case* (1926); *The 'Canary' Murder Case* (1927);

The Greene Murder Case (1928); *The Bishop Murder Case* (1929); *The Scarab Murder Case* (1930); *The Kennel Murder Case* (1931); *The Dragon Murder Case* (1933); *The Casino Murder Case* (1934); *The Kidnap Murder Case* (1936); *The Garden Murder Case* (1937); *The Gracie Allen Murder Case* (1938); *The Winter Murder Case* (1939).

Photonovel. See *Fotonovel.*

Pilgrim's Progress, The. This work by the English writer John Bunyan (1628–1688) (qv) was first published in two parts (Part I 1678; Part II 1684). Since then there have been many translations into foreign languages, and in terms of numbers circulated it is essentially a popular book. The largest number of reprints – notably cheap ones produced with an eye to the mass market – was published during Victorian times, when copies were frequently given as school or Sunday school prizes. Since this was a time of intense religious evangelism, it is hardly surprising that *The Pilgrim's Progress* should have been regarded as a book which could safely (though with some alterations to the text!) be put into the hands of the young.

So far, so good. E. P. Thompson, however, has argued in *The Making of the English Working Class* (1963, p. 31) that Bunyan's book was one of the two foundation texts of the English working-class movement (the other was Thomas Paine, *Rights of Man* (1791–92)). He may be right; and if he is, the notion of popularity as implying that the book was *read*, as opposed to being merely doled out as a reward for punctuality or proficiency at school, must be looked at again.

It is no accident that the period of 'cheap editions' coincided not only with the golden age of evangelism, but also with the formative years of the labour movement. Enthusiasm for the book may not have been enormous in the higher echelons of the established church, nor amongst the leaders of non-conformity; but Bunyan, with his zeal and eloquence, was seen as a writer who could be counted upon to inspire the young with a sense of Christian endeavour. At some point, however, a part of the book's radicalism (an element, curiously enough, entirely overlooked by clergymen and ministers who saw only religious significance in its pages) may well have been absorbed by its readers. Religious radicalism, as Bunyan knew, was contagious. What he could not know was that such feelings could, and often did, harden into secular political radicalism. In this sense, Thompson was almost certainly right. At the very least, no book can be popular for so long without having an effect upon at least some of those who read it; but of course, what we cannot be sure of is just how many of those who possessed a copy did in fact read it.

I know of no study dealing with cheap reprints of *The Pilgrim's Progress*, neither in terms of how many there were nor what impact they may have made upon readers.

One is certainly needed. So far as books about Bunyan are concerned, they are legion. Especially recommended is JACK LINDSAY, *John Bunyan. Maker of Myths* (1937). The Penguin English Library edition of *The Pilgrim's Progress* (1965 and reprints) contains an excellent Introduction by ROGER SHARROCK.

Pinder of Wakefield, The. Jestbook (qv) entered originally in the Stationers' Register on 4 February 1632. It tells the story of George A. Greene who has various adventures including a fight with Robin Hood (qv). Henslowe's *Diary* (ed. Greg, 1904–8, vol. i, p. 16) mentions a play about George A. Greene; and there was a popular ballad, 'Robin Hood and the Pindar of Wakefield', surviving fragments of which were printed in J. W. Hales and F. J. Furnivall (eds.) *Bishop Percy's Folio Manuscript* (vol. i, 1867) pp. 32–36.

E. A. HORSMAN, *The Pinder of Wakefield* (1956).

PINKERTON, Allan (1819–1884). Scottish-American writer and detective. Born in Glasgow, son of a police sergeant, Pinkerton went to Chicago in 1842. He discovered and captured a gang of counterfeiters, and as a result was made Deputy Sheriff of Cook County. He resigned from the Chicago Police in 1850 and opened The Pinkerton National Detective Agency, which specialized in railway theft and became extremely successful. Cases from the archives of the agency were used as material for several books about crime and detection published under Pinkerton's name. The narratives are so sensational that it is impossible to sort out fact from fiction. The books were extremely popular, and each one had on its cover the symbol of the agency, an open eye, and the motto 'We never sleep'.

These were the titles: *The Expressman and the Detective* (1874); *Claude Melnotte as a Detective and Other Stories* (1875); *The Molly Maguires and the Detectives* (1877); *The Spy and the Rebellion* (1883); *Thirty Years as a Detective* (1884).

Allan Pinkerton's son, A. Frank Pinkerton, wrote novels under the general title 'The Frank Pinkerton Detective Series'. Titles included: *Dyke Darrell, the Railroad Detective; or, the Crime of the Midnight Express* (1886); *Jim Cummings; or, the Great Adams Express Robbery* (1887). This last novel presents a problem: the text is practically identical with *Jim Cummings; or, the Crime of the 'Frisco Express* (1887) by Francis Farrars, which appeared before the other Jim Cummings tale. Was Farrars a pseudonym used by Pinkerton, or was the later book merely a piece of plagiarism?

PITTS, John (1765–1844). British printer and publisher, an important producer of street ballads and other ephemera. His premises, sometimes referred to as the 'wholesale Toy and Marble warehouse', were in Seven Dials, an area of London near Shaftesbury Avenue. It has been greatly redeveloped since about 1883, and is now hardly recognizable as the place where Pitts set up his first establishment in Great St Andrew Street in 1802. James Catnach (qv) had premises nearby, and there was considerable rivalry and bad feeling between the two firms.

The standard work is LESLIE SHEPARD, *John Pitts Ballad Printer of Seven Dials, London* (1969). It is more widely ranging than its title suggests and is, perhaps, the best and the most scholarly study to date of the early nineteenth-century street ballad, especially in terms of its production and the geography of the trade.

PLAIDY, Jean. See *Hibbert, Eleanor.*

POE, Edgar Allan (1809–1849). American author and creator of C. Auguste Dupin (qv), the first important fictional detective. Poet, fiction writer, critic and editor, Poe was the inventor of the detective story: in five stories he anticipated all the twists and types which later writers were to exploit in their various ways.

The tales were:

'The Murders in the Rue Morgue' (1841). A sensational thriller.

'The Mystery of Marie Rogêt' (1842). Fictional treatment of a real crime. Straightforward analytical exercise in detection.

'The Gold Bug' (1843). Mystery revolving around breaking a secret code.

'The Purloined Letter' (1844). Classic secret agent and detective story.

'Thou Art the Man' (1844). Narrator solves a small town murder mystery.

All these stories except the last one were published in *Tales* (1845) – now a book of extreme rarity.

Pop. British comic strip character created by John Millar Watt. He first appeared in the *Daily Sketch*, 20 May 1921, in a strip called 'Reggie Breaks it Gently'. A plump character, 'something in the city', he wore a top hat and striped trousers. He started out with a moustache and pince-nez, but these were later dropped. Henpecked by wife and family, he always came up with a witty retort; and there was often a pictorial twist as well, the fourth panel of the strip being used for this.

Pop was one of few British strips to be syndicated in the USA. A *Pop Annual* was published from 1924 to 1929. The strip came to an end on 23 January 1960.

Popeye. Spinach-eating, wise-cracking, omnipotent sailor created by E. C. Segar. He made his first appearance in a comic strip called *Thimble Theatre* on 17 January 1929. Popeye was an immediate success, and was soon joined by other characters including J. Wellington Wimpy (whose passion for the hamburger is commemorated in its synonym 'wimpy'), Olive Oyl, Swee'pea and others.

Popeye films began in 1932, and there were books featuring the hero. His creator died on 13 October 1938, and for a decade afterwards the characters prospered; but eventually they dwindled to near-disappearance, although the name of Popeye is still a household word.

BUD SAGENDORF, *Popeye the First Fifty Years* (1981).

Popular novelists. Biographical details of popular novelists (however defined) are often hard to come by. There are, of course, exceptions such as Florence Barclay (qv); but the fact remains that many writers who, in their own day, were remarkably prolific and gave a great deal of pleasure to their readers, remain elusive and often obscure figures.

This is a very brief list of works which the present writer has found of exceptional value in this connection:

S. AUSTIN ALLIBONE, *A Critical Dictionary of English Literature and British and American Authors* (3 vols., 1882). This contains details of 46,000 authors; and a Supplement (2 vols., 1891) contains details of 37,000 authors. This work is indispensable for authors up to the latter half-of the nineteenth century.

ALBERT JOHANNSEN, *The House of Beadle and Adams and its Dime and Nickel Novels* (2 vols., 1950). Supplementary volume (1962). The bulk of the second volume and part of the third is taken up with biographical details of the authors of dime novels (qv) and other popular fiction.

W. O. G. LOFTS and D. J. ADLEY, *The Men Behind Boys' Fiction* (1970). An unpretentious and invaluable guide to popular writers, many of whom wrote for Amalgamated Press (qv).

MONTAGUE SUMMERS, *A Gothic Bibliography*, ND (1940). The author index usually has dates of birth and death, and sometimes gives biographical details as well.

Popular prophecy. Fortune telling, prediction, dreams and omens as guides to the future have long been regarded as important. Popular prophecy of this kind is probably as old as human society itself, and there is no sign yet of any dwindling of interest in it. For more than 300 years it has formed an element in printed popular literature. Prophecy appeared in ephemera of the seventeenth century, and became an increasingly popular theme in eighteenth-century chapbooks (qv). The ancient prophecies of Merlin, Nostradamus, Nixon (a Cheshire worthy, according to tradition), Mother Shipton (qv), were all readily available, and there were also dream books and fortune tellers.

Such publications continued in one form or another during the nineteenth century, and the theme maintains a lively presence today as 'What the stars foretell' columns in widely read newspapers. The occult generally has enjoyed a considerable revival over the last 20 or 30 years. This has been reflected in popular literature, but the development still awaits, so far as I am aware, critical investigation. Certainly there is a paucity of material on early popular prophecy and occultism; but a pioneer study by Deborah M. Valenze, 'Prophecy and Popular Literature in Eighteenth-Century England', *The Journal of Ecclesiastical History*, vol. 29, No. 1, January 1978, is excellent. There are some pertinent comments in J. F. C. Harrison, *The Second Coming* (1979).

PORTER, Anna Maria (1780–1832). British popular novelist, sister of Jane Porter (qv). They collaborated in one book, *Tales Round a Winter's Hearth* (2 vols., 1826).

PORTER, Gene Stratton (1886–1924). Bestselling American romantic novelist whose three novels, *Freckles* (1904), *Girl of the Limberlost* (1909) and *Laddie* (1913) were extremely popular in the USA and in Britain.

PORTER, Jane (1776–1850). British novelist whose tale *The Scottish Chiefs* (5 vols., 1810) was extremely popular, reprinted in one-volume editions throughout the nineteenth century. Her sister Anna Maria Porter (qv) was also a writer of fiction.

Precinct, The 87th. Although Ed McBain (qv), writer of the series of detective stories set in this precinct, denies that the location is New York, the mythical island of Isola where the action takes place is obviously Manhattan.

So far, there have been 25 or more books featuring the 87th Precinct. The first of them, *Cop Hater*, was published in 1956. The chief characters are: Detective Steve Carella, whose beautiful wife Teddy is a deaf-mute; Lieutenant Peter

Byrnes; Detectives Cotton Hawes, Meyer Meyer, Andy Parker, Bert Kling; Desk Sergeant Dave Murchison; and a clerk, Alf Miscolo.

Several of the 87th Precinct novels have been made into films, quite often with an altered locale.

PREST, Thomas Peckett (*c*. 1810–1879). Prolific British author of more than 80 sensational novels, most of which were published by Edward Lloyd (qv). He was the creator of Sweeney Todd (qv), and as 'Bos' he produced a number of plagiarisms of work by Charles Dickens (see *Dickens imitations*). Prest also wrote plays for production at the Britannia, Hoxton, and was a talented musician.

Prince of Storytellers, The. See *Oppenheim, E. Phillips.*

Pulp magazines. These were so called because they were printed on untrimmed wood-pulp paper. By 1920 there was a standard format: with bright, glossy covers, they measured about 7 inches by 10 inches and usually contained around 120 pages.

The inventor was the New York publisher Frank A. Munsey (qv). In 1882 the first number of his eight-page magazine, *Golden Argosy. Freighted with Treasure for Boys and Girls*, made its appearance, and in 1891 he followed it with a low-priced general magazine for adults called *Munsey's* which was so successful – 700,000 of each number were sold at its peak in 1896 – that he revamped his earlier venture. *Argosy*

came out in 1896 with 192 pages of adult adventure fiction (about 135,000 words) plus 60 pages of advertisements, with thick yellow covers on which were printed details of the contents. It was an immediate success, and because it was printed on coarse wood-pulp paper it was eligible (as dime novels and better printed popular fare were not!) for cheaper second-class postal rates. By 1907 each number of *Argosy* was selling half a million copies. Munsey followed it up with *Cavalier* and *All-Story*, which were brought out during the First World War, and in the 1920s he introduced *Detective Fiction Weekly*.

Other publishers hastened to cash in on Munsey's success, and from 1905 there were many rival pulp magazines in circulation. Street and Smith, the New York publishers who had been involved with weekly fiction since the 1850s, brought out *Popular Magazine* in 1903 and *Top-Notch* in 1910. Later they published *Detective Story, Western Story, Love Story, Sea Stories* and *Sport Story*, the titles indicating that by the 1920s pulp magazines were tending each to specialize in one type of story. The growth of these magazines was extremely rapid. At the end of the war in 1918 there were perhaps two dozen titles: by the middle years of the Depression over 200 were on sale. Cheap fiction published in magazines, usually at 10 cents a time, had become big business.

The 1920s and 1930s saw the heyday of the pulp magazine, and the most celebrated of these was

Black Mask (qv). Among the firms active in this field were long-established publishers like the Butterick Company and Doubleday; while newcomers included William Clayton, who produced a number of successful titles which made him a million dollars before he went broke in 1932. He then sold all his magazines, one of which, *Astounding Science Fiction*, continued into the 1970s as *Analog*.

George T. Delacorte, who founded Dell Publishing in 1922, did better. His early magazines were pulps, the best known of which was *War Birds*. As early as 1929 he was experimenting with comic books (qv) printed in four colours – the kind of publication which would eventually supersede the pulp magazine. Wilford and Roscoe Fawcett also went into the pulp market, but they were not as successful as they later became with *Captain Marvel Comics* (qv). The Popular Library, which published a large number of pulp titles during the 1930s – one of them was *The Phantom Detective* – was started by Ned L. Pines and Leo Margulies, who had worked for Munsey. Another firm, Popular Publications, was founded by Henry Steeger and Harold S. Goldsmith in the 1930s. They featured the word 'Dime' in the titles of their earliest publications: *Dime Detective*, *Dime Sport*, *Dime Adventures*; and their success enabled Seeger and Gold-smith to buy up many of their competitors.

Many factors contributed to the decline of the pulp magazine, among them rising prices, labour troubles, changing social attitudes and the increasing popularity of comic strip stories published in book form (see *Comic books*). For Munsey perhaps the writing had been on the wall as early as 1920, for in that year *All-Story* merged with *Cavalier*, and then with *Argosy*, to become *Argosy-All-Story Weekly*, and in order to keep the price at 10 cents the number of pages was cut from 224 to 144 and the name was changed once more – to *Argosy*.

Pulp magazines represent one of the most flamboyant and widely selling elements in American popular literature, and vast numbers of them were imported into Great Britain during the 1930s. Their history has been splendidly told by Ron Goulart, *An Informal History of the Pulps* (New York 1973, first published as *Cheap Thrills*, New York 1972). There is also a substantial anthology with many facsimiles in colour, *The Pulps*, edited by Tony Godstone (New York 1970). More recently R. K. Jones, *The Shudder Pulps* (New York 1975 and 1978), explores with knowledge and black and white illustrations what the author calls 'the weird menace magazines of the 1930s'.

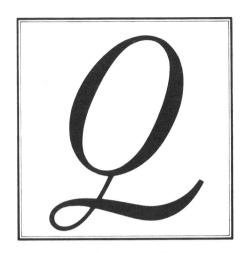

QUEEN, Ellery. See *Ellery Queen.*

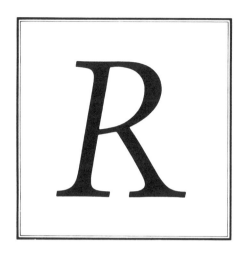

Race Williams. First 'hard-boiled' private eye, created by C. J. Daly (qv).

RADCLIFFE, Ann (1764–1823). British author whose first novel, *The Castles of Athlin and Dunbayne: A Highland Story*, was published in 1789; her best known work, *The Mysteries of Udolpho*, appeared five years later. It marked a significant stage in the development of the gothic novel (qv). At the end, the author offers rational explanations for the unusual and apparently supernatural events which occur in the story. In *The Italian; or, The Confessional of the Black Penitents* (1797) Mrs Radcliffe uses a convention which is still widely used by detective story writers – in conversation, a perceptive narrator explains events to a less intelligent, perplexed but interested companion.

She excelled in describing brooding, macabre landscapes in Italy, where her novels were set, and a mood of horror permeated her books. A bestselling author, she made a good deal of money from her novels, and unauthorized versions of her tales enjoyed a wide circulation. There is a full entry listing her works and the plays founded upon them in Montague Summers, *A Gothic Bibliography* (ND), pp. 135–142.

Ann Radcliffe (née Ward) should not be confused with a contemporary novelist Mary Ann Radcliffe, nor with Ann Sophia Radcliffe.

Radio Times **and *TV Times*.** Weekly papers giving details of radio and television programmes. *Radio Times* (commenced 28 September 1923) covers the British Broadcasting Corporation (BBC): TV Times (commenced 20 September 1955) covers the independent television companies. In addition to programme details, both publications are illustrated and publish articles on personalities, shows, sport, etc. As such each journal is an important and unique part of the popular literature of entertainment. I have come across no similar publications in the USA.

14 The first issue of The Radio Times,
September 28, 1923

Not much has been written about either publication. An article by L. CROCOMBE 'How Radio Times began' was published in *RT* 25 September 1953. S. BRIGGS, *Those Radio Times* (1981) is well illustrated. An exhibition entitled 'The Art of Radio Times' was held at the Victoria and Albert Museum London (October 1981–February 1982) and a book with the same title was issued simultaneously by BBC Publications. So far as *TV Times* is concerned, the only source known to me is the souvenir supplement published with the issue dated 16 September 1976, which celebrated 21 years of independent television in Britain.

Raffles. The gentleman cracksman created by E. W. Hornung (qv) and continued by Barry Perowne (qv). Raffles could have been outstandingly successful in any career he followed, but he chose crime. On one occasion, penniless and desperate in Australia, he realized that all he could do in the circumstances was to steal; but although forced into crime by necessity, he found that he loved it and never looked back. Once in England, his reputation as one of the best cricketers in the world, together with his dazzling intelligence and wit, to say nothing of his handsome appearance, made him a welcome guest in the homes of the wealthiest familes.

His adventures were told in four books written by E. W. Hornung: *The Amateur Cracksman* (1899) (Short stories); *The Black Mask* (1901) (Short stories – US title

Raffles: Further Adventures of the Gentleman Cracksman); *A Thief in the Night* (1905) (Short stories); *Mr Justice Raffles* (1909).

In 1932 Barry Perowne, with the consent of the Hornung estate, revived the character in a long series of stories written for *The Thriller*, a weekly magazine published in London by Amalgamated Press (qv). The outbreak of war in 1939 caused the suspension of this magazine and the temporary disappearance of Raffles; but he reappeared in the pages of *Ellery Queen's Mystery Magazine* and *The Saint Mystery Magazine* from 1950 onwards. 14 of the best of these stories were published in a book, *Raffles Revisited* (1974).

The new Raffles was rather different from the original one – the gentleman jewel thief had become a two-fisted adventurer. Continuity, however, was to some extent maintained by the fact that Raffles's associate, Bunny, whose life the cracksman had once saved, remained the narrator of the stories.

Raffles appeared in a short American film made in 1905, and was featured in an Italian serial in 1911. In 1925 there was another film featuring the thief, described as 'a gentleman by birth'. Ronald Coleman played the part in 1930, and there was a British *The Return of Raffles* two years later. The most memorable portrayal, however, was that of David Niven in a United Artists film in 1940.

REACH, Angus B(ethune) (1821–1856). British journalist and author of an early crime story, *Clement Lorimer; or, the Book with the Iron Clasps*, published in six monthly parts between October 1848 and March 1849, with illustrations by George Cruikshank. It came out as a hardbacked book in 1849. He wrote other books which were popular, including *The Natural History of 'Bores'* (1847) and *The Natural History of Humbugs* (1847).

Readers/Readership/Reading public. See *Literacy*.

REEVE, Arthur B(enjamin) (1880–1936). American author and creator of Craig Kennedy (qv), the scientific detective. After studying law, Reeve became a journalist. He wrote a series of articles on scientific crime detection, and out of his interest in this subject came his detective hero. He was the first American writer of mystery stories to become widely popular in Great Britain. There were only four which did not feature Craig Kennedy.

REEVE, Clara (1728–1807). British novelist whose most popular work, *The Old English Baron* (1778), was often reprinted.

Reggie Fortune. Created by H. C. Bailey (qv). Fortune is a practising physician and surgeon who acts as a special adviser to Scotland Yard. His associates there are Stanley Lomas, Chief of the CID, whose attitude to Fortune is grudgingly respectful, and Superintendent Bell, Lomas's assistant, who is devoted and admiring. Nine of the 21 Fortune books, published between 1920 and 1948,

were novels: the remainder were short stories. Three of the books had different titles when they were published in the USA.

Religious tracts. Short pamphlets, sometimes illustrated, dealing with religious and moral themes, designed for distribution to the widest possible public. They were mainly issued in Great Britain and in the USA by religious societies whose members paid a subscription to cover the costs of producing the tracts, which were then either distributed free to the poor, or given away to the needy, in lieu of money, so that they could be sold to those who stood in need of the comfort that such publications allegedly offered.

The chief British organizations were The Society for Promoting Christian Knowledge (founded 1698/99) and the Religious Tract Society (founded 1799 and now known as the Lutterworth Press). The Methodists were also active in this field – their interest dates from 1782, when John Wesley set up a society 'to distribute religious Tracts among the Poor'. None of their earlier tracts seems to have survived; but John Mason, who was Methodist Book Steward from 1827 to 1864, published a very large number of tracts (1,326,000 copies in 1841, for instance). In addition to these three major bodies, there were in Britain many small and sometimes provincial tract societies during the first half of the nineteenth century, although very little is known about them.

In the USA the Methodist Book

Concern, founded in Philadelphia, issued its first publication in 1789, moved to New York in 1804, and in 1824 opened its own printing office. The Massachusetts Society for Promoting Christian Knowledge was founded in 1803, and the New York Religious Tract Society in 1812. The New England Tract Society, founded at Andover in 1814, moved to Boston in 1823 and changed its name to the American Tract Society. There were also local groups and societies who issued tracts – in 1825, in New York, a merger of some 50 societies took place under the name of the American Tract Society.

Tracts in both countries were much the same in content and appearance. The extent to which they were read remains problematic; but the fact that they were produced in enormous numbers does not. The nineteenth century was the heyday of the religious tract; but towards the end of the twentieth one still comes across them – a tract was presented to me on the streets of Vancouver in the summer of 1981! The Protestant Truth Society (London) still issues fiercely polemical tracts, while other institutions publish gentler ones. The tradition is far from dead, though in its contemporary manifestations, still less in its historical ones, this kind of publication does not attract very much attention from historians, sociologists or others who are concerned with popular religion.

We know little about the authors who laboured over several centuries to popularize the message of Christ-ianity. Josiah Woodward, who wrote a number of bestselling titles for the Society for Promoting Christian Knowledge in its early days, remains a shadowy figure; but more is known about Grace Pettman (qv), whose writing career spanned the nineteenth and the twentieth centuries, and whose considerable output included tracts.

Closely connected with these ephemeral religious publications is the whole subject of popular Christian iconography. This remains an even more neglected area of study. The best book known to me is Martin Scharfe, *Evangelische Andachtsbilder* (1968). Virtually unknown in Britain and in the USA, it is a scholarly and pioneering exploration of a theme which is rich in possibilities for research.

The bibliography of material about religious tracts is meagre. The following titles are helpful, but rarely as detailed as one would wish:

W. K. LOWTHER CLARKE, *A History of the S.P.C.K.*

W. K. LOWTHER CLARKE, *Eighteenth Century Piety* (1944) contains a discussion of some early tracts.

GORDON HEWITT, *Let the People Read* (1949) covers the history of the Religious Tract Society.

FRANK CUMBERS, *The Book Room* (1956) is an account of Methodist publishing.

MICHAEL SHEARD, 'Methodist Tract-Visiting Societies in the Early Nineteenth Century', published in *Proceedings of the Wesley Historical Society*, vol. 39, 1973, pp. 34–40, is both original and illuminating.

V. E. NEUBURG, *Popular Literature* (1977) contains an Appendix, pp. 249–264, on 'Religious Tracts'.

See also *Colportage*; *More, Hannah*; *Pettman, Grace*; *Spurgeon C(harles) H(addon)*.

REYNOLDS, G(eorge) W(illiam) M(acarthur) (1814–1879). Bestselling British novelist – most published man of the nineteenth century. His works outsold those of Charles Dickens when Dickens's popularity was at its height (cf. Donald Kausch article noted at the end of this entry).

Reynolds was left a fortune by his parents, who died while he was in his early 'teens. He travelled throughout Europe and then settled in Paris, where unsuccessful literary ventures depleted his legacy. In 1837 he returned to London, worked as a journalist and began writing novels. As Editor of the *London Journal* (no. 1, 1st March 1845) he gradually achieved both fame and fortune.

Several of his best-known novels first appeared as serials in the *Journal*'s pages, and others were similarly published in *Reynolds' Miscellany* (1846–1869). His other periodicals were *Reynolds' Political Instructor* (1849–1850) and *Reynolds' Weekly Newspaper* (1850–1879); and this latter paper was still being published as *Reynolds' News* until 16 September 1962, surviving as the *Sunday Citizen* which ceased publication on 18 June 1967.

He specialized in lurid, sensational novels, in many of which his attacks upon the aristocracy and the clergy showed his radical and Chartist sympathies. He provided for his readers an escape into the past, horrors of all kinds, moral truths and sentimentality. For the mass reading public of the nineteenth century almost all the literary fashions of the novel between the 1830s and the 1860s were represented through Reynolds's pen, and

15 A twentieth century American religious tract

these included a number of stories derived from Charles Dickens (see *Dickens imitations*). After falling out with the publisher George Vickers (qv), Reynolds was published from about 1848 by John Dicks (qv), who issued a collected edition of Reynolds's works (? dates) comprising 28 titles in 36 volumes – this total is almost certainly incomplete.

As an example of his enormous popularity, an early novel, *Master Timothy's Bookcase* (1842), went through five editions in less than four years. It is, however, for two series of stories that he is best remembered. Both were constantly reprinted during the nineteenth century. Their publishing history is difficult to unravel, but in outline it is as follows: *The Mysteries of London*, Series 1 and 2 (1844–1848) were written by Reynolds, but after a quarrel with the publisher Series 3 and 4, of two volumes each, were written respectively by Thomas Miller and E. L. Blanchard. Reynolds meanwhile had gone over to the publisher John Dicks and began writing *The Mysteries of the Court of London* (1848–1856), which comprised four series of two volumes each, all written by Reynolds. Both titles were originally issued in weekly parts. In a postscript to the final volume of the latter title Reynolds wrote:

For *twelve* years, therefore, have I hebdomadally issued to the world a fragmentary portion of that which, as one vast whole, may be termed an Encyclopedia of Tales. This Encyclopedia consists of twelve volumes, comprising six hundred and twenty-four weekly Numbers. Each Number has occupied me upon an average seven hours in the composition ... four thousand three hundred and sixty-eight hours.

He went on to point out that the regularity of his routine 'will account to the public for the facility with which I have been enabled to write so many other works during the same period, and yet to allow myself ample leisure for recreation and for healthful exercise.' The 'other works' referred to number about 25!

Reynolds's wife, Susannah Frances Reynolds, was herself an accomplished novelist whose *Gretna Green; or, All for Love* (1847–1848) went through several editions. She wrote other novels, a cookery book (*Household Book of Practical Receipts*, 32 parts, 1847), and a popular song, 'The Belle of the Village'.

So far as I am aware, no full-length study of G. W. M. Reynolds exists; but the following items are useful:

MONTAGUE SUMMERS, *A Gothic Bibliography* (1940).

MARGARET DALZIEL, *Popular Fiction 100 Years Ago* (1957).

LOUIS JAMES, *Fiction for the Working Man* (1963, 1974).

DONALD KAUSCH, *George W. M. Reynolds: A Bibliography* (in *Transactions of the Bibliographical Society, The Library*, Fifth Series, vol. XXVIII, no. 4, December 1973).

RHODE, John and **BURTON, Miles.** Pseudonyms of Cecil John Charles Street (1884–1964). British author of 140 mystery novels. For 37 years he produced four detective stories a year; and he was also a career army officer, reaching the rank of major.

His first novel was *ASF* (1924 – US title *The White Menace*) – written under the pseudonym John Rhode; and it was under this name that he published 72 novels which featured Dr Lancelot Priestley, a mathematician, as the detective. As Miles Burton he wrote 61 novels about Desmond Merrion, intelligence agent and later private detective, and his friend Inspector Henry Arnold of Scotland Yard.

RICHMOND, Legh (1772–1827).

British author. Native of Liverpool, Cambridge graduate, ordained in 1798 and appointed Curate of Brading and Yaverland on the Isle of Wight in the same year. In 1805 he became Chaplain to the Lock Hospital, London, and Rector of Turvey in Bedfordshire, where he remained for the rest of his life.

While on the Isle of Wight he wrote several bestselling religious tracts (qv) which were published separately and later collected together and published as *Annals of the Poor* (2 vols., 1814). The individual titles are: *The Dairyman's Daughter*, of which it is said that four million copies in 19 languages were circulated by 1849; *The Negro Servant*; *The Young Cottager*; *The Cottage Conversation*; and *A Visit to the Infirmary*.

T. S. GRIMSHAWE, *The Life of Legh Richmond* (1828 and reprints).

There is a useful entry in the *Dictionary of National Biography* by G. F. W. MUNBY, who also wrote, in collaboration with THOMAS WRIGHT, *Turvey and Legh Richmond* (2nd Edition, 1894).

The five religious tracts under the title *The Dairyman's Daughter and other Annals of the Poor* were reprinted, with colour photographs, by the Gospel Standard Baptist Trust Ltd. in 1970.

Riddles. Riddles, like jokes, have a history that is older than printing. Both are probably as old as the use of language itself, and both have traditionally provided opportunities for verbal wit and for bawdiness. The first printed collection of riddles in English was *The Demaundes Joyous*, published by Caxton's successor, Wynkyn de Worde, in 1511. Two fragments, one in the Bodleian Library and the other in the Edinburgh University Library, originally rescued from the binding of an old book, provide evidence that William Rastell printed a collection of riddles about 20 years later. Some of these turn up in *The Booke of Merrie Riddles* (earliest known edition 1617), which was reprinted throughout the seventeenth century.

Riddles continued to be popular, and in the nineteenth century they were often cleaned up and new ones were devised for inclusion in children's books and magazines. Books of riddles are widely sold today, both in North American supermarkets and in bookstores. In Britain, they are to be found in bookshops!

No comprehensive study of the riddle is known to me. The following titles indicate some of the richness of the subject:

A. TAYLOR, *A Bibliography of Riddles* (1939). The same author's *English Riddles from the Oral Tradition* (1951) contains 1,749 entries.

JOHN WARDROPER (ed.), *The Demaundes Joyous* (1971) is a facsimile reprint of the first riddle book together with an Introduction and a Bibliography.

One of the earliest MS collections has been published as *The Exeter Book of Riddles* (1979). The Introduction and Notes by the translator, KEVIN CROSSLEY-HOLLAND, are excellent – as indeed are the riddles themselves.

HELENE HOVANEC, *The Puzzler's Paradise* (1978) sets riddles within the general context of puzzles, and has some unusual illustrations.

RITSON, Joseph (1752–1803). An irascible, meticulous British scholar and editor; a vegetarian; and a radical in politics. During his lifetime he engaged in learned, acrimonious controversies with contemporaries, and at the same time did some solid work in the field of early English popular literature.

Amongst his more important books in this connection are: *Select Collection of English Songs* (3 vols., 1783). *Gammer Gurton's Garland* (1783–84) – a collection of nursery rhymes. *Pieces of Ancient Popular Poetry* (1791). *Robin Hood* (1795) – a long essay on the famous outlaw

and a number of early ballads which recounted his adventures.

Letters of Joseph Ritson (2 vols., 1833).

H. A. BURD, *Joseph Ritson, a Critical Biography* (1916).

B. H. BRONSON, *Joseph Ritson, Scholar at Arms* (2 vols., 1938).

ARTHUR JOHNSTON, *Enchanted Ground* (1964). There is an excellent chapter on Ritson.

ROBERTS, Edwin F. (Dates unknown). Exceptionally prolific British writer of popular fiction, much of it published in penny weekly parts. He was active round about the middle of the nineteenth century, and was associated with G. W. M. Reynolds (qv).

Robin Hood. English outlaw and hero who lived with a band of followers known as his 'merry men' in Sherwood Forest, near Nottingham. Amongst them were Little John, Will Scarlett, Much the Miller's Son, Allen a Dale and Friar Tuck; and an important member of the group was Maid Marian. He is usually portrayed as protecting the poor against the tyranny and rapacity of King John, Norman knights, the Sheriff of Nottingham, and various prelates.

His earliest appearance in print was *A lyttel geste, of Robyn Hode and his meyne, and of the proude sheryfe of Notyngham*, printed in London by Wynkyn de Worde in about 1510. A unique copy survives in the University Library, Cambridge. His adventures have subsequently appeared in numerous books, and latterly he has featured in films and on television.

The first to gather together the old ballads about him was Joseph Ritson (qv), whose *Robin Hood: a Collection of all the Ancient Poems, Songs and Ballads* was published in 1795, and several times reprinted. A facsimile of an 1823 reprint was published by E.P. Publishing Ltd in 1972.

The best introduction to the outlaw is R. B. DOBSON and J. TAYLOR, *Rymes of Robyn Hood* (1976), which contains a critical introduction, texts and a bibliography. J. H. GABLE, *A Bibliography of Robin Hood* (Nebraska, 1938), is also useful.
Between 1958 and 1961 several articles dealing with Robin Hood appeared in the British journal *Past & Present*. These have been reprinted in R. H. HILTON (ed.), *Peasants, Knights and Heretics* (1976).

ROBINS, Denise (1897–). Bestselling British author of more than 170 romantic novels dating from 1924. Among the best are *Enchanted Island* (1956), *Put Back the Clock* (1962) and *The Other Side of Love* (1973).

Robinson Crusoe. Fictional sailor who was shipwrecked and settled on a tropical island, the creation of Daniel Defoe (?1661–1731) in *Robinson Crusoe* (1719) and *Further Adventures of Robinson Crusoe* (1719). Both narratives, almost al-

ways combined into one and endlessly rewritten or adapted, have been popular ever since – and they have also taken the forms of chapbooks (qv), children's books, films, pantomimes, and so on.

After some years alone on his island, Crusoe was visited by a party of cannibals who landed with a prisoner. He drove them off, and saved the captive from a horrible fate. Captive became faithful companion, and was given the name of Man Friday – Crusoe kept a record of the passage of time, and this was the day on which the rescue took place.

The term Man Friday (and its adaptation to Girl Friday) has been used in recent years to describe a secretary-cum-personal assistant, and advertisements have used the phrase. Today, in deference to the sensibilities of some, and indeed with legal sanction, a 'Person Friday' is asked for.

ROBINSON, Emma (1814–1890). British author of some 21 popular novels, the first *Whitefriars; or, The Days of Charles the Second* (1844) and the last *The Matrimonial Vanity Fair* (1868). One story, *The City Banker; or, Love and Money* (1856), was in fact begun as a serial in *The London Journal* by J. F. Smith (qv), and concluded by Emma Robinson after he had severed his connection with the journal.

ROCHE, Regina Maria (1773–1845). British author of some 20 gothic novels (qv). The most popular, *The Children of the Abbey* (4

169

vols., 1796), was originally published by the Minerva Press (qv), and was reprinted in cheap one-volume editions throughout the nineteenth century.

ROHMER, Sax (1883–1959). British novelist and short story writer who produced more than 50 books. Rohmer is best remembered, however, as the creator of Dr Fu Manchu (qv). Born Henry Arthur Ward in Birmingham, Rohmer had an unsettled family background. His father was a clerk in an office, but his mother was an alcoholic. He had little interest in school, and was unable to hold down a job requiring regular hours, so he determined to become a writer. His early stories were about the occult, in which he had an abiding interest. His first efforts at fiction were not successful; and it was not until 1910 that his first book, *Pause!*, a collection of short stories written in collaboration with George Robey and published anonymously, appeared.

During a newspaper assignment in Limehouse, East London's Chinatown, his search for 'Mr King', a local criminal, gave him the idea for Fu Manchu. He made his first appearance in book form in 1913. Rohmer also created Sumuru, a female counterpart of the Doctor, whose adventures were recounted in several books; and there were many other novels and short stories, together with a standard reference work on the occult, *The Romance of Sorcery* (1914).

Although he was an immensely successful writer, Rohmer was never a wealthy man because he was not able to handle money. Further, he was cheated by his agent over a period of 15 years, and a lucrative film contract brought him only $8,000 after a legal battle instead of the $4 million which was reported in the press.

Rohmer married Rose Elizabeth Know in 1909, and despite various marital crises they stayed together until his death 50 years later. His wife was a great help to him in his work.

ROLLINS, Hyder Edward (1889–1958). American scholar, Professor of English at Harvard University. His editorial contributions to ballad study are outstanding. Amongst them are:
'The Black-letter Broadside Ballad' in *P.M.L.A.*, 34 (1919), pp. 258–339.
Old English Ballads 1553–1625 (1920).
A Pepysian Garland. Black-letter Broadside Ballads of the Years 1595–1639. Chiefly from the Collection of Samuel Pepys (1922, reprint 1971).
Cavalier and Puritan. Ballads and Broadsides Illustrating the Period of the Great Rebellion 1640–1660 (1923).
An Analytical Index to the Ballad-Entries (1557–1709) in the Registers of the Company of Stationers of London (1924, reprint 1967).
The Pack of Autolycus or Strange and Terrible News ... as Told in Broadside Ballads of the Year 1624–1693 (1927, reprint 1969).

'Roman policier'. See *Gaboriau, E.*

Romantic fiction. General term for love stories with a happy ending which are free from sadism, violence and sex. Such stories usually revolve around a pretty young girl with a highly developed moral sense who meets, often in an exotic setting, a tall, dark, handsome stranger who is often aristocratic and not seldom arrogant as well. At first she hates him and then, against her will, she falls in love with him, learning eventually, to her surprise and delight, that he loves her too. They marry and live happily ever after. A variation which is increasingly popular features male doctors and female nurses in a hospital setting.

Romantic fiction is much criticized, both for its perpetuation of sexual stereotypes and for a middle class ethos which precludes any mention of social problems arising from money, class or race. Despite such criticism, stories with a happy ending remain enormously popular. Many publishing firms issue fiction of this kind, and Mills and Boon (qv) and Harlequin (qv) specialize in it.

See RACHEL ANDERSON, *The Purple Heart Throbs* (1974) – a rapid and entertaining survey. There is also a Romantic Novelists' Association, founded in 1960.

ROWLANDS, Samuel (1570?–1630?). Prolific British author who wrote an account in verse of the adventures of Guy of Warwick (qv). Its bibliography, like that of all Rowlands's work, is complex and obscure.

He typifies the miscellaneous popular writer of the period, who would turn his pen to pretty well any task. The Hunterian Club of Glasgow reprinted his works between 1872 and 1880, and a final volume appeared in 1886. Edmund Gosse wrote a general introduction to the edition which was reprinted in his *Seventeenth Century Studies* (1883).

RUCK, Berta (1878–1978). British popular novelist amongst whose novels were *Arabella the Awful* (1918), *The Bride Who Ran Away – Nurse Henderson* (1922), *Shopping for a Husband* (1967). In *A Story-Teller Tells the Truth* (1935) she is very explicit about her work:

I belong to the School of Thought (the Non-Thinking School, if you like) that considers 'compensating dream fiction', not as opiate, but as tonic, and prefers to leave the tale on a note definitely gay and hopeful. People condemn the story-teller's cheerfully tidied-up last chapter as the flight from reality. Personally I regard it as the entrance into the original real world. . . .

Berta Ruck's married name was Amy Roberta Onions.

RYMER, James Malcolm (1804–1884). Prolific British author of sensational novels which were mainly published by Edward Lloyd (qv) and John Dicks (qv). His best known novels were *Ada the Betrayed; or, the Murder at the Old Smithy* (56 numbers, 1842) and *Varney the Vampire; or, the Feast of Blood* (109 numbers, 1847). Both are sometimes attributed to T. P. Prest (qv).

It was said of Rymer that he had written ten novels simultaneously, and that he made a fortune out of writing popular fiction. At his death his estate was £8,000.

There is a possibility that he visited the USA to write for American publishers. Whether or not this is so, some of his stories were published there under the pseudonyms Nelson Percival, J. D. Conroy, Septimus R. Urban and Bertha Thorne Bishop. In Britain he used the pseudonyms Malcolm J. Errym and Malcolm J. Merry.

M. SUMMERS, *A Gothic Bibliography* (ND).
A. JOHANNSEN, *The House of Beadle and Adams* (vol. II, 1950).
LOUIS JAMES, *Fiction for the Working Man* (1974, (1963)).
Some of the details to be found in these reference books are conflicting.

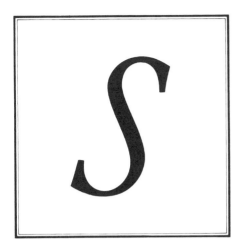

SABATINI, Rafael (1875–1950). British romantic novelist and short story writer whose work was published between 1904 and 1942. His most popular novel, *Scaramouche* (1921), was a best-seller in the USA.

Although he was born in Italy, Sabatini's mother was English and he settled in Britain as a young man, living there for the rest of his life.

SALE, 'Chic' (Charles Partlow) (1885–1936). American author of a bestselling book of 'lavatory' humour, *The Specialist*, which was first published by The Specialist Publishing Company, St. Louis, 1929.

Sam Spade. Fictional detective created by Dashiell Hammett (qv), and perhaps the first 'hardboiled' detective. Tough, confident, cynical, competent, Sam Spade made his appearance in *The Maltese Falcon* (1930). In the Warner Brothers film of the novel (1941) the part of Sam Spade was played by Humphrey Bogart. There was also a CBS radio series for which some of the scripts were written by Hammett. Sam Spade appeared in only three short stories and one novel, but is the best-known of Hammett's creations, partly because of the excellence of his writing and partly on account of Bogart's film portrayal of the character.

Sapper. See *McNeile, H. C.,* and *Bulldog Drummond.*

SAYERS, Dorothy L(eigh) (1893–1957). British scholar and author. Creator of Lord Peter Wimsey (qv), whose adventures were told in eleven novels, four volumes of short stories and one limited edition pamphlet. In collaboration with Robert Eustace (pseudonym of Dr Eustace Robert Barton) she wrote a non-Wimsey mystery, *The Documents in the Case* (1930).

Dorothy Sayers also wrote religious books, and was a distinguished translator of Dante. Despite the popularity of her mystery stories, the later ones were held by some critics to be snobbish. On her reputation, see C. STEINBRUNNER and O. PENZLER (eds.) *Encyclopaedia of Mystery and Detection* (1976).

Scarlet Pimpernel, The. Character created by Baroness Orczy (qv). To his contemporaries in the days of the French Revolution he is Sir Percy Blakeney, a foppish dandy who lives only for pleasure. In reality, however, he is a master of disguise and a daring secret agent who goes to France and rescues aristocrats from the clutches of revolutionaries. His dual identity is known only to a trusted few confidantes – and eventually to his French wife, Marguerite, and his arch-enemy, Chauvelin.

He first appeared in a play, *The Scarlet Pimpernel* (1905), written by Baroness Orczy and her husband, Montague Brastow, in order to get her novel of the same name published. The play was very successful, and the novel came out in the same year. It was followed by others featuring Sir Percy, including *The Elusive Pimpernel* (1908), *Sir Percy Hits Back* (1927), and *The Way of the Scarlet Pimpernel* (1933).

There have been several Pimpernel films, the best of which was made in 1935 and starred Leslie Howard, Merle Oberon and Raymond Massey.

Science fiction. This is the best documented genre in the entire field of popular literature. New novels and short stories are published in hardback, paperback, magazines and comic strips; much early material is reissued, and where it is not, out-of-print items are eagerly collected. There is, however, even amongst its keenest adherents, no readily agreed definition as to what science fiction is. It is more recognized than defined.

According to *Webster's New World Companion to English and American Literature* (1973) it is:

... a branch of speculative literature whose modern origins may be traced to Jules Verne and H. G. Wells. Strictly defined, it deals in extrapolations of the future based on scientific or pseudo-scientific hypotheses. Among its most popular themes are space flight, time travel, encounters with extraterrestrial beings, psychological or biological changes in human and alien life forms, and the effects of technology on social behaviour.

Probably not all Science Fiction enthusiasts would agree wholeheartedly with this definition, but it seems reasonably accurate and fairly comprehensive.

The basic themes are neatly tabulated in JAMES GUNN, *Alternate Worlds. The Illustrated History of Science Fiction* (1975), an excellent survey of developments. These themes are:

1 Travelling – world and universe; space travel; alternative worlds.
2 Wonders of science.
3 Man and machine.
4 Progress and regression. Utopias; anti-utopias.
5 Man and society.
6 Man and the future.
7 War – changing weapons; Armageddon.
8 Cataclysm.

9 Man and environment.
10 Superpowers – invisibility; immortality; mental control over people, things, events.
11 Superman.
12 Man and alien.
13 Man and religion.
14 Miscellaneous.

In addition to Gunn's book there are several other basic reference works: KINGSLEY AMIS, *New Maps of Hell* (1960). Brief and informative.

BRIAN ASH, *Who's Who in Science Fiction* (1976, Revised Edition 1977).

BRIAN ASH (ed.), *The Visual Encyclopedia of Science Fiction* (1977). Sub-titled 'A Documented Pictorial Checklist of the SF World', it covers every aspect of the subject, is copiously illustrated and has full bibliographies. An essential reference book. A great deal of science fiction has been published in magazines, and the section dealing with this aspect is of especial importance (pp. 305–311). There are also sections on the subject in the cinema and on television.

At the time of writing, the latest reference book is P. NICHOLLS, *The Encyclopedia of Science Fiction* (1981).

Over the years the subject has developed a striking and colourful iconography, and this has been documented by BRIAN ALDISS, *Science Fiction Art* (1975) and ANTHONY FREWIN, *One Hundred Years of Science Fiction Illustration* (1974).

Science fiction in comic strip form is covered in HUBERT H. CRAWFORD, *Crawford's Encyclopedia of Comic Books* (1978) and MAURICE HORN (ed.), *The World Encyclopedia of Comic Books* (1976).

SCOTT, Sir Walter (1771–1832). British novelist whose stories were enormously popular throughout the nineteenth century in both Great Britain and the USA. In the latter country his popularity is attested by the fact that when he died, the *Richmond Enquirer* published the sad news in an issue of the newspaper heavily bordered in black – a courtesy usually reserved for the death of a President.

Besides being a successful author, Scott had a deep interest in ballad literature. His *Border Minstrelsy* (3 vols., 1802–03) has often been reprinted; and in 1814 he contributed to *Encyclopaedia Britannica* essays on 'Chivalry' and 'Romance' which were reprinted in *Miscellaneous Prose Works* (3 vols., 1847).

The extent to which he drew upon popular tradition in the making of his novels is illustrated in an anonymous book, *Waverley Anecdotes* (1850).

Seventeenth century ballads. See *Furnivall, F. J.* and *Onley, W.*

Sexton Blake. Detective created by Harry Blyth. Blake first appeared on 20 December 1893 in a story called 'The Missing Millionaire', published in No. 6 of *The Halfpenny Marvel*, a boys' weekly. The story was credited to Hal Meredith, a pseudonym for Blyth. In April 1894 the *Union Jack* was launched, and published many Blake stories. The popularity of the detective was enormous and nearly 200 authors – including Edwy Searles Brooks (qv) who wrote 76 Blake stories – produced about 4,000 tales featuring him. There were translations into a number of European languages and also into Arabic, Hindi and Afrikaans.

Blake had an assistant named Tinker, a landlady called Mrs Bardell and a bloodhound, Pedro.

Amongst the Blake authors were Robert Murray; George Hamilton Teed; Gwyn Evans; Anthony Skene; Lewis Jackson; John Hunter; John G. Brandon; Mark Osborne; Coutts Brisbane; Andrew Murray; Cecil Hayter; Walter Tyrer; Anthony Parsons; Donald Stuart; Rex Hardinge; Gilbert Chester.

The earliest Blake film was produced in 1909, and the last seems to have been in 1945. In September 1978 the BBC launched a serial entitled *Sexton Blake and the Demon God*, written by Simon Raven.

It is worth recalling that Blake made his debut four years before Sherlock Holmes, and is probably the longest living detective in fiction.

E. S. TURNER, *Boys will be Boys* (1976 (1948)).
C. STEINBRUNNER and O. PENZLER (eds), *Encyclopedia of Mystery and Detection* (1976).

SHELLEY, Mary (1797–1851). British writer, daughter of Mary Wollstonecraft, an early feminist and radical; wife of the poet Percy Bysshe Shelley. She was the creator of Frankenstein (qv), who made his appearance in *Frankenstein: or, the*

Modern Prometheus (1818). Although she wrote other novels, none was so popular as this one.

Sherlock Holmes. Detective created by Sir Arthur Conan Doyle (qv). In his deerstalker hat, Inverness cape and with curved pipe, he is instantly recognizable all over the world.

Sherlock (he was very nearly called Sherrinford) Holmes was born in Yorkshire on 6 January 1854, and solved his first case while an Oxford undergraduate. After taking his degree he became a consulting detective. In 1881 he was introduced to Dr John H. Watson (qv) and the two men shared Holmes' flat at 221b Baker Street.

Besides possessing immense deductive powers which he used to solve criminal cases, Holmes had a mastery of some unusual subjects and wrote books with esoteric titles, for example *A Study of the Chaldean Roots in the Ancient Cornish Language*. Until his 4-volume study *The Whole Art of Detection* is published, his *Practical Handbook of Bee Culture with Some Observations upon the Segregation of the Queen* must be regarded as his *magnum opus*. He smokes a pipe, plays the violin like a virtuoso, and is addicted to cocaine – his fondness for which, however, he did not mention to Watson when the two men discussed their respective shortcomings before agreeing to share Holmes's flat. Holmes never married, though it is possible that he had an affair with Irene Adler, a former opera singer who was born in New Jersey in 1858. 'To Sherlock Holmes she is always *the* woman', remarked Watson ('A Scandal in Bohemia' (1891)). After Irene's death in 1903 Holmes retired to keep bees in Sussex with his old housekeeper, Mrs Martha Hudson. Just before war began in 1914 he came out of retirement for a brief period. . . . The Holmes stories were narrated by Watson, often to the detective's displeasure, for he did not like sensation or melodrama and felt that, if told at all, the stories should be recounted as exercises in logic.

The first Holmes story, *A Study in Scarlet*, was published in *Beeton's Christmas Annual* for 1887, and later appeared in book form. Altogether there were nine Holmes books comprising 60 tales featuring the detective, of which four were full length novels. Most of the Holmes adventures were first published in *The Strand Magazine*, London, with illustrations by Sidney Paget. In the USA they were published in *Lippincott's Monthly Magazine*; *Collier's*; *Liberty Magazine*; *Hearst's International Magazine*. Occasionally stories appeared in the USA a month or so before they were published in Great Britain.

Checklist of Books (* denotes a full length novel). *A Study in Scarlet*, 1887*; *The Sign of Four*, 1890* (American edition 1891); *The Adventures of Sherlock Holmes*, 1892; *The Memoirs of Sherlock Holmes*, 1894; *The Hound of the Baskervilles*, 1902*; *The Return of Sherlock Holmes*, 1905; *The Valley of Fear*, 1915*; *His Last Bow*, 1917; *The Case Book of Sherlock Holmes*, 1927.

Sherlock Holmes is also the most enduring of screen detectives. He first appeared in *Sherlock Holmes Baffled* in 1903, and numerous films have followed. He has also featured in radio and television series.

Holmes' methods are best summed up in a comment of his own:

'It is a capital mistake to theorize before one has data. Insensibly one begins to twist facts to suit theories, instead of theories to suit facts.' ('A Scandal in Bohemia', 1891)

There is a considerable Sherlock Holmes literature; but perhaps the most useful guide to the detective's career is MICHAEL and MOLLIE HARDWICK, *The Sherlock Holmes Companion* (1962).
See also W. S. BARING-GOULD, *The Annotated Sherlock Holmes* (2 vols., 1968).

SHIRLEY, John (?–1702). British writer of popular fiction. Amongst his works were *An Abridgment of the History of Guy of Warwick* (1681); *The Triumph of Wit* (1688) – 8th Edition 1724; *Great Britain's Glory: an Abridgment of the History of King Arthur*.

SIMENON, Georges (Joseph Christian) (1902–). Prolific Belgian author of more than 200 novels, creator of Maigret (qv). Simenon could, when he was young, write a book in three or four days, but later he restricted his output to about twelve books a year. Many of them have been successfully filmed.

Simon Templar. See *The Saint.*

Simple Simon. Nursery rhyme character who survives today in a poem, at most four verses long, although more usually only two are given. His history, however, goes back a very long way and is extremely obscure – neither origins nor authorship are known.

A tune 'Simple Simon' is mentioned in John Playford, *The Dancing Master* (1665 edition), and a ballad, *Simple Simon's Misfortunes and his Wife Margery's Cruelty*, dates from around 1685. Several chapbook versions were published during the eighteenth century. According to Francis Grose, *Classical Dictionary of the Vulgar Tongue* (Revised and Corrected by Pierce Egan, London, 1823), he is 'a natural, a silly fellow'; and this gives a clue to the archetypal nature of this character. The fool has long been a well-known figure in literature, and while explorations into the nature of Simple Simon are rare to the point of virtual non-existence, there is a considerable literature on fools, some of which casts light, occasionally oblique but often illuminating, upon this character.

A pioneer study is w. a. CLOUSTON, *The Book of Noodles* (1888). There is also OCTAVE DELEPIERRE, *Histoire Littéraire des Fous* (1860). The standard work, however, with its ample documentation and full bibliography, remains ENID WELSFORD, *The Fool* (1935).

SIMS, George R(obert) (1847– 1922). British journalist, novelist, short story writer, playwright, poet. Sims was a voluminous writer, much of whose work described the life of the poor. His best known novels were *The Case of George Candlemas* (1890) and *The Mystery of Mary Ann* (1907). He also created the first female detective in a collection of short stories, *Dorcas Dene, Detective* (1897), and a further collection of stories with the same title was published in 1898. Dorcas Dene (née Lester) gave up her career as an actress to earn money as a detective when her young husband went blind. She was popular with the reading public.

Sir Henry Merrivale. See *Carr, John Dickson.*

SMITH, E. E. (1890–1965). American writer. 'Doc' Smith – he was a genuine Ph.D. – was in turn a lumberjack, bus conductor and chief chemist in a doughnut-mix factory. His first novel, written between 1915 and 1920, was serialized in *Amazing Stories* eight years later. When it appeared in book form as *The Skylark of Space* (1946) it was an immediate success, and sequels followed: *Skylark Three* (1948), *Skylark of Valeron* (1949); and *Skylark Du Quesne* (1967), completed shortly before the author's death. The backdrop of these novels was prodigious – mile-long starships, battles in space and a host of hostile aliens. The action ranged across the galaxy: the Skylark novels were a saga of space.

The other major group of novels

by Smith were the 'Lensman' tales: *Triplanetary* (1948); *First Lensman* (1950); *Galactic Patrol* (1950); *Gray Lensman* (1951); *Second-Stage Lensman* (1953); *Children of the Lens* (1954); *The Vortex Blaster* (1960). These two monumental series have been often reprinted. Smith did write other novels – *The Spacehounds of IPC* (1947); *Subspace Explorers* (1965); *The Galaxy Primes* (1965) – but his fame rests upon the Skylark and Lensman titles.

RON ELLIK and BILL EVANS, *The Universes of E. E. Smith* (1966) – a guide to his imaginary worlds and the characters who inhabit them.

SMITH, John Frederick (1803–1890). Prolific British author of popular novels and melodramas. He worked at one time or another for Edward Lloyd (qv), George Vickers (qv) and John Cassell (qv). His output was enormous, and many of his books, with slightly different titles from their English ones, were published in New York by Dick and Fitzgerald as 'J. F. Smith's Celebrated Novels'.

Soap opera. Radio/television serials so called because the original American ones, begun in the early days of broadcasting, were said to have been sponsored by soap manufacturing companies. They are, in fact, popular fiction in a non-printed form.

In the USA more than a dozen are currently running, with episodes transmitted during the day from Monday to Friday. In Britain the three major television soap operas are not transmitted every day, and go out during the early evening period, though this is subject to change. A radio serial, *The Archers* ('an every day story of country folk', commenced 1951), is broadcast by the BBC round about seven o'clock on week-day evenings; there is a repeat on the following day, and an omnibus edition on Sundays. It is the only surviving radio soap opera – the other two, both British, which overlapped the television era were *Mrs Dale's Diary* (1948–1969) and *Waggoner's Walk* (1969–1980).

The following is a reasonably complete list of current American television soap operas, with date of commencement: *All my Children* (1970), *Another World* (1964), *As the World Turns* (1956), *Days of our Lives* (1965), *The Doctors* (1963), *The Edge of Night* (1956), *General Hospital* (1963), *The Guiding Light* (1963. This serial, almost a national institution in the USA, commenced on radio in 1937, and transferred to television in 1956), *Love of Life* (1951), *One Life to Live* (1968), *Ryan's Hope* (1975), *Search for Tomorrow* (1951), *Somerset* (1970), *The Young and the Restless* (1973).

The major British television serials are: *Coronation Street* (1960), *Crossroads* (1964), *Emmerdale Farm* (1972).

A critical history of radio/television soap operas in Britain and the USA remains to be written. In both countries, but notably the latter, many have begun but have not survived for long; and the reasons

179

for failure would be interesting to explore. It must be said that soap opera rarely, if ever, translates successfully from one country to the other. Comic strip characters, on the other hand, do so easily and often. In Britain the BBC has consistently failed to sustain a long-lasting television soap opera, despite various attempts to do so. Its most successful effort, *Compact* (1961), did not last long. The commercial companies have been very much more successful in this field.

The phenomenon of the soap opera has produced a distinctive ephemeral sub-literature in each country. In the USA, *Soap Opera Digest* is typical of several magazines. Originally a monthly when it commenced publication in the mid-seventies, the issue dated 1 May 1979 announced that in future it would appear every three weeks. Besides synopses of televised episodes, there is chat about the stars; hints for aspirants ('So you want to be a soap star?'), interviews and other features make up each issue. Several daily newspapers, too, run a weekly column summarizing the stories for the benefit of those who have missed an episode.

In Britain, things are rather different. Articles in newspapers and periodicals have tended to proliferate, and the television companies themselves have issued souvenirs and special feature publications in magazine format. These have included *Coronation Street 2000* (1980); *Crossroads Special Souvenir Issue* (1978); and *The Secrets Behind Emmerdale Farm* (1979). In 1961

TV Times (see *Radio Times and TV Times*) issued a two-part guide to *Coronation Street* as a pull-out supplement, with a detailed plan of the area and notes on the main characters. Finally, all three serials have spawned a number of novels. *The Archers*, too, has been the subject of numerous newspaper and magazine articles. In addition, in 1958, 1959, 1961 and 1966, the BBC published copies of the 'local newspaper' read by the Archers, *The Borchester Echo*. Although there is no advertising on BBC channels, in 1959 the family was used to promote a brand of soup.

Reference material on soap opera is sparse. So far as the US is concerned there are two useful paperbacks: ROBERT LA GUARDIA, *The Wonderful World of TV Soap Operas* (1974); RON LACKMAN, *TV Soap Opera Almanac* (1976). There was also an unsigned article in *Time* of 12 January 1976 entitled 'Sex and Suffering in the Afternoon'.

In England there is: NORMAN PAINTING, *Forever Ambridge* (1975. The author was one of the original members of the cast of *The Archers*); WILLIAM SMETHURST (ed.), *The Archers. The First Thirty Years* (1980. This is the latest and most comprehensive book on the serial); NOELE GORDON, *My Life at Crossroads* (1975. The author was a star of the serial; and the book contained a Foreword by the wife of the Prime Minister of Great Britain!).

The most recent additions – at the time of writing – to what will probably be an increasing number of titles are: RICHARD DYER *et al.*, *Coronation Street* (1981). H. V. KERSHAW, *The Street Where I Live* (1981. This is the best 'inside' view of *Coronation Street* to date).

Solar Pons. Detective created by August Derleth (qv). He became known as 'The Sherlock Holmes of Praed Street', and his adventures were recounted by a companion, Dr Lyndon Parker.

When Sir Arthur Conan Doyle stopped writing Sherlock Holmes stories, Derleth asked whether he might write pastiches of the detective. Since nobody opposed the idea he went ahead and created Solar Pons, whose first adventure was told in a short story published in 1929. Like Holmes, Pons wears an Inverness cape and a deerstalker hat, and his methods of detection are the same. There were altogether ten Pons books, all except one containing short stories published between 1945 and 1973. There are 'factual' essays about Pons, Parker and their background in *Praed Street Papers* (1965) and *Praed Street Dossier* (1968).

SOUTHWORTH, Emma **Dorothy Eliza Nevitte** (1819–1899). American author of more than 60 novels, many of them reprinted in Britain by the firm founded by William Milner (qv). Her first publication, *Retribution*, was written as a short story for the magazine *The National Era*, and grew into a novel entitled *Retribution; or The Maiden's Dower: A Tale of Passion*, published in 1849.

SPILLANE, Mickey (1918–   ). American mystery writer, creator of Mike Hammer (qv). He was born Frank Morrison Spillane in Brooklyn, New York, began writing for magazines in 1935, and turned to pulp magazines and comic books. He has also been a circus performer, served with the United States Air Force during the Second World War and worked with federal agents to break a narcotics ring. In 1952 he became a Jehovah's Witness.

With a blend of violence and sex, Spillane has sold more copies of his books than any other American author except Erle Stanley Gardner. When his books first appeared in the 1950s he dealt with sex more realistically than most of his contemporaries. Today, however, such treatment of the subject does not appear outrageous, and the abiding impression left by his novels is that they are tales of violence redeemed only by the fact that his heroes Mike Hammer and Tiger Mann are totally incorruptible. The latter, who seems to be engaged in a permanent vendetta against Russian agents, appears in the following novels: *Day of the Guns* (1964); *Bloody Sunrise* (1965); *The Death Dealers* (1965); *The By-Pass Control* (1966). Other Spillane books are *The Long Wait* (1951); *The Deep* (1961); *Me, Hood!* (1963 – two novelettes); *Killer Mine* (1964 – two novelettes); *The Flier* (1964 – two novelettes); *The Delta Factor* (1967); *Tough Guys* (1970); *The Erection Set* (1972); *The Last Cop Out* (1973).

Many Spillane books have been turned into successful films.

SPURGEON, C(harles) H(addon)
(1834–1892). Famous British preacher, writer, Christian activist and temperance advocate. A man of phenomenal energy, he wrote some 50 books, a number of them reprinting the sermons that he had preached to packed congregations. For many years he was the guiding light of the Metropolitan Tabernacle, for the building of which he raised considerable sums of money. He was also instrumental in founding a Pastor's College and the Stockwell Orphanage in South London.

In 1866 he founded the Colportage Association, for, as he said, 'the sale of vicious literature can only be met by the distribution of good books: these can only be scattered in rural districts by carrying the books to the doors, and even in towns the book-hawker's work greatly stimulates their sale.' Spurgeon took this part of his work as seriously as anything he undertook, because he realized the crucial importance of the printed word in spreading ideas, both religious and otherwise.

Several of his books were described in the publisher's catalogue as 'popular'. Among them were the following titles, with the numbers sold by the time of his death: *John Ploughman's Talk*, 380,000 copies; *John Ploughman's Pictures*, 130,000 copies; *All of Grace*, 40,000 copies; and *According to Promise*, 30,000 copies.

I do not know of any satisfactory modern biography or critical assessment of Spurgeon. The Rev. R. SHINDLER, *From the Usher's Desk to the Tabernacle Pulpit* (1892), is rather fulsome, but does have some value because it conveys the atmosphere – sometimes stifling – of nineteenth-century evangelism. Spurgeon's own book, *The Metropolitan Tabernacle. Its History and Work* (1876), is as fascinating as the personality of its author.

See also *Religious tracts*.

Spy thrillers. Thrillers are books about crime or mystery which thrill or excite the reader. Spy thrillers are just that, but with the added ingredient of espionage. The appeal of the spy story in the last decades of the twentieth century is closely connected with the cold war and great power rivalry. Equally, widely publicized news stories about defection to 'the other side' and speculations about a 'third man' have all helped to create a climate for this kind of fiction. Some of its most notable exponents are Len Deighton (qv), Ian Fleming (qv) and John le Carré (qv).

There is one excellent study of the genre: BRUCE MERRY, *Anatomy of the Spy Thriller* (1977). See also D. MCCORMICK, *Who's Who in Spy Fiction* (1977).

Stationers' Company. See *Company of Stationers of London, The*.

STEWART, Mary (1916–).
British romantic novelist whose first book, *Madame Will You Talk*, was an immediate success when it was published in 1954. Other successful

novels blended mystery and romance.

STOKER, Bram (1847–1912). Irish creator of the vampire Count Dracula (qv). Born Abraham Stoker in Dublin, he went to the university there, subsequently becoming a civil servant, an unpaid dramatic critic and a lawyer. Then he became secretary and business manager to the English actor, Sir Henry Irving; and both in his service and after Irving's death in 1905 he wrote 17 novels. The only other vampire book was *Dracula's Guest and Other Weird Tales* (1914).

DANIEL FARSON, *The Man who wrote Dracula. A biography of Bram Stoker* (1975).

STOUT, Rex (Todhunter) (1886–1975). American detective story writer. Creator of Nero Wolfe (qv), who appeared in 47 books published between 1934 and 1975, and of other detectives. Theodolinda ('Dol') Bonner, who ran an agency in New York, appeared in several Wolfe stories, and she and her assistant Sally Colt are featured in *The Hand in the Glove* (1937). Tecumseh Fox featured in three books: *Double for Death* (1939), *Bad for Business* (1940) and *The Broken Vase* (1941). *Alphabet Hicks* (1940) is about a disbarred lawyer of that name who became a cabdriver and private detective; *Red Threads (1939)* features Inspector Cramer, who is also in several Wolfe stories; and in *Mountain Cat* (1939) the murderer is caught by Delia Brand. Stout

published one thriller, *The President Vanishes* (1934), anonymously.

STOWE, Harriet Beecher (1812–1896). Prolific American writer who is remembered for one book, *Uncle Tom's Cabin* (2 vols., 1852). This had previously appeared in a Washington magazine, *The National Era*, in weekly parts from 5 June 1851 to 1 April 1852. In the USA the book sold 100,000 copies in eight weeks, 200,000 within a year, and 313,000 by April 1856. In Britain some 30 editions were published within six months of its first appearance in the USA. The demand was phenomenal. It was translated into 17 European languages, and several versions were available in French, German and Dutch.

Only one of her other books enjoyed great popularity – though nothing like that of *Uncle Tom's Cabin*. This was *Dred: a Tale of the Great Dismal Swamp* (1856), which sold 150,000 copies in the USA and 125,000 copies in Britain within two years of publication.

STRATEMEYER, E. L. See *Keene, Carolyn.*

Street and Smith. American publishing firm founded in 1855 under the direction of Francis Smith. Its first publication was *The New York Weekly*, a small tabloid which contained romantic fiction, short stories and humorous articles.

In 1856 the firm published *Tip Top Weekly*, which featured Frank Merriwell, athlete, Yale graduate, adventurer. He went out West, there successfully taking on outlaws and Indians; he travelled round the world, and occasionally visited Britain where he helped Scotland Yard to defeat international smugglers; he also worked as an undercover agent assisting police in the USA. Between 1856 and 1915 *Tip Top Weekly* published more than 500 of his adventures, and in 1936 there was a Frank Merriwell film serial.

Street and Smith published widely for the popular market, and a detailed study of the firm would be well worth undertaking – so far as I know it has never been attempted. In 1949 they discontinued pulp magazines (qv) and comic books (qv) in order to specialise in more sophisticated family magazines.

SUE, Eugène (1804–1857). Pseudonym of Marie Joseph Sue, French author of *Les Mystères de Paris* (4 vols., 1842–43). Translated into English as *The Mysteries of Paris*, it was published in 90 parts between 1844 and 1846, reissued in three volumes, and much reprinted in various editions. The ten-volume *Le Juif Errant* came out in 1844–45. As *The Wandering Jew* the English translation was immensely popular, reprinted in various forms and abridged for the cheap market. Both these works show the author's sympathy for radical causes, a political outlook that was blended with sensationalism and melodrama.

Superheroes (American). The success of Superman (qv), who made his appearance in 1938, and of Batman (qv), who followed a year later,

brought a number of imitations. Amongst these superheroes who had superhuman powers and were devoted to America and to the endless fight against crime were the following names, with their year of origin: Aquaman (1941), Captain America (1941), Captain Marvel (1940), Captain Marvel Junior (1941), Captain Midnight (1941), Captain Wings (1941), Flash (1940), Green Lantern (1940), Hawkman (1940), Human Torch, The (1939), Iron Man (1963), Plastic Man (1941), Spectre, The (1940), Spider-Man (1962), Spirit, The (1940), Supergirl (1959), Wonder Woman (1941).

Superman. Created by Jerry Siegel and Joe Schuster, this omnipotent American hero first appeared in the initial number of *Action Comics* in June 1938.

Superman, born on the doomed planet Krypton and launched into space as a baby, landed on earth where he was adopted by an elderly couple, Jonathan and Martha Kent. As he grew up, discovering his special abilities, he decided to devote his life to combating crime and evil and to fighting for 'truth, justice and the American Way'. Living his everyday life as the mild-mannered, bespectacled newspaper reporter Clark Kent, he adopts his Superman guise at will, when there is need for his services.

He has been enormously popular on radio, television and stage, and in a series of animated cartoons. There have also been innumerable toys, games and giveaway novelties connected with him. In January 1939 a

Superman newspaper strip was commenced, with stories very much more adult than the comic book versions.

See M. L. FLEISCHER, *The Great Superman Book* (1978).

SWANN, Annie S. (1859–1943). Best-selling British author of more than 250 books, some of which remained in print for 50 years or so. For her first novel, *Aldersyde* (1883), she was paid £50 for the copyright – and copies were still being sold in 1934.

All her work was characterized by a strongly Christian outlook. Her autobiography, *My Life* (1934), was itself a bestseller, reprinted eleven times by 1937 when the first cheap edition appeared; and it stresses the evangelical nature of her fiction.

Her married name was Burnett Smith.

Sweeney Todd. Demon barber of Fleet Street, London. He used to cut the throats of customers while he was shaving them, and propel their bodies direct from the barber's chair into a cellar below, where they were cut up and made into pies by Mrs Lovett, who had a shop next door. Her pie shop was renowned for its products. The theme probably originated in Paris, and became extraordinarily popular in Britain.

Sweeney Todd made his first appearance in a story called 'The String of Pearls' by Thomas Peckett Prest (qv). It was published in one of Edward Lloyd's (qv) journals, *The People's Periodical* (No. 1, 21 November 1846), and ran to 37 chapters serialised in the first 18 numbers. In 1850 it was reissued and expanded to a lengthy romance published by Lloyd in 92 weekly parts. It was subsequently often reprinted.

The demon barber took the fancy of the public and was translated to the stage as a melodrama. The first version, *The String of Pearls or the Fiend of Fleet Street*, opened on 1 March 1847 at the Britannia Theatre, Hoxton. Other stage versions followed, and there have been revivals in the twentieth century – a musical based upon the story was staged in London during the late 1970s. At the same time a junior version, 'Sweeney Toddler', was popular in a British comic called *Whoopee!*

PETER HAINING, *The Mystery and Horrible Murders of Sweeney Todd the Demon Barber of Fleet Street* (1979).

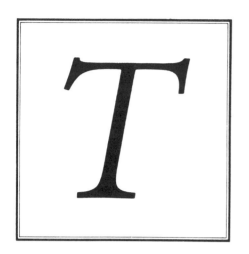

Tarlton, Richard (*d.* 1588). British comic actor who enjoyed considerable fame during his lifetime. He was the subject of two jestbooks (qv), *Tarltons Jests* (before 1600?) and *Tarltons Newes out of Purgatorie* (before 1590?). Both were reprinted, the former title in an edition of 1611, in James Orchard Halliwell (ed.), *Tarlton's Jests and News out of Purgatory with Notes and Some Account of the Life of Tarlton* (1844). There is an entry on Tarlton in the *Dictionary of National Biography*.

Tarzan. Member of the British nobility, Lord Greystoke, created by Edgar Rice Burroughs (qv). He was orphaned in the African jungle and brought up by apes, whose undisputed leader he became. *Tarzan of the Apes* (1914), which sold over 25 million copies, was the first of more than 30 stories which were printed and sold in 56 languages, amounting to something over 90 million copies.

Tarzan appeared in 42 films and 57 television adventures. He also starred in some 500 radio broadcasts and more than 12,000 comic strips.

The best study of Tarzan is in French: F. LACASSIN, *Tarzan* (Paris, 1971). In over 500 pages the Tarzan myth is discussed and its various forms analysed. There is also an excellent bibliography.

TAYLOR, John (1580–1653). Prolific British writer of prose and verse in pamphlet form for a popular market. He is sometimes referred to as 'The Water Poet' because he earned his living as a Thames waterman for several years. Unlike his contemporaries, he did not revamp traditional material, but produced original work. He hit upon a novel scheme for bringing some of this to the attention of the public: he would advertize the fact that he was about to undertake a journey and invite subscriptions to pay for the publication of an account of it to be written upon his return. One such undertaking was to walk to Edinburgh and back 'not carrying any Money to or fro, neither Begging, or Borrowing, or Asking Meate, drinke or Lodging'. His narrative was published as *The Pennyles Pilgrimage* in 1618. Taylor had a talent for doggerel and controversy.

All the Workes of John Taylor the Water Poet (1630) was reprinted by Scolar Press in 1973. This is the most accessible edition of his work although, despite the title, it is by no means complete.

TEGG, Thomas (1776–1845). British publisher. One of the earliest men to realize the importance of the mass market. He published numerous cheap reprints and abridgements of works which had sold well.

HENRY CURWEN, *A History of Booksellers* (ND, *c*. 1875).
F. A. MUMBY, *Publishing and Bookselling* (New and Revised Edition, 1949).
V. E. NEUBURG, *Popular Literature* (1977).

Temperance. The temperance movements of the nineteenth century created a vast popular and propagandist literature, much of which seems to have become lost to posterity. The difficulty in finding it seems to have caused historians of the movement to disregard it altogether. T. S. Arthur (qv), the American novelist, was the most prolific writer in the temperance cause, and his novels were widely circulated both in his own country and in Great Britain.

Other writers included Harriet A. Glazebrook (married name Beavan; *b*. 1847), whose poem 'The lips that touch liquor shall never touch mine' had a great vogue in temperance circles. J. W. Kirton wrote, amongst other things, a minor classic of the movement, often issued as a tract, called 'Buy your own cherries!'. Writers like this enjoyed great popularity, and there were magazines such as *The National Temperance Mirror*, *The Good Templars' Watchword*, *The Juvenile Templar*, and others. Also much in demand were anthologies like *The Temperance Reader* and *The Abstainer's Companion*. In London there was a National Temperance Publication Depot, and temperance works were also issued by religious publishers.

Why should the literature of temperance be thought worth rediscovery? There are two reasons. First, any popular literary enterprise linked to a social cause is interesting for its own sake; and secondly, the history of the temperance movement in Britain and the USA can never be adequately written just in terms of institutions and organizations. Its moral economy can be understood only if we know something about the books and the magazines that were read, the tracts that were written and distributed, and the poems that were recited at meetings.

The key to temperance literature is to be found in PETER T. WINSKILL, *Temperance Standard Bearers of the Nineteenth Century* (2 vols., 1897, 1898). Containing just over 1,000 pages, international in scope, with most probably all of the temperance writers of Britain and the USA included in it.

Terry and the Pirates. US adventure strip created by Milton Caniff, first published in October 1934. The story took place in China and featured Pat Ryan, a tall, handsome adventurer, and Terry, his young companion. They were soon joined by a comic Chinese character called Connie.

The strip became increasingly authentic and the dialogue wittier and pithier. Pat and Terry met and overcame a colourful series of villains who included Pyzon, General Klang and Baron de Plexus. The stories were most memorable for the women in them. The most deadly of their enemies was the Dragon Lady; Burma and Normandie Drake vied with each other for Pat's affections; while Terry was soon involved with April Kane.

The entry of the USA into the war changed the character of the strip. Terry became a pilot in the USAAF in China, and his commanding officer Colonel Flip Corkin took over as father figure. By this time Terry had become the star of the feature. On 29 December 1946, after a dispute with Tribune-News Syndicate, Caniff signed his last Terry strip and it was taken over by George Wunder. Although it went on for another 25 years, finally disappearing on 25 February 1973, the strip lost much of its attraction, humour ebbed away and the personality of the characters was much diminished. Terry himself became an Air Force Major expressing conventional cold war views.

Under Milton Caniff the popularity of the strip built up slowly and reached its climax during the war. There was a comic book version; a film *Terry and the Pirates* was made in 1940; and there was a radio adaptation and a television series during the 1950s.

TEY, Josephine (1896–1952). Pseudonym of Elizabeth Mackintosh, British creator of Inspector Alan Grant of Scotland Yard, who appears in all but two of her mysteries.

Her best known book is *The Franchise Affair* (1948), based in a much altered form upon an eighteenth-century case concerning the disappearance of a girl named Elizabeth Canning.

Several of Josephine Tey's novels have been filmed.

'Elizabeth is Missing' or, Truth Triumphant (1947), by LILLIAN DE LA TORRE, is useful and has a good bibliography.

The Saint. The Saint (otherwise Simon Templar) was created by Leslie Charteris (qv). An adventurer, a latter-day Robin Hood, the Saint frequently breaks the law, but his motives for doing so are always impeccably pure – hence his nickname. His main aim in life is to bring criminals to justice when the law is powerless to act. In pursuit of this objective he often comes up against Chief Inspector Claud Eustace Teal of Scotland Yard (in New York his police adversary is Inspector John Fernack).

Templar has all the physical expertise that a successful adventurer requires, and has mastered the art of knife-throwing, bare-back riding and driving racing cars. It goes almost without saying that he is an expert air pilot. In addition to all this, he dresses well and is a connoisseur of food and wine. Although attracted to women, he returns most often to Patricia Holm who appeared in the first Saint book, *Meet the Tiger*, in 1928. Whenever he is involved in a case Templar leaves his calling card – there is no lettering upon it, merely a stick figure with a halo which has become internationally famous as the emblem of the Saint.

Between 1928 and 1975, 46 Saint books were published. Amongst the eight which have appeared since 1964 only one was completely written by Leslie Charteris. The other seven were written by collaborators with Charteris, in some cases, making the final revision.

Also connected with Simon Templar was *The Saint Detective Magazine*, retitled *The Saint Mystery Magazine*, finally appearing as *The Saint Magazine*, published between Spring 1953 and October 1967. The first Saint film was made in 1938 with Louis Hayward in the starring role. Many other films followed, with George Sanders most often playing Templar. There have also been radio and television series. The best known of the latter was made in England, with Roger Moore starring as the Saint in 120 hour-long episodes.

See C. STEINBRUNNER and O. PENZLER (eds.) *Encyclopedia of Mystery and Detection* (1976) for a complete listing of Saint novels and films.

The Thin Man. See *Hammett, Dashiel*, and *Nick and Nora Charles*.

The Toff. Created by John Creasey (qv). The Honorable Richard Rollison, gentleman adventurer – similar to The Saint (qv) – is known to the police as The Toff. He has a valet, and an aunt, Lady ('Old Glory') Gloria Hurst, who help his investigations; and his official contact with the police is Inspector Gryce.

The Toff made his first appearance in print in a story called 'The Black Circle' published in a British weekly magazine, *The Thriller*, in 1933. The first of 55 books recounting his adventures was *Introducing The Toff* (1938).

Thomas (or Jack) Hickathrift. Character in an ancient legendary tale which was popular as an eighteenth-century chapbook (qv), and which had a strong East Anglian connection. In an encounter with a giant he used the wheel and axletree of a cart which he was driving as a shield and club with which he defeated his adversary.

Thorn Birds, The. Best-selling novel published in 1977. See *McCullough, Colleen*.

Tiger Tim. British comic character created by Julius Stafford Baker. Published initially in the *Daily Mirror* on 16 April 1904, it was the first newspaper comic strip in Britain. The opening caption set the tone: 'Hooray! Mrs Hippo has left the schoolroom! Now is our time to peep into that treacle jar!' – and the fun went on for more than seventy years.

The original Hippo Boys were Tiger Tim and Willy Giraffe, Peter Pelican, Billy Bruin, Jumbo Jim, Jacko the Monkey and some unnamed animals. After publication in various journals they moved to *The Rainbow*, a weekly children's comic which started on 14 February 1914. By now the characters were at a new school, Mrs Bruin's Boarding School, and they were known as The Bruin Boys. Later they went over to *Tiger Tim's Weekly*, published by Amalgamated Press (qv), which began on 31 January 1920. Meanwhile Mrs Hippo had reopened her school, and her new pupils were Tiger Tilly and the sisters of the other Bruin Boys. They were published in another Amalgamated Press comic, *The Playbox*, which started on 14 February 1925.

Tiger Tim and his friends outlasted their sisters and were still about in the 1970s. There are some excellent facsimiles of the comics in Dennis Gifford, *Happy Days*, 1975.

Titbits. Family magazine founded by George Newnes (later Sir George Newnes – 1851–1910) in 1881, and still going strong. Newnes raised the capital for his venture by opening a vegetarian restaurant, which made a profit of £400 in a few weeks. This was enough to start the magazine, so he sold the restaurant.

The first number of *Tit-bits from all the most interesting books, periodicals and newspapers in the world* was dated 22 October. The aim of the magazine was to provide amusement and information for the emerging middle classes of industrial towns; but its success suggests strongly that it reached, in fact, a much wider public.

Newnes's success prompted several rival publications, but none of them proved to be so lasting. Among them were: *Answers to Correspondents*, 1888–1950; *Pearson's Weekly*, 1890–1939; *John Bull*, 1906–1964; *Blighty*, 1916–1930; *Everybody's*, 1930–1959. Rather more remote descendants of *Titbits* included: *Picture Post*, 1938–1957; *Illustrated*, 1939–1960; *Reveille*, 1940–1979.

Titbits is the sole survivor of a genre which died out gradually as radio, and then television, began to take its place. Today in Britain the 'colour supplements' published by several Sunday newspapers represent a tenuous link with these earlier periodicals.

Tom and Jerry (I). A film cartoon featuring this cat and mouse team, *Puss Gets the Boot*, was produced by Fred Quimby, directed by William Hanna and Joseph Barbera, in 1939. Over the next 25 years Tom and Jerry starred in well over 100 films. In 1948 they appeared in a comic book, and went on doing so fairly continuously until 1974.

Tom and Jerry (II). Tom and Jerry, however, have other connotations. As Corinthian Tom and Jerry Hawthorn, they were the chief characters in *Life in London* (1821) by Pierce Egan (qv), a book which took the reading public of the 1820s by storm. First published in serial parts, with coloured illustrations, it was reprinted in various forms and inspired a number of imitations. There were authorised and unauthorised stage versions, some of the songs from which became 'hits'. Their 'rambles and sprees through the metropolis' made Tom and Jerry household names.

Tom Thumb. Diminutive legendary hero, said to be the offspring given by Merlin the Wizard to the childless ploughman. He was first mentioned in Reginald Scott, *The Discoverie of Witchcraft* (1584). According to a broadside ballad, *Tom Thumb his life and death . . .* , printed for John Wright in 1630, he was a Knight at King Arthur's court.

Another tradition equates him with Tom-a-lin, otherwise Tamlaine, a Scot of Scandinavian descent. Tom Thumb's adventures appeared in an eighteenth-century chapbook whose contents were largely adapted from the ballad mentioned. France, Germany and Denmark have similar tiny heroes.

According to legend, Tom Thumb was buried in Lincoln Cathedral, but the blue flagstone marking the place was lost during repairs in the early part of the nineteenth century.

TV Times. See *Radio Times and TV Times.*

Tyll Eulenspiegel (English: Howleglas/Owlglass). Peasant hero of a series of fictional episodes in which, through wit or cunning, he always outsmarts the innkeepers, tradesmen, farmers, nagging women, priests and officials with whom he comes into contact. The book became very popular when first published in German at Strasburg in 1519 (there may have been an edition in 1483), and was soon translated into English.

Although his popularity in several English versions did not last into the seventeenth and eighteenth centuries, Tyll Eulenspiegel is an important comic hero because he demonstrates triumphantly that when faced with an authority which was often pompous and insensitive, the 'little man' could win. It was this sort of humour that Charlie Chaplin and Norman Wisdom were to exploit so brilliantly in the twentieth century. Within the European tradition, Jaroslav Hasek's 'Good Soldier Svejk' is the most direct descendant of Tyll Eulenspiegel.

K. R. H. Mackenzie, *The Marvellous Adventures and Rare Conceits of Master Tyll Owlglass* (1860), contains a bowdlerised version of the German text. There are also appendices which discuss the possible authenticity of Tyll Eulenspiegel, and speculations about Thomas Murner, who may have been the original author. Mackenzie's book is more than one hundred years old, and the fact that it has not yet been superseded underlines the need for critical texts of early popular prose.

See also C. H. HERFORD, *Studies in* *the Literary Relations of England and Germany in the Sixteenth Century* (1886), Chapter V.

Uncle Tom's Cabin. See *Stowe, Harriet Beecher.*

Underground press. See *Alternative press.*

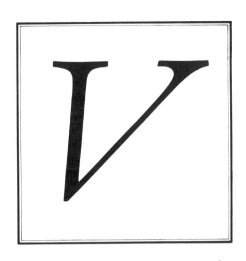

VACHELL, Horace Annesley (1861–1955). British writer. His most famous book, *The Hill* (1905), was about public school life. *Loot: From the Temple of Fortune* (1913), *Quinney's Adventures* (1924), *The Enchanted Garden and Other Stories* (1929) and *Experiences of a Bond Street Jeweller* (1932) are collections of mystery and detective short stories, and represent the best of his work. He also wrote several novels, one in collaboration with Archibald Marshall, *Mr Allen* (1926) – US title *The Mote House Mystery*. Others include *The Yard* (1923) and *The Disappearance of Martha Penny* (1934).

Valentine and Orson. Twins and heroes, probably French in origin (fifteenth century), who were adopted and brought up by a bear. In England their adventures were told in an eighteenth-century chapbook.

ARTHUR DICKSON, *Valentine and Orson* (1929).

VAN DINE, S. S. (1888–1939). Pseudonym of Willard Huntington Wright, American writer. Creator of Philo Vance (qv), whose exploits were recounted in books which became phenomenally successful. He was also the Editor of *The Great Detective Stories* (1927), the introduction to which is one of the classics of detective fiction scholarship.

JOHN TUSKA, *Philo Vance. The Life and Times of S. S. Van Dine* (Bowling Green University Popular Press; 1971) is a useful monograph.

VERNE, Jules Gabriel (1828–1905). French writer, one of the founding fathers of science fiction – H. G. Wells (qv) was the other.

Verne's first novel was *Five Weeks in a Balloon* (1863); and he became established as a writer of scientific stories with *From the Earth to the Moon* (1865) and its sequel *Round the Moon* (1870). Other novels in the scientific vein were *Twenty Thousand Leagues under the Sea*

(1870), featuring Captain Nemo; and *The Clipper of the Clouds* (1886), about a 100 foot long airship powered by 74 rotor blades, each mounted on a mast. It was owned by Robur, who appeared in a sequel, *Master of the World* (1904).

Round the Moon was filmed in 1902, and there have been later film versions of other novels.

I. O. EVANS, *Jules Verne and his Work* (1967).
JEAN CHESNEAUX, *The Political and Social Ideas of Jules Verne* (1972).

VERNER, Gerald (1896–1980). British writer. Real name Donald Stuart, but almost always known by his pseudonym. Author of more than 100 thrillers, translated into 35 languages.

Verner became a writer in the 1920s after a very mixed career as an actor, night club cabaret producer, worker in Billingsgate Fish Market, calendar designer and pavement artist. At the end of the First World War, while living as a down-and-out in London, he wrote *The Embankment Murder*, for which he was paid £70. He also wrote for the stage, radio and television.

VICKERS, George (?–1846). British publisher of cheap fiction. G. W. M. Reynolds (qv) was connected with him for the first volume of *The Mysteries of London*, but nothing further seems to be known.

VICTOR, Mrs Metta V. (1831–1885). Prolific American writer of dime novels for the firm of Beadle and Adams (see *Dime novels*), of which her husband, Orville J. Victor, was Editor from 1861 to 1896. She also wrote poems, sketches and stories for other publishers. Her first novel for Beadle was *Alice Wilde*, published in 1864. Besides writing under her own name, Mrs Victor used the following pseudonyms: 'Seeley Regester'; 'Mrs Mark Peabody'; 'Walter T. Gray'; 'Corinne Cashman'; and 'Eleanor Lee Edwards'.

VIDOCQ, François Eugène (1775–1857). French writer. Detective as well as author, Vidocq had an adventurous career as a soldier, policeman and spy. His four-volume *Mémoires* (1828–1829), much of which was fiction, was a sensational ghostwritten account of his life. It was published in England as *Memoirs of Vidocq, Principal Agent of the French Police Until 1827; and now Proprietor of the Paper Manufactory at St. Mandé; Written by Himself* (1828–29). The US edition had a shorter title: *Memoirs of Vidocq, French Police Agent*.

Volksbücher. German traditional stories published in book form similar to chapbooks (qv).

The standard work is JOSEPH GÖRRES, *Die Teutschen Volksbücher* (1807, reprint 1925). There is an excellent modern study in German: H. J. KREUTZER, *Der Mythos vom Volksbuch* (1977).

WALLACE, (Richard Horatio) Edgar (1875–1932). British writer. Probably the most popular thriller writer, Wallace was also a journalist, dramatist and poet. Because he could not find a publisher to back him, he founded the Tallis Press in 1905 and published his first mystery story, *The Four Just Men*, in the same year. He advertised it widely and offered a £500 reward to any reader who could guess how the murder of the British Foreign Secretary was committed. The advertising campaign and the competition resulted in tremendous sales – and in financial loss, because several readers guessed the correct solution and had to be paid.

He wrote several sequels to this first book: *The Four Just Men: The Council of Justice* (1908); *The Just Men of Cordova* (1917); *The Law of the Four Just Men* (1921) (US title *Again the Three Just Men* (1933)); *The Three Just Men* (1925); *Again the Three Just Men* (1928) (US title *The Law of the Three Just Men* (1931)).

Wallace was an extraordinarily prolific writer, and more than half of his 173 books were mystery stories. He once dictated an entire novel during a week-end, and on one occasion worked out the plots of six novels simultaneously. His popularity was tremendous – it is said that during the 1920s and 1930s in England one in four of all books read was written by Wallace. He made a great deal of money from his writing, and lost even more because of his extravagant lifestyle and his predilection for backing the wrong horses. Horse racing was a life-long passion, and he often lost £250 in a day at the race track. He was racing editor for a newspaper, and several of his stories had racing themes and backgrounds.

When he died he left considerable debts, although his books continued to make money. His style was slapdash and full of clichés, but in spite of this he was, and perhaps still is, enormously readable, with a shrewd ear for convincing dialogue. His characters are clearly defined, and the pace of his writing, however complex the plot, carries the reader along to a usually surprising climax.

Two of Wallace's characters were memorable. One was J. G. Reeder (qv): the other District Commissioner Sanders, who maintained law and order in West Africa. The latter epitomized those attitudes of unassailable white supremacy, with paternal attitudes to the subject people whom he regarded as savage children, which would now be regarded as highly offensive. Because of this, the novels about him – *Sanders of the River* (1911) was the first of several – have a curiously remote, period quality.

Hundreds of films have been made from Wallace's novels and short stories. There were plays, and there was a television series in 1959.

The standard life is MARGARET LANE, *Edgar Wallace, the Biography of a Phenomenon* (1938, New Edition 1964).
The complexities of Edgar Wallace's publishing history are to some extent unravelled in w. o. g. LOFTS, *The British Bibliography of Edgar Wallace* (1969).
His own autobiography, *People* (1926), reprinted some years later in an undated edition entitled *Edgar Wallace. A Short Biography*, is interesting, but curiously unrevealing.

WATERS (Dates unknown). Pseudonym of British writer William Russell, although in some early American editions of his work, his name is given as Thomas Russell. He

wrote detective short stories, the first of them published in Chambers' Edinburgh Journal, 28 July 1849. They were later published in New York as *The Recollections of a Policeman* (1852) and then in England as *Recollections of a Detective Police-Officer* (1856). A second volume with the same title was published in 1859. Both volumes were frequently reprinted, often with changes of title.

'Waters' wrote in the first person as a member of the Metropolitan Police who became so successful that he had two assistants – one of whom was a ventriloquist.

Amongst his other books were: *The Game of Life* (1857); *Leaves from the Diary of a Law Clerk* (1857); *A Skeleton in Every House* (1860); *Recollections of a Sheriff's Officer* (1860); *The Experiences of a French Detective Officer. Adapted from the MSS of Theodore Duhamel* (1861); *Experience of a Real Detective* (1862) (By 'Inspector F'); *Autobiography of an English Detective* (1863); *Mrs Waldergrave's Will and Other Tales* (1870). Under the pseudonym 'Lieutenant Warneford, R.N.', Russell wrote a number of sea stories.

Many (?all) of his books were issued initially in cheap form as 'Yellowbacks' (qv). Nothing, however, seems to be known about this author's life.

Weary Willie and Tired Tim. Almost the longest-lived of British comic strip characters. These two tramps, one fat and the other thin, were created by the artist Tom

Browne (1870–1910). They began life in a weekly comic, *Illustrated Chips* (see *Comics*) in May 1896. A few weeks later, as 'Weary Willy [Willie came later] and Tired Tim', they took over the front page and remained there until they were retired to the mansion of Marmaduke Pump, Millionaire, when *Chips* ceased publication in 1953.

Browne gave up drawing the tramps in 1900, and was followed by several artists. In about 1912 Percy Cocking took over, and continued to draw the strip until its end.

WEBSTER, Jean (1876–1916). American novelist and short-story writer whose principal works appeared between 1903 and 1914. Her most popular book, *Daddy Long-Legs*, was published in 1912, and a sequel, *Dear Enemy*, two years later.

WELLESLEY-SMITH, Mrs F. A. (1874–1962). British author of much popular fiction – she was writing until she was well past 80. Most of her life was spent in Beckenham, Kent, to which she came as a young bride in 1893. In her early days as a writer she produced several hundred short stories and serials for periodical publications. Just before the outbreak of war in 1939, Mills and Boon had begun to publish her work; while in the 1920s, and probably earlier, Amalgamated Press had been one of her publishers. She used both her own name and, for over 100 novels, the pseudonyms Frances Braybrooke and Cecily Colpitts.

I am grateful to her son, C. Wellesley-Smith, for most of these details.

WELLS, H(erbert) G(eorge) (1886–1946). British writer, one of the founding fathers of science fiction (qv) – Jules Verne (qv) was the other. Wells was a writer of extraordinary range and fertility. Science fiction was only one of the themes which he tackled successfully.

As a young man he resisted attempts to make him a tailor's, then a chemist's, apprentice, and won a scholarship to the Normal School of Science (now Imperial College of Science and Technology). Afterwards he became a teacher, but ill health prevented his following this career, so he turned to writing – and won immediate success. Until his death he enjoyed a considerable reputation in intellectual circles, and probably even more widely, both as a prophet and as a popular educator.

The Time Machine (1895) was the first of his science fiction works. It was followed by *The Island of Dr Moreau* (1896); *The Invisible Man* (1897); *The War of the Worlds* (1898); *When the Sleeper Wakes* (1899); *The First Men in the Moon* (1901); *The Food of the Gods* (1904); *A Modern Utopia* (1905); *In the Days of the Comet* (1906); *The War in the Air* (1908).

Many of his stories were filmed, and notable among these was *The Shape of Things to Come* (1933), which was filmed in 1935.

Wells also wrote some 70 short

stories, many of which – 'The Country of the Blind', 'The Empire of the Ants', 'The Crystal Egg', for example – were science fiction.

BERNARD BERGONZI, *The Early H. G. Wells: a Study of the Scientific Romances* (1961).

Western novels and stories ('Westerns'). The fictional West, sometimes called the Wild West, is a creation of the last years of the eighteenth century. Early colonists, assailed by starvation, illness, accident, climate and Indians, regarded North America as mostly wilderness. From the point of view of the British government, anything west of the Appalachian Mountains was simply a blank. By the mid-eighteenth century, however, the land to the West was beginning to be thought of in rather different terms – it offered the possibility of unlimited expansion and opportunity. After the Revolution, the great push westwards began; emigrants moved across the plains beyond the mountains, and the first overland crossing to California, led by Jedidiah Smith, took place in 1826.

Accounts of such journeys, real or imagined, soon found their way into books, and by the 1840s there existed a considerable popular literature of the West. The first great character in Western fiction was Daniel Boone (1734–1820), whose adventures in real life were related and augmented until he achieved the status of a mythical hero. Several biographies of him were written,

and eventually Boone, with his fabulous rifle Tick-licker, became a standard character in fiction.

Next came Davy Crockett (1786–1836), frontier scout and hunter. Before his death amongst the defenders of the Alamo, Crockett had been presented in fiction as a wise, honest, humorous, plain-speaking man of the people: after his death he was practically canonized, and was a major figure in both fiction and drama for something like 100 years. He enjoyed a brief, though intensive, revival in the cinema and on the television screen in the 1950s.

Novels about the West were made even more popular by James Fenimore Cooper (1789–1851) (qv), whose story *The Deerslayer* (1941) featured Natty Bumppo (also known as Leatherstocking, Hawkeye, Deerslayer and Pathfinder). He was the prototype of the cowboy hero.

There were others whose adventures in real life, retold and imaginatively enhanced, contributed to the making of the Western novel. Amongst them was Kit Carson (1809–1868), frontier scout and guide, of whom several biographies were written and whose fictional adventures were told by several authors. William F. Cody (1846–1917), better known as 'Buffalo Bill', after leading an adventurous life in the West, became a theatrical entrepreneur and a legend in his own lifetime. He wrote a number of novels about his experiences, but it is impossible to distinguish them from others written in his name by Prentiss Ingraham (qv). The literature on Buffalo Bill is considerable. See especially his *Autobiography* (1888); Helen Wetmore Cody and Zane Grey, *Last of the Great Scouts* (1899); and Richard J. Walsh, *The Making of Buffalo Bill* (1928).

W. H. Bonney (1859–1881), who passed into legend as 'Billy the Kid', was little more than a ruffian with a talent for quick shooting who, like Dick Turpin (qv), was glamorized after his death and was the subject of numerous books and articles. See J. C. Dykes, *Billy the Kid. The Bibliography of a Legend* (1952).

With the coming of dime novels (qv – see also *Beadle and Adams*), there was a flood of Western fiction which featured cowboys, Indians, sherriffs, dudes, outlaws, miners, judges, dance-hall girls, scouts, soldiers, gamblers and others. Railroads, covered wagons, stage coaches, Wells Fargo, the Pony Express, to say nothing of Custer's last stand, all became the mainstays of fiction. Backgrounds included the gold rush, range wars, cattle rustling, with landscapes which ranged from prairie, river and lake to mountain and forest. There was, in effect, more real historical background than the writer could use.

The two outstanding American writers of Westerns were Zane Grey (qv) and Clarence E. Mulford (qv). In Britain, J. T. Edson (qv) has specialised in novels of this kind. Apart from these authors there is a host of nineteenth and twentieth-century practitioners of this genre.

Reference material on the Western is patchy. The following are useful:

J. G. CAWELT, *The Six-Gun Mystique* (ND ?1970).

J. B. FRANTZ and J. E. CHOATE, *The American Cowboy, Myth and Reality* (1955, English Edition 1956).

R. W. ETULAIN, *The Popular Western* (1974).

DARYL JONES, *The Dime Novel Western* (1978).

A. LENNIGER (ed.), *Western Writers of America. Silver Anniversary Anthology* (1977).

R. B. NYE, *The Unembarrassed Muse* (1970).

H. N. SMITH, *Virgin Land. The American Myth as Symbol and Myth* (1950) – see Chapter 2.

Western novels have an obviously close connection with the cinema. In this connection see G. N. FENIN and W. K. EVERSON, *The Western. From Silents to the Seventies* (Revised Edition, 1973).

WEYMAN, Stanley John (1855–1928). British writer of popular historical novels published between 1890 and 1928. The best known of his books is probably *Under the Red Robe* (1894), a stage version of which was put on at the Haymarket Theatre in London in 1896. It was produced as a musical in New York in 1927.

WHEATLEY, Dennis (Yeats) (1897–1977). British writer. Once described as a 'Prince of Thriller Writers', Wheatley fought in the Great War, and in 1918 entered the family business as a wine merchant. He was the author of more than 60 books, many of them still in print. His works have been translated into

29 languages, and have sold more than 37 million copies.

His first book, *The Forbidden Territory* (1933), was an immediate success, and was reprinted seven times in seven weeks. One of the themes which he exploited skilfully was the occult: *The Devil Rides Out* (1935) and *The Haunting of Toby Jugg* (1948) dealt with Satanism and black magic.

When asked why his novels were popular, Wheatley replied: 'I think it is because I always write two books. First of all I write a straightforward thriller. Then I write information. People know when they read one of my books that they're going to learn something.'

WHEELER, Edward L(ytton) (?1854–1885). American, self-styled 'sensational novelist', creator of the famous young outlaw and desperado 'Deadwood Dick', said to have been based upon a real character of the West, Richard W. Clark.

Wheeler began writing for story papers in the 1870s, and his first novel was probably *Hurricane Nell, the Girl Dead-Shot; or the Queen of the Saddle and Lasso*, published as No. 1 of Starr's 'Ten Cent Pocket Library', 4 May 1877. He followed this up with other stories, and in the same year began the Deadwood Dick series. Altogether he wrote 33 of these, the last one appearing in the year of his death. They were all published as 'dime novels' (qv).

About 97 'Deadwood Dick, Jr' stories were written by someone else.

WHITTAKER, Frederick (1838–1889). American, turned to writing after active service during the American Civil War. He wrote more than 170 novels of the swashbuckling adventure type, nearly all of them published by Beadle and Adams (qv). He used the pseudonym Launce Poyntz.

WILLETT, Edward (1830–1889). American author of about 200 novels, most of them published by Beadle and Adams (qv). For some of his stories he used the pen name J. Stanley Henderson.

WINSOR, Kathleen (1919–   ). Bestselling American author whose novel *Forever Amber* (1944), set in Restoration England, was immediately popular. Her later work, which included *The Lovers* (1952), *America With Love* (1957), and *Calais* (1979), was not so successful.

WINTER, John Strange (1856–1911). British writer. Pseudonym used by Eliza Vaughan Stannard, prolific author during the 1880s and 1890s of military romances. Titles included *Cavalry Life* (1881); *Regimental Legends* (1882); *In Quarters* (1885); *Army Society* (1886); *A Born Soldier* (1894). She also wrote romantic novels: *That Imp!* (1887); *That Mrs Smith!* (1889); *Three Girls* (1892); and others.

Her most unusual novel was a love story which turned upon the 'problem' of the Thirty-Nine Articles of the Church of England. *The Soul of a Bishop* (1893) is set against a background of society life in Blankhampton, and follows the romance of Miss Cecil Constable and the Reverend Archibald Netherby.

WODEHOUSE, P(elham) G(renville) (1881–1973). Prolific British humorous writer of bestselling novels, short stories and plays. His publishing career extended over more than 70 years – the first book, *The Pothunters*, came out in 1902, and the last, *Aunts Aren't Gentlemen* in 1974.

Amongst his memorable creations were Ukridge, Lord Emsworth, Psmith and Mr Mulliner; but his best-known character was Jeeves, manservant and valet to Bertie Wooster – the quintessential gentleman's gentleman whose name has passed into the English language. He appears in many of Wodehouse's novels, from *Thank You, Jeeves* (1934) to *Much Obliged, Jeeves* (1971) – this last as sparklingly funny as ever. The only book in which he appears without Bertie Wooster is *Ring for Jeeves* (1953).

The reputation and enduring popularity of Jeeves has, to some extent, overshadowed some of Wodehouse's early writing. His school stories, in particular, are excellent.

Quite the best book on P. G. Wodehouse is RICHARD USBORNE, *Wodehouse at Work to the End* (1976). This is a revised edition of a work which was first published in 1961; and there was a Penguin edition in 1978. GEOFFREY JAGGARD, *Wooster's World* (1967) and *Blandings the Blest* (1968), are directories

which make it easy and pleasant to trace people and places in two very different Wodehouse worlds. Inevitably there are critical studies. OWEN DUDLEY EDWARDS, *P. G. Wodehouse* (1977), is good: for the collector, DAVID JASEN, *Bibliography and Reader's Guide to the First Editions of P. G. Wodehouse* (1971), is essential. Wodehouse's own autobiographical *Performing Flea* (1953), *Bring on the Girls* (1954) and *Over Seventy* (1957) have been reissued as *Wodehouse on Wodehouse* (1980). The latest book at the time of writing is BENNY GREEN, *P. G. Wodehouse. A Literary Biography* (1981).

Women's magazines. Magazines produced specifically for women date from the end of the seventeenth century. The first of them was *The Ladies Mercury*, founded by the publisher ('bookseller' as he would have been called in his own day) John Dunton in 1693. At first it was a monthly, and then it appeared fortnightly. Sixteen women writers contributed material on 'All the nice and curious questions concerning Love, Marriage, Behaviour, Dress and Humour in the Female Sex, whether Virgins, Wives or Widows.' One of the features was an 'Answers to Correspondents' section.

In 1710 *Records of Love, or Weekly Amusements for the Fair Sex* made its appearance. The tone was mostly sentimental, and it was probably the first women's periodical to carry serial fiction. 'The Generous Heiress' was published in two parts in numbers 6 and

7; 'The Wandering Dancing Master' was serialized in three subsequent issues. During the reign of Queen Anne, publications for women readers proliferated. There was a *Female Tatler*; likewise *Spectator*, *Whisperer*, *Guardian*, *Delight*, *Tea-Table*, *Repository*, *Visitor*, as well as *Gazettes*, *Mercuries* and *Intelligences*. The word 'magazine' itself was first applied to a women's periodical by Edward Cave, who published *The Ladies Magazine or Monthly Intelligence* in 1732.

After this brisk eighteenth-century development the women's magazine was well established, and many more were published during the following century. It was during this period that magazines aimed at working class women began to appear – in the eighteenth century the reading public for such periodicals had been seen entirely in middle class terms. There were also magazines, several founded at the end of the century by Amalgamated Press (qv), which specialized in publishing fiction. In general, though, the contents of women's magazines in both Britain and the USA were varied. Practical assistance in running a home and bringing up children was offered; there were features on cookery, needlework, knitting and other home activities; usually there was a 'Letters to the Editors' section; and more often than otherwise, the proportion of fiction outweighed that of non-fiction.

Two dates are of especial importance, in Britain at least. One is 1911. On the 4 November of that year *The Woman's Weekly* made its first appearance. It cost one penny (old style) and announced on its cover that it was 'the paper for every woman. The paper for every home.' A shirt blouse pattern was given away with every copy. It was an immediate success, and is still going strong. Its significance lay in the fact that it was the first periodical to break through the class barrier of readership and to aim for a mass circulation amongst women. This practice has since become much more widespread, as the continuing success in Britain of magazines like *Woman's Own* (1932) and *Woman* (1937) demonstrates.

The other date was 1972, when the feminist journal *Spare Rib* was launched. Its predecessors had been *The Woman Worker* (1908) and the Suffragette periodical *Dreadnought* (1915). The standards of *Spare Rib* are high. It tackles all kinds of problems which the more conventional women's press is content to ignore. The question which arises with this magazine is the extent to which it can properly be described as popular literature. Feminists would probably admit that this publication has not yet succeeded in striking a responsive chord amongst working class women: nonetheless, *Spare Rib* remains the most serious attempt to provide a feminist popular journal to date.

The tradition of women's magazines in the USA has been rather different, and there has been little that resembled the 'domestic' tradition which remains an established element in the mass magazines designed for a female readership in Britain. At the lower end of the market, the American tradition of comic strip stories has virtually taken over in fictional magazines designed for teenage girls. Strictly speaking these are not 'women's magazines', but the decline of prose narrative and the substitution for it of picture stories seems to represent a portentous change in popular taste.

CYNTHIA L. WHITE, *Women's Magazines 1693–1968* (1970).
ALISON ADBURGHAM, *Women in Print* (1972).
CYNTHIA L. WHITE, *The Women's Periodical Press in Britain 1946–1976* (1977).
IRENE DANCYGER, *A World of Women* (1978).
The Times has published two supplements on the subject. One was dated 16 September 1965 and the other 28 July 1972. Newspaper and periodical articles on aspects of the women's magazine appear more often than one might think.

WOOD, Mrs Henry (1814–1887). Bestselling British novelist. It was said that two and a half million of her books had been sold by the turn of the nineteenth and twentieth centuries. Born Ellen Price in Worcester, she had several years of ill-health during her childhood. At the age of 22, however, she was in sufficiently good health to marry Henry Wood, a banking and shipping agent. For the next two decades they lived in France, and towards the end of this period she began contributing stories and articles anonymously to magazines in London. When her husband lost his job through some undisclosed indiscretion, she had to put her talent to the test. She entered a Temperance League novel-writing competition, and her entry, *Danesbury House*, written in a month, won the prize of £100.

Meanwhile she began writing *East Lynne*. After magazine serialization it appeared in book form in three volumes (1861), and was an immediate success. Sales by the end of the century had reached the half million mark. Her other novels included *The Channings* (1862); *The Shadow of Ashlydyat* (1863); and *Roland Yorke* (1869).

Mrs Henry Wood dealt in sensation. She told a good story, with a strong plot and well-defined characters. Her themes of murder, bigamy, and even adultery, were acceptable to her reading public because wickedness – and, of course, virtue – always received its due reward.

WOOLRICH, Cornell (George Hopley) (1903–1968). American author of 36 volumes of crime and mystery novels and collections of short stories, many in the tradition of Dashiell Hammett (qv) and Raymond Chandler (qv). Some of his early work was published in *Detective Fiction Weekly* and *Dime Detective*.

Several of Woolrich's stories were made into successful films.

WREN, P(ercival) C(hristopher) (1885–1941). British writer. Born in Devon, P. C. Wren was educated at Oxford, and then spent five years working his way across the world, serving for a time as a soldier in the French Foreign Legion. At one stage he lived in India, and he saw Army service during the Great War until he was invalided out in 1917.

His first book was *Dew and Mildew* (1912), and others followed; but it was not until 1924, with the publication of *Beau Geste*, that he achieved fame and success. This story of the Foreign Legion quickly became a bestseller, and was adapted for the stage and the screen. There were several sequels – *Beau Sabreur* (1926), *Beau Ideal* (1928), *The Good Gestes* (1929); but none was as successful as the first of the series. His last book, *Odd But Even So: Stories Stranger than Fiction*, appeared in the year following his death.

WYNDHAM, John (1903–1969). British writer. Pseudonym of John Wyndham Parkes Lucas Benyon Harris (all his forenames have at one time or another been used as pseudonyms).

Wyndham's first story, 'Worlds to Barter', was sold to *Wonder Stories* in 1925, and nearly all his early work appeared in similar American magazines. His first novel was *The Secret People* (1935), and the second *Planet Plane* (1936) – later retitled *Stowaway to Mars*. His best-known and best-selling novel was *The Day of the Triffids* (1951). Also successful were *The Kraken Wakes* (1953 – US title *Out of the Deeps*), and *The Midwich Cuckoos* (1957). The latter was filmed in 1960 as *The Village of the Damned*, and there was a sequel, *The Children of the Damned*, in 1963. There are many collections of his short stories, including some of the earlier ones in *Sleepers of Mars and Wanderers of Time* (1973) written under the name of John Benyon Harris.

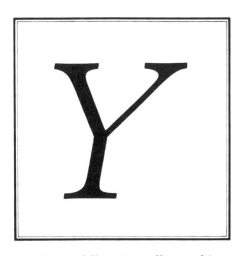

Yankee peddlers. Broadly speaking, the American equivalent of chapmen (qv). The distances they had to travel were, of course, very much greater than they were in Britain, and the range of goods that they carried and the services that they offered were, perforce, much wider too. By about 1860 railroads, and to a lesser extent roads and river transport, made it possible for factories to supply the increasing need for their goods more quickly to a growing population, so that the importance of the peddler declined sharply. Like his counterpart in Britain, he had played a vital part in the inland trade, and like him too, he continued his existence as a streetseller in towns.

RICHARDSON WRIGHT, *Hawkers and Walkers in Early America* (1927, 1955).
J. R. DOLAN, *The Yankee Peddlers of Early America* (1964).
Both books have useful bibliographies.

YATES, Dornford (1885–1960).

Pseudonym of Cecil William Mercer, British author of adventure and secret service fiction. His first novel, *The Courts of Idleness* (1920) was followed by 33 others. Amongst the best known characters created by Yates were Berry, Boy Pleydell and Jonah Mansel; and there is a sympathetic study of these characters, together with a nostalgic look at the writer, in Richard Usborne, *Clubland Heroes* (1953, reprinted 1974).

A. J. SMITHERS, *Dornford Yates, A Biography* (1982).

Yellow-back. Name given to a particular kind of cheap edition which began to appear round about the middle of the nineteenth century for display and sale on railway bookstalls. Most of it was fiction, the price was usually two shillings, and yellow was nearly always the predominant colour – supported by red and black – of the boards in which the books were bound.

Yellow-backs represented an important innovation in cheap publishing. At a level above that of penny dreadfuls/penny bloods (qv), they were designed for a mass market. For the most part they were reprints; but an influential forerunner of yellow-back publishing, the Irish firm Simms and McIntyre, inaugurated their 'Parlour Library' in 1847 with an original work of fiction, *The Black Prophet*, by William Carleton. Priced at one shilling a volume, the series with its original works and reprints, was so successful that a London office was soon opened. By 1863, when the 'Parlour Library' came to an end, it had been responsible for nearly 300 titles.

The decorated boards in which the Simms and McIntyre books were bound paved the way technically for the yellow-back proper. Among the many yellow-back series the 'Railway Library' launched by Routledge in 1849 was the largest and the best known. Output was considerable – 327 titles in 1862, for example, and 860 in 1880.

MICHAEL SADLEIR, 'Yellow-Backs', published in John Carter (ed.), *New Paths in Book Collecting* (1934).
The catalogue of Sadleir's collection, *XIX Century Fiction* (2 vols., 1951, reprinted 1969) is invaluable, especially vol. II.

Yellow Kid, The. Hero of the first true comic strip created by Richard Felton Outcault (1863–1928). He first appeared as one of several slum children in a coloured panel called 'At the Circus in Hogan's Alley' in the Sunday paper *New York World* on 5 May 1895. By January 1896 he had become more prominent and wore a yellow nightshirt. He caught the public fancy and was referred to as 'The Yellow Kid'. Through the medium of messages emblazoned on his garment he would talk to the public – the messages would be cheeky and generally related to the theme of the panel.

The career of this character was short and bedevilled by legal battles over rights after Outcault had left the *New York World* in 1896. He was much irked by this, and by criticism of his creation; and it was finally dropped in 1898.

The memory lingered on for a time, kept alive by novelties such as games, buttons, puzzles and statuettes. Today The Yellow Kid is part of the folklore of the comic strip.

16 A typical yellow-back